SWITZERLAND

A GUIDE TO THE

CAPITAL AND MONEY MARKETS

SWITZERLAND

A GUIDE TO THE

CAPITAL AND MONEY MARKETS

Dr. Henri B. Meier

and

Dr. John E. Marthinsen

Published by Euromoney Publications

in association with

The Julius Baer Group
JP Morgan
Swiss Bank Corporation

Published by
Euromoney Publications PLC
Nestor House, Playhouse Yard
London EC4V 5EX

Telephone: +44 (71) 779 8888

Jacket design by PW Reprosharp Ltd, London
Typeset by Julie Foster
Printed by in England by Balding+Mansell, Peterborough

This book is dedicated to all those who kept
Switzerland out of wars – this most demeaning,
cruel and senseless of all human disgraces –
thereby creating the precondition for
Switzerland's international capital market

PREFACE

The first edition of this book appeared in 1983. Over the following two years, the Swiss capital markets underwent such important structural changes that a second edition was required. It has been over a decade since the 1985 edition appeared, and the financial landscape in Switzerland has changed dramatically. However, the main pillars that made Switzerland a leading financial centre remain unaltered. Among them are the nation's: saving capacity, currency strength and convertibility, freedom of capital transfers, political, social and economic stability, neutrality, well-organized and well-funded financial institutions, simple legal principles and international environment. These pillars are as important in the 1990s as they ever were, and are the foundation for Switzerland's position as the world's largest private banking centre.

Both the rules of the game and the framework of the international capital markets have undergone drastic changes, driven by the liberalization and globalization of the financial markets, as well as the revolution in information technology. In spite of the changes that have occurred in most areas, it is clear that there are sectors where *plus ça change, plus ça reste pareil*. Significant negative characteristics of the international macroeconomic environment and, in particular, the action or inaction of governments within that environment continue to haunt both developed and developing nations.

The most constant part of the international financial landscape has been governments' weakness for managing and balancing their budgets. In nations where there is no significant counteraction, such as a strict monetary policy, budget deficits have significantly increased domestic inflation rates and weakened international currency values. Government deficits have produced persistent competition for capital. Necessitous financing has diverted spending toward consumption and away from employment-generating, productive investments. Moreover, the supply of funds to the domestic and international capital markets has been skewed detrimentally by restrictive rules (eg, the set of regulations governing pension fund investments favours domestic debt instruments over both domestic equity and foreign investments).

Since the early 1990s, the markets, institutions, systems and laws influencing the Swiss financial markets have changed at speeds atypical for Switzerland. The outstanding characteristics of these changes have been:

- enhanced transparency and investor protection,
- tougher competition,
- greater efficiency and
- more novel financial instruments to manage risk.

Enhanced transparency, better investor protection and an improved ability to compete have been the direct result of both a trend by Swiss corporations toward complying with international accounting standards and a string of recently passed and pending legislation, such as Switzerland's Company-, Stock Exchange-, Investment Fund- and Banking Laws.

After a decade of debating, Swiss Company Law requires companies, inter alia, to publish consolidated and audited financial statements and to report the dissolution of hidden reserves. The Stock Exchange Law should regulate the newly created Swiss Stock Exchange, oversee public takeovers, and protect the rights of minority shareholders. The Federal Law on Investment Funds (Mutual Funds Law) is one of the most modern in Europe. It was designed to protect investors and greatly liberalizes investment fund rules, enabling Swiss funds to compete more effectively in the international marketplace. Finally, the new Banking Law addresses issues related to cantonal supervision, 'foreign controlling interests', international reciprocity and the international transmission of information between supervisory bank authorities.

The recent Swiss Stamp Tax revision should also strengthen Switzerland's ability to compete. In a September 1992 referendum, the Swiss electorate voted to abolish the stamp duty on money market transactions. The old tax was one of the major reasons for the flow of mutual fund business from Switzerland to other countries (especially Luxembourg). Its repeal changes the incentives that were previously so clearly biased against Switzerland.

Domestically, tougher competition – especially in the banking and insurance areas – has been the direct result of deregulation and the abolition of price agreements and conventions. Increased competition in the banking sector led to approximately one hundred take-overs, mergers and major participation agreements in just a few years. In the insurance sector, competition was so stilted that changes meant abolishing agreements imposed by law! The effect of this intensified competition has been evident not only in the hectic merger activity in banking and insurance sectors but also in the closer cooperation among regional banks and an actual and proposed sale of cantonal banks.

Simultaneous with the intensified competition between banks and insurance companies, the Swiss Postal System (PTT), the largest clearing institution in Switzerland, has started to play a more active role in the Swiss financial markets. PTT has begun to pay interest on account balances to attract savings and in 1993, it offered federal deposits with maturities of 1 to 3 years, making it a new participant in Switzerland's money markets. The PTT also competed by introducing Postcard-Eurocards and postal checks, as well as disbursing cash in automatic "Postomats".

Greater efficiency has been the result of both competition and technological improvements. Rapid computer developments and advances in information technology have helped change the profile and *modus operandi* of the Swiss securities markets. The Swiss electronic stock exchange (EBS) and the integration of all prominent aspects of Swiss security markets, made fully operational in 1996, are visible improvements in efficiency.

Less visible, but equally important, has been the revolution in the back-office. Fully integrated automatic systems have been developed to handle delivery, settlement and global custody. Ten years ago, Switzerland's seven stock exchanges and the services of SEGA, the clearing system for Swiss securities, were praised as unique. Today there is only one Swiss stock exchange behind which stands the Swiss Electronic Stock Exchange, SECOM, Swiss Interbank Clearing, and Intersettle. These institutions handle the provision of market information as well as effecting fund transfers, trades, delivery, custody, control and management for all securities: shares, bonds, options and futures.

A proliferation of novel financial instruments was introduced in Switzerland and throughout the world to manage the increased volatilities of currencies and interest rates. With the creation of the Swiss Financial Futures and Options Exchange (SOFFEX) in the late 1980s, financial derivatives have been fully integrated into the new electronic stock exchange system. Quickly becoming the third largest derivatives exchange in Europe (in terms of contracts), SOFFEX is an example of how an institution can make a quantum leap by using modern information technology. In Switzerland, the remarkable growth of standardized, exchange-traded contracts on SOFFEX was overshadowed by the development of the covered options market.

Switzerland will introduce in 1996 the world's first, nation-wide, fully integrated, electronic security network. Many institutional, legislative and technological changes were required to effect the changes, and though refinements will continue to be made, Switzerland's new financial marketplace provides a solid foundation for the nation's global financial position in the twenty-first century.

This book is organized in thirteen chapters that cover the gamut of Swiss capital- and money markets. The transformation and present status of the Swiss capital market are described in such a way that every chapter is self-contained for easy reference. Chapter 1 (Switzerland and its success factors) identifies and explains the major causes of Switzerland's economic success – prominent among which is the nation's well-developed, efficient and safe financial system. In discussing these factors, the chapter also provides a demographic profile of Switzerland within the context of both historical and contemporary developments.

Chapter 2 (Recent economic and political history) provides an overview of recent economic and political developments in Switzerland, focusing on the main barometers of the nation's economic health; namely, unemployment and inflation. Swiss fiscal policy and the nation's relationship to the European Union are also discussed.

Chapter 3 (Swiss industry, agriculture and trade) identifies and describes Switzerland's major non-financial economic sectors. It goes on to provide a profile of the nation's international trade in goods and services, as well as its main trading partners.

Chapter 4 (Swiss banks and other financial institutions) focuses on the structure, conduct and performance of the Swiss banking industry in the domestic and international markets. Both on- and off-balance sheet activities are discussed. Chapter 5 (Swiss banking secrecy and related Swiss laws) complements Chapter 4 by focusing on Swiss banking secrecy laws. Perhaps no area of the Swiss financial system has received as much attention and as little understanding as these laws. This chapter separates myth from reality and explains current Swiss practice within the context of its historical development. The chapter also highlights Switzerland's rules pertaining to certain 'white-collar crimes', such as insider trading, money laundering and organized crime.

Chapter 6 (Swiss insurance and institutional investment markets) discusses the major financial institutions that compete with banks. The structure and conduct of the Swiss institutional investment market (eg, insurance companies, mutual funds and pension funds) are emphasized along with the competitive, financial activities of the Swiss Postal, Telephone and Telegraph service (PTT).

Chapter 7 (Swiss National Bank and monetary policy) discusses philosophy, tools and goals of the Swiss National Bank, the regulator of the Swiss money supply. It goes on to review the evolution of monetary policy from the collapse of the Bretton Woods system (1971-1973) to the 1990s, with particular emphasis on the years between 1984 and 1995.

Chapter 8 (The Swiss franc) discusses the size and structure of the foreign exchange market for Swiss francs, as well as the reason for the franc's strength (focusing on the 1984 to 1995 period). The connection between Switzerland's money supply growth and the international value of the franc, as well as the currency's gold backing and the likely impact the European Union's common currency will have on the Swiss franc are also covered.

Chapters 9, 10 and 11 discuss the major investment instruments and practices in the Swiss capital and money markets. Chapter 9 (Swiss debt markets) describes the domestic, foreign and Euro-markets for private and public Swiss franc debt. Among the major industrial nations, Switzerland has some of the most (long-term) and least (short-term) developed debt markets in the world. Chapter 9 highlights the major types of Swiss franc debt instruments, security issuing practices, taxes and (the newly proposed) listing requirements.

Chapter 10 (The Swiss equity market) is the equity counterpart to the discussion in Chapter 9. The size, structure and forces changing Switzerland's equity markets are the focus of this chapter. International comparisons, foreign participation, the (newly proposed) listing requirements, stock price indices, as well as the costs and taxes borne by investors are discussed.

Chapter 11 (Swiss derivative markets) explores financial derivatives, one of the fastest growing and most exciting segments of the Swiss financial system. The discussion centres on the size and structure of the Swiss derivative markets (OTC and exchange-traded), the important derivative instruments, their major users and the (newly proposed) listing requirements.

Chapter 12 (Major Swiss taxes on investors) explains the major taxes facing individuals investing in Switzerland. US Supreme Court Justice John Marshall once said 'The power to tax involves the power to destroy'. Perhaps no market better typifies this maxim than the international financial markets. Because taxes can discretely change investor returns, participants in the highly mobile international capital markets respond to these taxes by moving business elsewhere. Swiss politicians have been slow to learn that higher tax rates in these markets are usually accompanied by lower tax revenues and a diminished ability to compete.

The final chapter (A revolution in automation: "Finanzplatz Schweiz") is in many ways the most important chapter of all. It explains the extensive reforms that have taken place in Switzerland over the 1988 to 1995 period and culminated in the world's first, fully integrated, electronic security network. Starting in 1996, the network will link all salient parts of the Swiss securities markets. The Swiss reforms needed to realize this goal have been without parallel in the nation's history, requiring dramatic changes in laws, technology and institutions.

This book benefits greatly from the contributions of Professor John Marthinsen, a long time partner on many projects. Dr. Marthinsen is a Professor of Economics and International Business, Chairman of the Economics Department at Babson College in Wellesley, Massachusetts, which he has helped to make one of the leading business schools in the United States. Professor Marthinsen has spent much time on special assignments in Switzerland and learned from the inside many of the nuances of the Swiss financial markets.

An undertaking of this scale required the support and cooperation of many people. John Marthinsen and I offer special thanks to all those who helped to improve and avoid mistakes by critically reading the draft or parts thereof. To start, for a change, near the end of the alphabet, thanks are extended to: Mr. J. Wicks, an 'insider' who has covered this market as a journalist and editor for many years and who is now with Swiss Business; Dr. A. Foellmi, Director of Swiss National Bank, a humanist, diplomat and central banker who reviewed the respective chapters in his field of expertise; Dr. M. Gmünder, an international corporate lawyer who examined the legal aspects; Mr. M. Büttler, a Swiss tax expert, who reviewed tax issues and Mr. D. Biedermann, a successful portfolio manager, all three with Roche, and Ms. Dagmar Schulz, my secretary who coordinated the information flow among experts.

Special thanks are also extended to Babson College's competent and friendly library staff who helped to uncover many facts, articles and books, and to Babson College for its commitment to linking theory to practice and for its support in this undertaking. My ultimate 'thank you' goes to Brigitte, my wife, who has had to sacrifice 'just a few more minutes' for over 30 years. I join John Marthinsen in his gratitude to Laraine, his wife, and sons, Eric and Nils, for their support, patience, encouragement and understanding.

Henri B. Meier

AUTHORS' BIOGRAPHIES

Dr. Henri B. Meier – Dr. Meier earned his M.A. and Ph.D. degrees at the University of St. Gall, after working for Williams Brothers Company under what was meant to be his "Prakikunt". After promotion from bookkeeper to general accountant, he returned to the University of St. Gall and carried out post-graduate work at Columbia University, New York. Thereafter, he worked at the World Bank where his main responsibilities included financial and coporate analysis, country economic and risk analysis, negotiating loans (mainly with Latin American countries), supervising financing programmes and managing the Bank's lending programme for Central America and the Caribbean as Division Chief – one of the youngest – under Robert McNamara.

After leaving the World Bank, Dr. Meier joined the management team at Motor Colombus Cons. Eng. where he was in charge of international marketing and financing the company's own projects. In 1979, he joined Handelsbank NW Zurich to build up its investment banking activities, including public and private issues, project finance, syndication, mergers and acquisitions. As a member of the management committee, he was also responsible for securities and foreign exchange trading; money market and treasury operations.

Dr. Meier joined Roche in 1986 assuming responsibility for treasury, accounting/controlling, corporate planning, acquisitions/divestitures and investments reporting to the Chairman/CEO. He is responsible for implementing Roche's state-of-the-art management information system for top management and treasury MIS, and introducing a group strategic plan and a global cash management system. In 1988–99, the Group's legal and financial structures were completely overhauled under his direction and its shares listed on the stock exchange. In 1990, Roche was one of the first Swiss companies to introduce International Accounting Standards and a group audit. During his first 10 years at Roche, Dr. Meier managed the purchase and sale of some Sfr14 billion of operating businesses and was able to tap international capital markets at exceptionally low financing costs. Dr. Meier is the recipient of many awards for his accomplishments as CFO.

Dr. John E. Marthinsen – Dr. Marthinsen is Professor of Economics and International Business at Babson College, Wellesley, MA, an independent business school, ranked as the "Best Business Specialty School in the US" for the seventh consecutive year. He earned his B.A. *magna cum laude* at Lycoming College. His M.A. and Ph.D. were earned at the University of Connecticut, where he was awarded a National Science Foundation scholarship and was inducted into the Phi Beta Kappa and Phi Kappa Phi academic honour societies.

Dr. Marthinsen has gained extensive consulting experience working for domestic and international companies and banks, and the US government. His consulting assignments have included projects on derivative risk evaluation and management, strategic planning, corporate financial analysis, mergers, acquisitions and divestitures, international cash management systems, financial planning models, treasury transfer pricing, financial engineering and project finance. Dr. Marthinsen has been a member of the United Nations Association's Economic Policy Council, has lectured at the University of Bern, Switzerland and was co-founder of the *Interest Rate Monitor*, a monthly investment newsletter.

Since 1974, Dr. Marthinsen has taught at Babson College, where he has served since 1992 as Chairman of the Economics Division. He has won three distinguished teaching awards at Babson, lecturing in the areas of international finance, banking and global macroeconomic analysis. He is co-author of *Entrepreneurship, Productivity, and the Freedom of Information Act*.

CONTENTS

CONTENTS

CONTENTS

SWITZERLAND AND ITS SUCCESS FACTORS

Switzerland is a federal state composed of 20 cantons and 6 half cantons (see Appendix 1-A.1). Although it is one of the smallest countries in the world in terms of surface area (41,300 km²) and population (7 million), Switzerland generates one of the world's largest Gross National Products (US$260.4 billion in 1994) and has a thriving international sector (exports of goods and services, excluding investment income, and imports amounted to US$93.5 billion and US$80.9 respectively in 1994). Switzerland is also one of the top actors in international financial markets.[1]

The source of these achievements is not an abundance of natural resources, wide access to seaports or superior climate. On the contrary, only 26,651 km² are productive (9,458 km² meadows and arable land, 709 km² orchards and vineyards, 5,646 km² pastures and 10,838 km² forests).[2] The nation is covered with mountains, and its limited arable regions are densely populated. Swiss soil is generally not best suited for agricultural purposes. Moreover, Switzerland is landlocked with no direct access to the sea and few navigable rivers.

Switzerland's economic success is tied directly to a number of interrelated characteristics that are relatively easy to identify but difficult to imitate. Among them are:

- a reliable and well-trained labour force,
- an emphasis on quality rather than quantity,
- a stable constitutional, democratic political system and a respect for individual liberties and freedom of action,
- international political neutrality,
- conservative monetary and fiscal policies,
- a high rate of personal saving and capital surplus,
- a modern infrastructure, and
- a well-developed, efficient and safe financial system.

Overview of Switzerland and its success factors

---

[1]   Union Bank of Switzerland, *Switzerland in Figures:* 1995 Edition pp. 1-2.
[2]   Union Bank of Switzerland, p. 1.

1. Swiss labour force

The role of immigration for acquired skills

In 1994, Switzerland's population was 7,037,800, of which 19.2% were foreigners.[3] Its civilian labour force totalled 3,330,000 people of which almost 30% were foreigners.[4] For centuries, foreign workers have played an important role in the Swiss economy. Many of the comparative international advantages the nation enjoys today are connected to the skills brought by immigrants who were persecuted in foreign lands. From France came watchmakers and precious metal craftsmen. Italy supplied ribbonmakers and weavers. The Dutch brought expertise in the production of cotton and silk band weaving. A cursory look at the major Swiss industries (eg, chemicals, pharmaceuticals, machinery and watches) reveals that virtually all of them are rooted in skills that were imported, modified and improved.

The role of education for perpetuating, renewing and developing skills

Switzerland's ability to perpetuate and improve its basic skills can be attributed in large part to a national emphasis on education. Since 1874, the Swiss Constitution has provided free and compulsory schooling. As a result, illiteracy is virtually non-existent. The cantons have been in charge of education at all levels: elementary, secondary (both technical and college-preparatory) and universities[5], while the federal government has focused its attention on ensuring the quality of higher technical education[6], special education institutions (eg, vocational, agricultural and teacher training) and apprenticeships.[7]

Table 1.1

Swiss educational levels & enrollments: 1993/1994

Levels	Total students	% of total
Nursery school level	149,250	11.18
Compulsory school level	751,974	56.34
Secondary school level II	278,207	20.84
Higher (tertiary) level	148,664	11.14
University	91,037	6.82
Technical college	16,419	1.23
Technician school	5,475	0.41
Preparation for higher study or professional examinations	17,762	1.33
Other	17,971	1.35
Uncertain	6,703	0.50
Total	**1,334,798**	**100.00**

Source: Bundesamt für Statistik, *Statistisches Jahrbuch der Schweiz 1995* p. 336.

[3] Union Bank of Switzerland, p. 1.
[4] OECD, *Economic Surveys: 1994-1995: Switzerland* p. vii.
[5] Universities exist in Basel, Bern, Fribourg, Geneva, Lausanne, Neuchâtel, Zürich and St. Gallen, the latter being the University for Business Administration, Economic Law and Social Sciences. Both Lucerne and Chur have theological institutes. (See Appendix 1, Table 1-A.2)
[6] Federal Technical Schools are the ETH in Zürich and EPUL in Lausanne.
[7] The 26 school systems with their differing curricula, books and standards are an example of excessive federalistic forces and institutions in Switzerland.

For residents of most cantons, a minimum of nine years of education is required. Typically, after primary school (4 to 6 years), students must choose whether to take a technical education path that combines formal classroom education with apprenticeships, or to enter the gymnasium in order to pass their Matura examination and gain entry into a Swiss university. Only about 8 per cent of all Swiss students attend university-level schools (see Table 1.1). The Swiss apprenticeship system, which is supervised by the federal government, is widely considered a decisive comparative advantage. It is credited for integrating young people into the work process. The high quality levels of university entrants are due to the impressive hurdle that the Matura examinations represent. Teachers/professors are well paid in international comparison and the public[8] school system has a high average standard of teaching and performance.

An accent on language education

Four national languages are recognized in Switzerland. Excluding foreigners, German is spoken by about 65 per cent of the population, mainly in the northern, central and eastern regions. French is the language of approximately 18 per cent of the Swiss population that lives in western Switzerland. Concentrated in Ticino, the southern-most canton, Italian is spoken by 8 per cent of the Swiss population, and Romansch, a Latin derivative and the oldest of four official languages of Switzerland, is spoken by a very small segment of the population (less than 1 per cent) in the canton of Graubünden.[9]

Dialects vary from canton to canton and from town to town, a phenomenon typical of the alpine region of Europe, but in Switzerland, "Schwyzertütsch", an unwritten Swiss German dialect, was even encouraged and promoted. Because of its size, the strong influence of bordering nations and the limited range of its regional dialects, the Swiss have put great emphasis on multilingual skills. Leading newspapers, magazines and advertisements are written in the mother language (German, French, Italian and Romansch), and most radio and television broadcasts are delivered in the same, but increasingly the dialect is finding its way into the mass media.

The versatility and ease with which the Swiss are able to communicate in many languages has been a valuable asset in establishing banking, investment and trade relationships throughout the world. Because their local dialect is spoken and/or understood by so few people, the Swiss educational system is oriented to accommodate the rest of the world rather than expecting the rest of the world to accommodate the Swiss language and culture.

The role of immigration for menial skills

Most highly educated individuals expect above average salaries. At the same time, within any nation there are occupations, such as crop harvesting, road construction and sanitation, that do not require advanced learning and generally offer relatively low salaries. Since the beginning of this century, the Swiss have increasingly filled these labour needs by using foreigners (ie, Gastarbeiter or guest workers). After World War II, when most major nations abided by the Bretton Woods agreement, the undervalued Swiss franc

---

8 The word, "public", stands for what it really means.
9 Considerable amounts of tax funds are spent each year to keep this language alive.

made investments in Switzerland so attractive that the resulting labour shortage enticed large numbers of foreign labourers to immigrate. Since the 1960s, when foreigners accounted for approximately 30 per cent of total labour force, the Swiss government has tried to contain further immigration. The current level of unskilled foreign labour in the work-force (about 18 per cent) and the threat of more to come have created internal social frictions. Labour mobility issues were central to the Swiss decision against joining the European Economic Area in 1992.

Unions

In general, the relationship between Swiss unions and management is constructive. Businesses, unions and the government have worked together to keep the unemployment rate at very low levels. Consequently, unions rarely strike and seldom resist technological innovations or fight for excessive salary increases (see Table 1.2). They seem to have a preference for job security over wage increases, but have fared extremely well with this policy over the past decades. Throughout the 1990s, Swiss workers have been among the highest paid labour forces in the world.

The two largest blue collar unions, the Trade Union Federation and the Christian National Trade Union, and the largest white collar union, the Union of Swiss Employees' Associations, are umbrella organizations representing many industries. Their role is to provide a united labour front for negotiations and discussions with the government. Wage and salary negotiations for organized labour are handled at the industry or company level.

Table 1.2

Strikes and lock outs in Switzerland: 1980-1992

	1980	*1985*	*1990*	*1991*	*1992*
Cases	5	3	2	1	3
Affected businesses	330	10	2	1	18
Workers involved (maximum)	3,582	366	578	51	220
Lost workdays (approximately)	5,718	72	4,090	51	673

Source: Bundesamt für Statistik, *Statistisches Jahrbuch der Schweiz 1995* p. 110.

2. Research and quality

Due to its diminutive size and lack of raw materials, Switzerland is not able to compete in areas that require low resource costs and significant economies of scale. The only way the country has been able to compete at international levels has been to provide value added in the form of quality and product differentiation. Research, development, training through apprenticeships, greater attention to detail, refined quality control processes and innovation have been the keys to success in Swiss manufacturing.

In 1992, Switzerland devoted 2.7 per cent of its GDP to research and development.[10] Most of these expenditures (over 70 per cent) were conducted by the private sec-

---

[10] Bundesamt für Statistik, *Statistisches Jahrbuch der Schweiz 1995* (Verlag Neue Zürcher Zeitung, 1994) p. 348.

tor. Of them, chemicals, electronics, machinery and metallurgy accounted for the overwhelming majority (approximately 80 per cent). Investments in R&D sacrifice current consumption for uncertain future rewards, but Switzerland has been able to reap huge dividends from them, and it is clear that their continuation is essential to the nation's economic vitality.

Two outstanding characteristics describe Switzerland's unique political system:

- extreme federalistic tendencies have resulted in the total diffusion and decentralization of power in the formal structures, and
- consensus politics on the part of the leading parties has developed as a result of the "magic formula" under which the four largest parties rule the country.

3. Switzerland's political system

Characteristics

Switzerland's executive branch of government is run by a seven member coalition of representatives from the four largest political parties. This magic formula is a recipe for peace and freedom, but it takes away some citizens' power, since consensus must be reached ultimately at the top level among the four parties (see pages 1-6 and 1-7, Federal Government). In quiet times of economic growth and wealth, this formula has proven to be beneficial and easy to administer, but in the early 1990s, the formula seemed to be lacking a few ingredients.

Switzerland had to adjust, making structural changes and liquidating many privileges. Politicians found it increasingly difficult to agree on cuts and there were few favours available to distribute. The heavily protected domestic sectors (eg, agriculture) were extremely well-represented politically and able to maintain generous privileges. Government became increasingly the distributor of favours in the form of subsidies. In 1993, over half of the federal government's revenues were distributed as subsidies.[11]

Hardly any other people show such a deep-rooted mistrust of any power accumulation as the Swiss. It is no wonder that a monarchy or dictatorship failed to take root. All political institutions and procedures seem to be geared toward diffusing political power. A review of the tax situation, for instance, shows that roughly one-third of the nation's fiscal income goes to the municipalities, a little more than one-third to the cantons and the remaining portion to the federal government.

Typically, at the top of each political unit, one finds councils with a presiding speaker. "Beware of strong men" is the rule everywhere. The institutions of *initiative* and *referendum* reflect the same basic mistrust. Any law issued by the parliament has to be submitted to public vote if a relatively small number of people request it. The same is true for any new draft law proposed by citizens. As the world gets more complex and interrelated, this system poses great challenges to its politicians.

---

[11] Bundesamt für Statistik, p. 394.

Constitution and democracy

After its foundation in 1291, Switzerland functioned as a loose alliance – a defence pact[12] – of autonomous cantons. Only in the 19th century was it subjected to centralist forces, but the constitution of 1848 still left most of the powers in the hands of the cantons by creating a confederation. The constitution set up a federal state, established a free trade area among the cantons and divided power between the federal and cantonal governments. All powers that were not specifically designated for the federal government remained with the cantons. To the federal government went the responsibility for such functions as postal and telegraph services, coinage and paper currency issuance, mass transportation (ie, railroad, aviation and navigation), negotiations with foreign countries and defence.

Ultimate power in Switzerland resides with the people, and Swiss citizens 18 years and older have the right to vote.

The Swiss Constitution is constructed so that:

- any legislative change in the constitution must be brought before the public,
- a relatively small number of citizens have the right to bring any new laws and treaties to a popular vote (ie, a referendum) and
- citizens have the right to initiate changes in the constitution.[13]

If a referendum is signed by at least 50,000 voters (or eight cantons), legislation passed by parliament is brought to a nationwide vote. If at least 100,000 voters sign an initiative (or if at least one of the Houses of the Federal Assembly votes affirmatively), a nationwide vote is held to change the Constitution or federal law.[14]

In some cantons and half cantons (specifically, Glarus, Appenzell Innerrhoden, Appenzell Ausserrhoden, Obwalden and Nidwalden), true visible, direct democracy still reigns. Elections and decisions on pending issues are conducted at open-air meetings (Landsgemeinde) with votes registered via a show of hands.

Federal government

The Swiss form of government is a combination of direct and indirect democracy. Parliament, the Federal Assembly, is a bicameral body with both houses (the National Council and the Council of States) having equal power. The National Council (Nationalrat) has membership limited to 200 members, with representation apportioned according to relative cantonal populations. Representatives are part-time officials with four-year terms of office.

The Council of States (Ständerat) is composed of 52 members, two from each of the twenty full cantons and one member from each of the six half-cantons. These representatives are also part-time, but their terms vary depending on the wishes of each canton. The Swiss system of checks and balances requires that bills be debated and passed by both chambers before they can be enacted into law.

---

[12] Each canton had its own laws, foreign policies, currency, army and measures.

[13] An initiative is a popular proposal for a new law or new articles in the Constitution. A referendum is a popular vote on a law passed by Parliament (federal or cantonal).

[14] The relative ease of changing their Constitution is one reason Switzerland has made nearly five times the number of amendments as the US.

The Federal Council (Bundesrat) is the executive arm of the government, responsible to parliament and composed of seven members who are elected for four-year terms by a joint session of both councils. Each Federal Council member is responsible for a federal department (ie, Finance, Foreign Affairs, Interior, Justice and Police, Defence, Economics, Transport and Energy). The President is responsible only for chairing the Federal Council meetings.[15] This position carries no constitutional powers and is alternated among Federal Council members on a yearly basis, with no president serving consecutive terms. Decisions are taken as a team, and the majority determines the Federal Council's view.

For over 35 years, the composition of the Federal Council has been shared by the four major political parties with the following unwritten allocation rule: two Social Democrats, two Liberals, two Christian Democrats and one Swiss People's Party representative. This concordance, as it is known, has brought stability to the government, but many feel that it has also bred a certain degree of inertia and sluggishness in the executive branch. That may be permissible when times are good but is less popular when times are hard. In the 1990s, rising federal deficits have induced citizen resistance to generous spending plans sufficient to fulfil the wishes of the politicians of all four parties.

The judiciary

Justice is administered primarily at the cantonal level. Each canton has its own independent system of civil and criminal justice, another example of excessively federalistic tendencies. The country's supreme court, the Federal Court, is located in Lausanne and composed of thirty judges who are appointed for six-year terms by the Federal Assembly. The Federal Court's jurisdiction has been deliberately limited. Its main responsibilities are in the areas of adjudicating suits between the cantonal governments and the federal government, between corporations and individuals, and between cantons. Railway cases and treason are also handled by the Federal Court. The Federal Court can review cantonal court decisions that involve federal laws and can review administrative rulings of federal departments, but it has no power to review the constitutionality of federal legislation.

Cantonal legislatures

Each canton has a unicameral, elected legislature with a legislative council and an administrative executive council. As previously mentioned, five of the smaller half-cantons vote by means of Landsgemeinde, a form of direct democracy where citizens vote in an open forum. Since the 1970s, women have had suffrage rights in all but one canton and in 1990, the last bastion fell when Appenzell Innerrhoden gave women this right.

4. Swiss neutrality

Since the opening of the Gotthard Pass in the 13th century, Switzerland's location has been of strategic value for north-south European transport and travel (ie, from the Mediterranean

---

[15] In a recent poll, over 50% of the Swiss did not know who the President of the Swiss Federal Council was.

to Germany). The threat of invasion was the basis for the 1291 mutual assistance treaty between the cantons Uri, Schwyz and Unterwalden that created Switzerland.

Prior to the industrial revolution, Switzerland was a poor country. Internal job prospects were so scant that for centuries it gained a world-wide reputation as a supplier of mercenary soldiers. For many prominent Swiss families, the recruitment and the organization of Swiss mercenary armies for foreign powers became their main source of income. Nevertheless, following a public outcry after the Battle of Marignano in 1515 when 12,000 Swiss mercenaries lost their lives, mercenary services were forbidden in Switzerland. Thereafter, the nation adopted a policy of neutrality. Three hundred years later, this policy was internationally recognized by the Congress of Vienna.[16]

Over the past century and a half, the position of armed neutrality has helped to fuel Switzerland's economic growth. During periods of conflict, it has enabled Switzerland to supply goods and services equally to all warring factions and to provide safe haven for people and international capital fleeing from economic, political or other threats. Moreover, the absence of war has allowed Switzerland to keep its infrastructure intact. During World Wars I and II, Switzerland's industrial capacity remained unscathed because of its neutral position.

5. Conservative monetary and fiscal policies

The Swiss central bank (hereafter called Swiss National Bank) is independent from the federal government and has a tradition of keeping inflation low. Since the end of World War II, the Swiss franc has been a role model for the international financial community. Positive current account surpluses and the gold backing of the Swiss franc have helped to stabilize prices and strengthen the domestic currency, but the main key to the Swiss franc's strength can be directly tied to the conservative financial policies enacted by the Swiss National Bank. Its anti-inflationary policies enjoy the backing of all political parties and most public interest groups.

The Swiss franc has floated relative to other currencies since 1973 giving the Swiss National Bank greater control over the domestic monetary base. At the same time, due to the nation's vulnerability to large international capital flows and its dependence on international trade, the Swiss National Bank has intervened to ensure the nation's exchange rate did not deviate too far from what it considered to be relative norms.

The Swiss National Bank's monetary philosophy is one of pragmatic monetarism, where monetary rules are preferred over human discretion. Believing there is a direct link between money growth and inflation, the Swiss National Bank has been able to maintain price stability by keeping a tight rein on money supply.[17] In fact, the only time this policy has been substantially altered was in the face of what were perceived to be destabilizing international capital flows.

Swiss monetary policy is generally not relied on as the basis for stimulating eco-

---

[16] Since 1815, it has been unconstitutional for the federal government to form political alliances or declare war except for self-defence.

[17] The Swiss National Bank controls the money supply by targeting the medium-term monetary base. See Chapter 7.

nomic growth. By contrast, fiscal policy is potentially more stimulative (or restrictive), but is inflexible and unpredictable in its implementation. Any federal tax decision can be challenged by popular referendum that may take months to decide, whereas money supply changes can be made instantly.

The biggest challenge to the Swiss National Bank's monetary policy in recent years has been monopolistic price increases imposed in the public-sector and higher taxes. To prevent the inefficiencies of the public sector from destabilizing the Swiss franc, the central bank felt obliged to impose highly restrictive monetary policies.

Switzerland has a well-earned reputation for acting as a conduit for international finance – taking deposits from investors world-wide and lending them outside Switzerland. Less well understood is the Swiss penchant for saving and its role as a net capital exporter. For decades, the Swiss have consumed much less than they earned. The fruits of this abstention from consumption are the nation's first class domestic infrastructure and its position as one of the world's largest net international investors. These investments earn billions of Swiss francs each year and contribute toward current account surpluses in its balance of payments.

Figure 1.1 compares the rate of saving as a percentage of GDP between Switzerland and other industrial countries. Of these nations, only Japan has, in recent years, been consistently above Switzerland in its willingness and ability to save.

6. A high rate of personal saving and a capital surplus

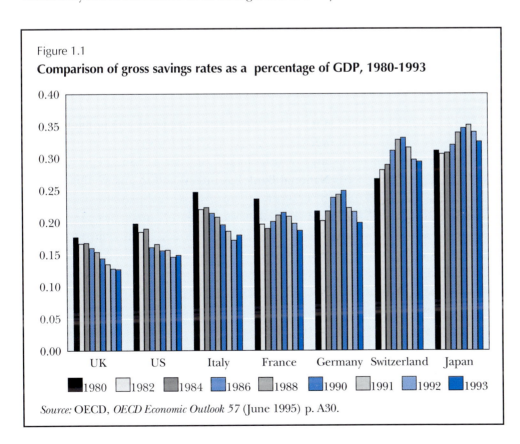

Figure 1.1

Comparison of gross savings rates as a percentage of GDP, 1980-1993

Legend: ■ 1980 ☐ 1982 ■ 1984 ■ 1986 ■ 1988 ■ 1990 ☐ 1991 ■ 1992 ■ 1993

Source: OECD, *OECD Economic Outlook 57* (June 1995) p. A30.

7. A modern and efficient infrastructure

Transportation

Switzerland has one of the world's most highly developed and efficient transportation and communication systems. Over 5,000 kilometres (3,100 miles) of railroad tracks (nearly 60 per cent federally owned), as well as 71,000 kilometres (44,000 miles) of roads criss-cross the nation. The Swiss railways have been electrified for decades, thereby reducing pollution and creating a significant demand for electricity. Nearly 40 per cent of Switzerland's electricity consumption is produced by nuclear power plants. "Rail 2000", an initiative begun in 1985, aims to improve, upgrade and expand domestic rail services.[18]

Because of Switzerland's central location, international travellers between Germany, Italy, France and Austria are likely to travel Swiss highways or railways. The network of national expressways is free of tolls, but a nominal fee is charged to foreign travellers for a *vignette* (permission sticker) to travel them. In addition to roads, the nation has a well-developed tunnel and bridge system that has significantly reduced north-south and east-west travelling times. In 1881, the Gotthard Tunnel (14.9 km) was built linking the cantons of Uri in the north and Ticino in the south of the Alps. In the early 1900s, the Lötschberg Tunnel (1911 – 14.6 km) linking Brig to Bern and Basel, and the Simplon Tunnel – I and II – (1906 and 1922 – 19.8 km) connecting Brig and Domodossola (Italy) were constructed. The latest major railway tunnel, the Furka (15.4 km) was opened in 1982.

At present, Switzerland, in an agreement with the EU, has undertaken to construct two transalpine railway tunnels by the year 2005 in order to accommodate the rising demand for north-south transport services. Approved in 1992 by popular referendum, the initiative commits Switzerland to building a 57 kilometre tunnel under the Gotthard and a 33 kilometre tunnel through the Lötschberg.[19] Work was to start as soon as the means of financing these projects were secured.

In addition to its railways and roads, Switzerland has four international airports – Zurich, Geneva, Basel and Bern, and its national carrier, Swissair, is owned jointly by the federal government, the cantons and private investors.

8. A well-developed financial system

In 1992, banking services accounted for about 6.5 per cent of the Swiss GDP, and in 1994, Swiss banks employed a little over 121,000 people, 3.6 per cent of the nation's total employment.[20] Because Switzerland is a small country with limited investment opportunities, the net inflow of international investment funds has always created a challenge. If all this foreign capital were combined with internally-generated saving and invested inside Switzerland, domestic rates of return would soon plummet below international levels. Over the years, institutions and competencies have been developed to efficiently and effectively invest these surplus funds abroad. Switzerland has thus become a financial turntable, importing funds and subsequently exporting them to profitable opportunities in other financial centres.

---

[18] Bundesamt für Statistik, *Statistisches Jahrbuch der Schweiz 1995* (Verlag Neue Zürcher Zeitung, 1994) pp. 199 & 240.

[19] OECD, *Economic Surveys 1993-1994: Switzerland* p. 72.

[20] See Chapter 4.

The origins of Swiss banking developed in the international trade fairs of Geneva, the Alpine north-south trade and the 15th century church council of Basel. During this early period, Geneva, Basel and Zurich became important financial centres. The growing volume of European trade created the need for a developed financial sector to support merchant and trade companies' requirements for commercial financing, fund transfers and capital procurement. Private banks – Marchands-Banquiers – arose to fill these needs and because of the problems and practical details surrounding collections, reimbursements and defaults, their affiliations spread to leading global centres.

Switzerland is one of the most intensively banked countries in the world. The competition for banking offices has been fierce and current concerns about efficiency and profitability are being carefully analyzed to determine whether, how and where to cut back. As a consequence, the number of establishments is gradually shrinking.

9. Natural resources

Switzerland has no natural resources worth mentioning. The strip of rich agricultural soil on the Swiss Plateau which lies between the Alps and the Jura is quite modest. Going beyond the traditional definitions, water is a resource that has been thoroughly exploited. Without the rivers and the difference in altitudes, industrialization in the mid-19th century would not have been possible. Today, 83 per cent of Switzerland's energy needs are met by imports.[21] Electricity from hydropower accounts for 16 per cent of total energy consumption with nuclear power contributing 23 per cent.[22] A sophisticated system of pump storage plants allows the Swiss to import electricity when it is cheap (eg, off-hours and during the summer) to pump water to dams in the mountains and utilize it for high tariff exports at peak hours/seasons.

Similarly, Swiss lakes, rivers, mountains and scenic cities are carefully managed as a resource for promoting tourism, an economic sector that is the third largest export industry, accounting for approximately 13 per cent of all export revenues (almost 8 per cent of GDP) and 360,000 jobs.[23] In 1993, Swiss tourist earnings amounted to Sfr 12.8 billion and Swiss tourists' expenditures abroad were estimated at Sfr 10.6 billion leaving a net positive balance of Sfr2.2 billion (ie, 11 per cent of Switzerland's current account surplus).[24]

Switzerland's geographic position in the heart of Europe is a potential resource that provides opportunities for transfer traffic which has been exploited since historic times. Having no obvious natural resources may be a blessing in disguise, because it forces nations like Switzerland and Singapore to utilize what they have.

---

[21] Bundesamt für Statistik, *Statistisches Jahrbuch der Schweiz 1995* (Verlag Neue Zürcher Zeitung, 1994) p. 195.
[22] Bundesamt für Statistik, p. 200.
[23] Bundesamt für Statistik, pp. 223 & 237.
[24] Bundesamt für Statistik, p. 233.

Appendix 1-A

Table 1-A.1

Swiss Cantons: population and income, 1992

Number	Canton	Population	Income (Sfr millions)	Status
1	Aargau	511,979	20,643	Full Canton
2	Appenzell Ausserrhoden	53,449	1,907	Half Canton
3	Appenzell Innerrhoden	14,548	462	Half Canton
4	Basel-Land (Bâle)	233,151	10,266	Half Canton
5	Basel-Stadt	196,634	11,845	Half Canton
6	Bern	953,458	38,431	Full Canton
7	Fribourg (Freiburg)	214,555	8,000	Full Canton
8	Genève (Genf)	383,911	21,973	Full Canton
9	Glarus	38,976	1,804	Full Canton
10	Graubünden (Grisons)	179,279	7,226	Full Canton
11	Jura	68,323	2,157	Full Canton
12	Luzern (Lucerne)	331,830	12,018	Full Canton
13	Neuchâtel (Neuenburg)	162,586	5,985	Full Canton
14	Nidwalden	34,866	1,456	Half Canton
15	Obwalden	30,247	1,006	Half Canton
16	St. Gallen	432,819	16,456	Full Canton
17	Schaffhausen	73,028	2,744	Full Canton
18	Schwyz	116,090	4,345	Full Canton
19	Solothurn	234,878	8,936	Full Canton
20	Thurgau	213,167	7,231	Full Canton
21	Ticino (Tessin)	294,108	10,307	Full Canton
22	Uri	35,544	1,250	Full Canton
23	Valais (Wallis)	262,389	8,392	Full Canton
24	Vaud (Waadt)	593,007	24,233	Full Canton
25	Zug	87,065	5,884	Full Canton
26	Zürich	1,158,007	67,387	Full Canton

Source: Taschenstatistik der Schweiz, Bern/Schweiz (1994) pp. 2 & 11.

Table 1-A.2

Major Swiss universities and graduate schools

Universities	Enrollment	Type	Founded
University of Basel	6,600	Cantonal	1460
University of Bern	8,600	Cantonal	1528
University of Fribourg	5,300	Cantonal	1889
University of Lausanne	6,400	Cantonal	1537
University of Genève	11,400	Cantonal	1559
University of Neuchâtel	2,200	Cantonal	1838
University of Zürich	18,600	Cantonal	1833
Federal Institute of Technology in Zurich (ETH)	8,600	Federal	1855
School of Technology in Lausanne (EPUL)	3,800	Federal	1853
University of St. Gallen	3,200	Cantonal	1899
IMD (Institute for Management Development)	83*	Private	1947

* Number represents the number of full-time students. IMD's primary focus is on short-term executive education programs.

Source: Pro Helvetia: Arts Council of Switzerland, "Education and Training," *Information Sheets on Switzerland* (Zurich: 1987).

RECENT ECONOMIC AND POLITICAL HISTORY

By virtually any measure, Switzerland enjoys one of the highest standards of living in the world (see Table 2.1). Yet, a little over 150 years ago, this nation was one of the poorest in Europe. The industrial revolution gave Switzerland the opportunity to escape from the limits that the paucity of arable land had imposed on its capacity to produce.

Overview of the Swiss standard of living

Over the period between 1984 and 1995, Switzerland came full cycle from expansion to recession and then back again to expansion. The years from 1983 to 1990 (inclusive) were ones of uninterrupted economic growth averaging 2.6 per cent a year (see Figure 2.1). This performance was solidly above the 1.7 per cent growth experienced over the previous cyclical upturn from 1976 to 1981, but milder than the 3.3 per cent average annual rate attained by the OECD nations (see Figure 2.2).

Near the end of the 1980s, Switzerland experienced an unusually high level of inflation. Starting in 1987 (at 1.4 per cent), the consumer price index climbed to 5.8 per cent in 1991 (see Figure 2.3).

1. Recent economic developments

Table 2.1

International comparisons of living standards (US$)

	Switzerland	US	Japan	France	Germany
GDP per person[a] (1992)	35,041	23,228	29,460	23,043	27,770
Per capita consumption (1992)	13,043	15,637	11,191	11,144	11,186
Passenger Cars[b] (1990)	441	568	282	413	480
Telephones[b] (1990)	905	509	421	482	671
Televisions[b] (1989)	406	814	610	400	506
Doctors[b] (1991)	3.0	2.3	1.6	2.7	3.2
Infant Mortality[c] (1991)	6.2	8.9	4.6	7.3	7.1

[a] Using current purchasing power parity
[b] per 1,000 inhabitants
[c] per 1,000 live births

Source: OECD, *Economic Surveys: 1994-1995, Switzerland* Basic Statistics: International Comparisons, p. 146.

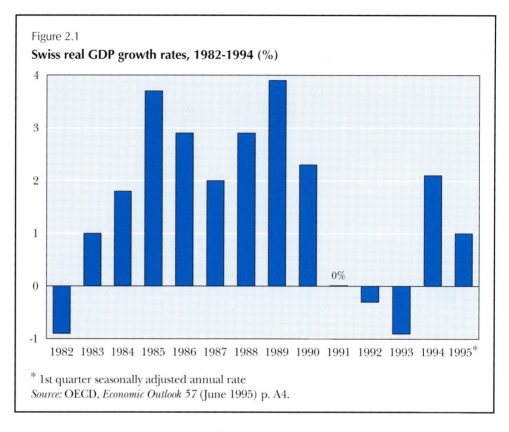

Figure 2.1

Swiss real GDP growth rates, 1982-1994 (%)

* 1st quarter seasonally adjusted annual rate
Source: OECD, *Economic Outlook 57* (June 1995) p. A4.

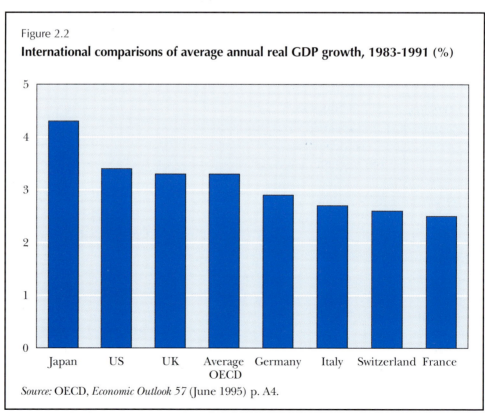

Figure 2.2

International comparisons of average annual real GDP growth, 1983-1991 (%)

Source: OECD, *Economic Outlook 57* (June 1995) p. A4.

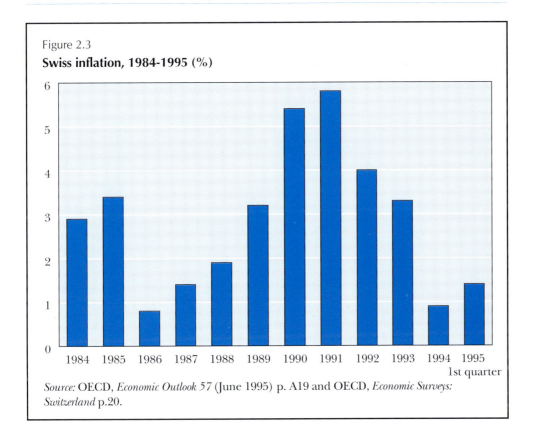

Figure 2.3

Swiss inflation, 1984-1995 (%)

Source: OECD, *Economic Outlook 57* (June 1995) p. A19 and OECD, *Economic Surveys: Switzerland* p.20.

In response to rising inflation, in 1988 the Swiss National Bank began to reduce the growth of the money supply, causing a recession that began in the first part of 1991 and lasted nearly three years to 1993 (see Figure 2.1).

Unemployment

For years, the Swiss unemployment rate was below 1 per cent and the envy of most OECD countries (see Figure 2.4). Residents were rarely threatened with job dismissals and typically, the unemployed could find jobs within a few days. The 1991-1993 recession significantly increased unemployment to 2.5 per cent in 1992, 4.5 per cent in 1993 and 4.7 per cent in 1994.

Two complementary but disturbing remnants of the recession were a worsening of Switzerland's structural unemployment rate and a rise in the nation's long-term (ie, over one year) unemployment rate. Recent studies estimate that Switzerland's structural (ie, natural) rate of unemployment increased from 1 per cent to 3.5 per cent indicating that future solutions to the unemployment problem could be in prudent microeconomic policies influencing incentives rather than macroeconomic policies influencing growth of GDP.[1]

In 1990, approximately 1,000 Swiss residents (7 per cent of the total unemployed) were out of work for more than one year compared to over 49,000 Swiss residents (about 29 per cent of the total unemployed) in 1994.[2] Equally disturbing was the uncharacteris-

---

[1] OECD, *Economic Surveys 1994-1995: Switzerland* p. 14.
[2] OECD, *Economic Surveys 1994-1995: Switzerland* pp. 11-14.

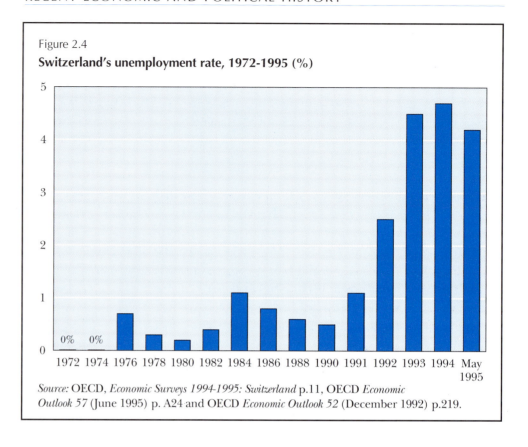

Figure 2.4

Switzerland's unemployment rate, 1972-1995 (%)

Source: OECD, *Economic Surveys 1994-1995: Switzerland* p.11, OECD *Economic Outlook 57* (June 1995) p. A24 and OECD *Economic Outlook 52* (December 1992) p.219.

tic response of employment to improving economic conditions. After the recessions of 1976 and 1983, employment began to rise after two quarters of expansion. By contrast, it took over one year (4 quarters) for the Swiss employment rate to reverse direction and rise after the 1991-1993 recession.

The changes in employment were not distributed equally among industries. Total employment peaked in 1991 at 3.87 million workers and then fell 2.4 per cent (losing approximately 94,000 jobs) until 1994. Most of this decline was suffered by the manufacturing industry where employment fell 12 per cent (representing 100,000 jobs) between 1990 and 1993. Over the same period, the services industry actually increased employment by about 26,000 jobs.[3]

The impact of a stronger Swiss franc and high wages on unemployment

The increase in unemployment during the early 1990s was atypical because it grew at a faster rate than real GDP fell, indicating that other causes besides the cyclical downturn were at work. High Swiss wages and the strong Swiss franc appear to be two of the most important reasons. A 1995 study by the Association of Machinery Manufacturers reported that between 1985 and 1995, its members had increased their employment in foreign countries by 57 per cent while simultaneously cutting employment in Switzerland by 21 per cent. The survey went on to show that in 1985, its members had 87 per cent of their capital located in Switzerland, but that, by 1995, this figure had fallen to 78 per

---

[3] OECD, *Economic Surveys 1994-1995: Switzerland* See footnotes 13, 14 and 15 on p. 10.

cent. In short, for many companies, Switzerland had become too expensive a place to do business.[4]

Watchmaker SMH and apparel manufacturer Calida were good examples of the growing trend to locate production overseas. SMH decided to transfer much of its production to Thailand and Malaysia, eliminating nearly 260 subcontracting jobs in the French- and Italian-speaking sections of Switzerland. Similarly, Calida announced plans to reduce its production of underwear in Switzerland to 20 per cent of total production from 65 per cent by the year 2000.[5]

Institutional causes of unemployment and structural unemployment in Switzerland

Other institutional and structural factors have also caused Switzerland's unemployment rate to rise. For instance, job opportunities have been increasingly unsuited to the pool of available Swiss skills and the location of these jobs has often been at variance with the areas of unemployed workers. A lack of responsiveness in the foreign and female work force has also been an ingredient behind the rise in Swiss joblessness. In the past, unemployment was managed by reducing the number of foreign work permits and counting on female participation rates to drop as jobs became harder to find. With the rise in permanent worker status for many foreign workers and the increased full-time participation rate of women, these traditional patterns have changed.

A final element in the unemployment equation was Switzerland's introduction in 1977 of compulsory unemployment insurance. In earlier years, approximately 80 per cent of the Swiss labour force had no unemployment insurance.[6] The new legislation provided incentives for the unemployed to register and also gave liberal benefits to the unemployed.[7] Both changes caused an increase in the official unemployment statistics.

In reaction to the rise in structural unemployment, the Swiss Parliament passed in June 1995 a law that makes the continued receipt of unemployment insurance benefits contingent, after a certain period, dependent upon the recipients attending employment and training programs.[8] Furthermore, the waiting period for unemployment benefits has been extended to one year (from 20 days) for school leavers.[9]

The 1991-1993 recession was long, but not especially steep (see Figure 2.1). As a result, inflationary pressures, particularly at the consumer goods level, diminished at an uncharacteristically slow pace. The battle to reduce inflation was improved by a strengthening Swiss franc, but was made more difficult by the services industry where productivity

Inflation

[4] Economic Intelligence Unit Limited, *EIU Country Report 2nd Quarter 1995* p. 14.
[5] Economic Intelligence Unit Limited, p. 23.
[6] IMF, *IMF Survey: Swiss Economy Faces Unaccustomed Challenges* (April 18 1994) p. 127.
[7] Unemployment benefits in Switzerland are now more liberal than in the US, Germany or France. Moreover, between 1977 and 1994 their duration has doubled and their rate of increase has outstripped the increase in Swiss nominal wages. See IMF, *IMF Survey: Swiss Economy Faces Unaccustomed Challenges* (April 18 1994) p. 127.
[8] OECD, *Economic Survey 1994-1995: Switzerland* p. 66.
[9] An emergency decree in 1995 temporarily raised the unemployment insurance contribution rate from 2 per cent to 3 per cent and suspended benefits for the first week of unemployment. These emergency provisions were instituted to reduce the unemployment insurance deficit and were effective only for 1995. See, OECD, *Economic Survey 1994-1995: Switzerland* p. 66.

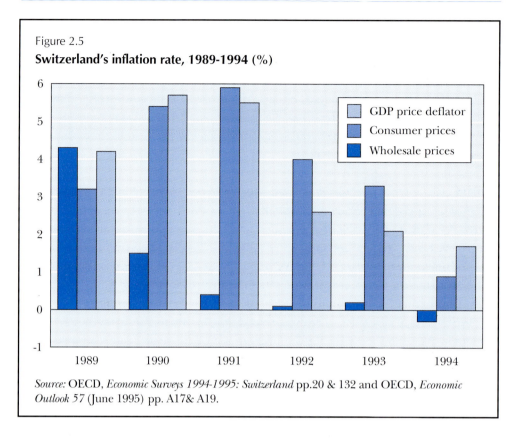

Figure 2.5

Switzerland's inflation rate, 1989-1994 (%)

Source: OECD, *Economic Surveys 1994-1995: Switzerland* pp.20 & 132 and OECD, *Economic Outlook 57* (June 1995) pp. A17& A19.

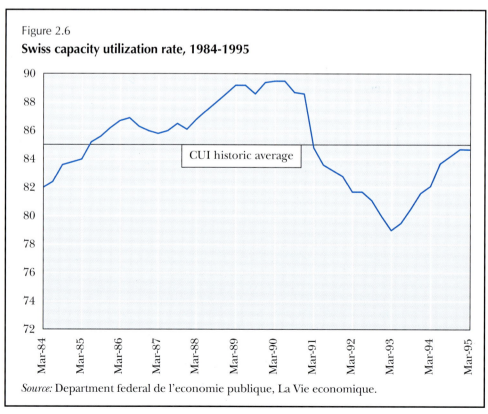

Figure 2.6

Swiss capacity utilization rate, 1984-1995

Source: Department federal de l'economie publique, La Vie economique.

increases were meagre and businesses were sheltered from foreign competition.[10] From 1991 to 1994, inflation in the services sector declined much more slowly than in the real goods sector. Moreover, the inflationary momentum built up at the end of the 1980s was difficult to reverse since contractual wages in Switzerland were often adjusted automatically to compensate for the preceding year's inflation. In the government sector, price increases were not restrained by competition.

As slow as it was to subside, the Swiss National Bank successfully reduced the consumer price index below its 1 per cent target by 1994.[11] There were good reasons to believe that inflation would stay under control for some time to come. Unemployment had curtailed union demands for pay increases, reducing the threat of cost-push inflation. An ever-strengthening Swiss franc had kept import prices low and restricted the price increases of import-competing Swiss goods.[12] Moreover, the rate of capacity utilization had increased after 1993, but still remained below the historic long-term average rate of 85 per cent (see Figure 2.6). Finally, price increases in the service industry, which accounts for 56 per cent of the Swiss consumer price index, slowed in 1994 to 1.4 per cent.[13]

During the first six months of 1995, the Swiss (12 month) CPI increased from 0.5 per cent to 2.1 per cent. The short term blip in prices was anticipated and did not affect the Swiss National Bank's medium-term monetary policy.[14] A large part of this surge was attributed to Switzerland's January 1 introduction of the value added tax (VAT). On most goods, the VAT produced only a small inflationary effect, raising taxes from 6.2 per cent to 6.5 per cent. Inflation was mildly reinforced by a 2 per cent VAT on some previously untaxed necessities (eg, food and medication). The largest impact was on services where taxes rose from 0 per cent to 6.5 per cent. Partially offsetting these inflationary influences was the reduction in company costs of production due to the elimination of turnover tax on real investments and intermediate products.

Government fiscal policy and the budget

Switzerland's general government expenditures (ie, federal, cantonal and municipal spending) are below most European nations, but have increased over the 1990s to levels that are above the US and Japan and much closer to the OECD average (see Table 2.2).

As a percent of GDP, Switzerland divides government spending fairly evenly among the federal, cantonal and municipal governments (see Figure 2.7). Over the first four years of the 1990s, each of these three levels of government ran budget deficits requiring financing from the Swiss capital markets (see Table 2.3).

Swiss fiscal policy at the federal level has neither the flexibility nor the power found in most developed nations. It lacks timeliness because any major tax policy in Switzerland can be challenged by a nationwide referendum. Moreover, its revenues are vulnerable because of the volatility of the stamp tax and withholding tax which together comprise

---

[10] OECD, *Economic Surveys: 1993-1994: Switzerland* p. 26.
[11] At the wholesale level, inflation had been brought under control as early as 1991.
[12] The Swiss total supply index (ie, the price of producer and import goods) fell from 4.3 per cent in 1989 to 1.5 per cent, 0.4 per cent, 0.1 per cent, 0.2 per cent and -0.3 per cent over the 1990 to 1994 period. OECD, *Economic Survey 1994-1995: Switzerland* p. 20.
[13] OECD, *Economic Surveys 1994-1995: Switzerland* p. 19.
[14] OECD, *Economic Surveys 1994-1995: Switzerland* p. 22.

Table 2.2

Current government outlays as a % of GDP, 1994

Country	Consumption	Social security	Other	Total
Japan	9.8	12.8	5.5	28.2
Iceland	19.9	6.2	7.0	33.0
US	17.4[a]	14.2	1.9	33.5[a]
Australia	17.7	12.7	5.7	36.2
Switzerland	**14.2**	**17.7**	**8.5**	**40.4**
United Kingdom	21.6	13.9	5.2	40.6
Ireland	15.6	16.6	8.4	40.7
Spain	17.0	16.7	9.0	42.7
Portugal	16.7	12.0	14.8	43.6
Greece	13.8	16.2	14.9	44.9
Germany	19.3	17.7	8.8	45.8
Canada	20.2	15.5	10.5	46.3
Austria	19.0	15.2	13.5	47.7
Italy	17.3	19.5	14.0	50.8
France	20.0	23.3	7.7	51.0
Netherlands	14.3	20.5	17.1	52.0
Norway	21.9	20.6	11.3	53.8
Belgium	15.3	22.4	17.2	54.9
Finland	22.4	24.9	10.2	57.5
Denmark	25.3	21.4	14.7	61.3
Sweden	27.3	19.7	20.4	67.4
Total	16.8	15.8	6.5	39.1
EU (15)	19.2	18.7	10.3	48.3

[a] Includes investment outlays.

Source: OECD, *Economic Surveys 1994 - 1995, Switzerland* p. 72.

Table 2.3

Government deficits, 1991-1995

	1991	1992	1993	1994[a]	1995[b]
Confederation	-4,044	-5,040	-9,199	-6,706	-7,051
Cantons	-3,781	-4,159	-5,390	-3,700	-4,200
Communes	-2,151	-2,730	-1,750	-1,250	-2,000
Total	-9,976	-11,929	-16,339	-11,656	-13,251
Social security	+2,917	+27	+3,070	+991	–
Total incl. social security	-7,059	-11,902	-13,269	-10,665	–

[a] Budgeted
[b] Projected

Source: OECD, *Economic Surveys 1994-1995, Switzerland* p. 53.

Figure 2.7

Federal, cantonal & commune spending as a % of GDP, 1993

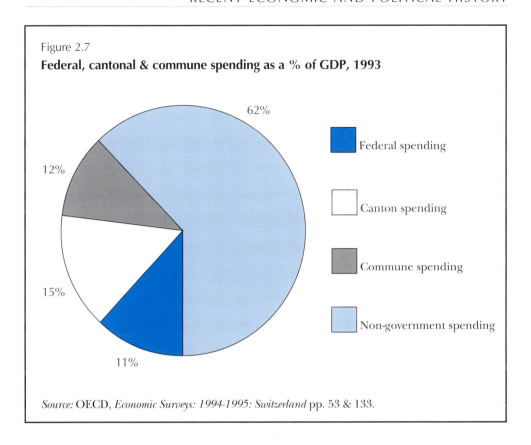

Federal spending

Canton spending

Commune spending

Non-government spending

Source: OECD, *Economic Surveys: 1994-1995: Switzerland* pp. 53 & 133.

slightly over 13 per cent of federal taxes.[15] Finally, its spending power is relatively small because Switzerland's federal government consumes, typically, between 10 per cent and 12 per cent of the nation's GDP.

Traditionally, Swiss fiscal policy has been conservative. Budget deficits are considered the exception rather than the rule, but the 1990s have been the exception (see Figure 2.8). Federal government deficits have occurred in each of the first four years of the 1990s, causing the debt-to-GDP ratio to rise above desired levels.[16]

During 1994, a healthier than expected economy caused the federal budget deficit to drop below projected levels (ie, to Sfr5.1 billion or 1.4 per cent of GDP) as both expenditures to support unemployment fell with lower unemployment and tax receipts increased with the higher level of income. In 1995, the federal government has tried to reduce further the federal deficit to 1 per cent of GDP by cutting its expenditures and raising taxes. Projections in 1995 (assuming a real annual growth rate of 2 per cent, inflation of 1.5 per cent, government expenditure growth of 3.1 per cent and government revenue growth of 6.8 per cent) indicated that the confederation deficit would fall from Sfr6.5 billion (1.8 per cent of GDP) in 1995 to Sfr1.9 billion (0.5 per cent of GDP) in 1998.[17]

---

[15] OECD, *Economic Survey 1994-1995: Switzerland* p. 58.

[16] Nevertheless, the debt-to-GDP ratio in 1993 was 47.5 per cent, below the 60 per cent level set by the European Community as a goal in the Maastrich Treaty.

[17] OECD, *Economic Surveys 1994-1995: Switzerland* p. 63.

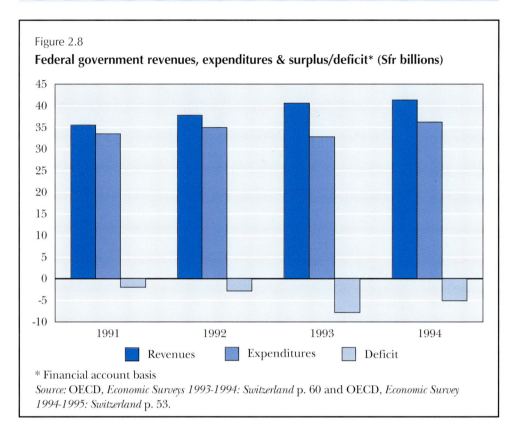

Figure 2.8

Federal government revenues, expenditures & surplus/deficit* (Sfr billions)

* Financial account basis

Source: OECD, *Economic Surveys 1993-1994: Switzerland* p. 60 and OECD, *Economic Survey 1994-1995: Switzerland* p. 53.

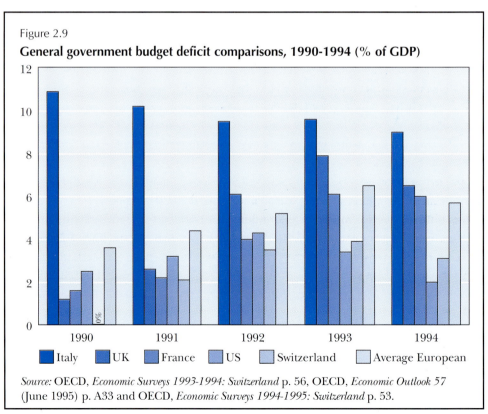

Figure 2.9

General government budget deficit comparisons, 1990-1994 (% of GDP)

Source: OECD, *Economic Surveys 1993-1994: Switzerland* p. 56, OECD, *Economic Outlook 57* (June 1995) p. A33 and OECD, *Economic Surveys 1994-1995: Switzerland* p. 53.

Recent increases in the federal deficit have been caused more by a decline in economic activity and changes in unemployment compensation than a worsening of the government's structural deficit. Though general government deficits have been larger than Swiss authorities would like, and look alarming to Swiss taxpayers, they are still low relative to many other developed nations (see Figure 2.9). Most Swiss voters feel it is unfair in view of the worsening relationship between the active population and the retirees to shift the burden for today's expenses to future generations.

The 1995 implementation of the new value added tax (VAT) (at a rate of 6.5 per cent), replacing the old turnover tax of 6.2 per cent, will help to raise the tax base. The tax reforms will also make the system more balanced. Under the old sales tax system, many areas that should have been taxed (eg, services, energy, medicine, books, newspapers, and non-alcoholic beverages) were not, and many areas that were taxed (eg, business investment and intermediate goods) should not have been. Economic distortions resulted.

The size of the public sector in Switzerland (and throughout Europe) along with its perceived inefficiencies and non-responsiveness to consumer demands has set into motion a wave of critical review. Reforms (under the banner 'New Public Management') have sought to improve public sector efficiency by separating the determination of public policy from its administration. Government managers are being given more flexibility and discretion for deciding how to accomplish objectives rather than having the means dictated to them.[18]

As a consequence, government functions are increasingly being out-sourced to private companies (with overview by public officials) when it is cost effective to do so.[19] The option to out-source has induced efforts to separate government functions into their various components so as to understand which parts are best provided by the government and which are best handled by the private sector. In 1995, the Swiss government's ownership of domestic infrastructure (eg, Postal, Telephone and Telecommunications Service – PTT, the railway system – Chemins de fer fédéraux (CFF), electrical power generation and delivery, cantonal banks and fire insurance) was large[20] relative to other OECD nations and its out-sourcing was relatively small.[21]

In 1992, after years of controversy, the Swiss parliament submitted Switzerland's application for membership in the European Union (EU). In December of the same year, Swiss voters returned a 'No' vote in a referendum determining whether Switzerland should join the European Economic Area (EEA), effectively a free trade zone between the seven Nordic and alpine members of the European Free Trade Area (EFTA) and the twelve members of the European Community (EC). As a result, Switzerland's EU application

2. Switzerland and the European Union

---

[18] See OECD, *Economic Surveys 1994-1995: Switzerland* pp. 68-113.

[19] Some of the main areas for out-sourcing are waste collection, road maintenance and school transportation.

[20] Fire insurance is mandatory in 19 of 26 cantons. In virtually all cantons, fire insurance must be purchased from the monopoly cantonal fire insurance company. OECD, *Economic Surveys 1994-1995: Switzerland* p. 100.

[21] It amounted to approximately 25 per cent of all services for cantons with over 5,000 residents. OECD, *Economic Surveys 1994-1995: Switzerland* p. 76.

has been put on hold, and further consideration has been postponed until the Swiss public demonstrates a clear mandate for membership.

The 'No' vote was important on many levels and has critical implications for Switzerland's economic future. It called into question the means by which the nation will be able to maintain or improve its position as one of the richest countries in the world. From virtually any perspective, international trade has played and will continue to play a significant role in Switzerland's economic activities. It is the international sector that has created the most value for Switzerland, and the EU nations are by far the largest component of this activity.

Reasons for the 'No' vote

Many citizens were afraid that voting 'Yes' for EEA would almost inevitably compel the nation to join the EU. Many 'No' votes were in fact directed against membership in the EU rather than against the EEA. Becoming a member of the EEA had obvious economic advantages, but there were trade-offs the Swiss were unwilling to make.[22] The most important are summarised here.

- Switzerland is a direct democracy with supreme powers vested in the people. The powers of the national government are restrained by individuals' rights to call referenda on important draft laws. Even taxes cannot be imposed against the will of the majority. Opponents felt that membership in the EU could compromise this style of government – a fundamental, unacceptable course of action for many Swiss.

- By its constitution, Switzerland must remain neutral. Many Swiss residents feared the nation's autonomy and geopolitical neutrality would be compromised by the union. For this reason, membership in the United Nations has been consistently rejected, although Switzerland collaborates and finances non-political activities of the UN and other multilateral organizations. Financial contributions in 1992 amounted to approximately US$1.1 billion (0.46 per cent of GDP).[23] Comparative figures for other developed nations are shown in Table 2.4.

- Major fears were associated with Switzerland being overrun by foreign workers seeking employment. At present, foreigners comprise almost a fifth of Switzerland's population, and a third of the domestic labour force, the largest proportion in any European country. Many residents felt that the current level was already straining the social fabric of the nation and represented a political risk. They were willing to join only if restrictions (eg, immigration quotas) could be put on the flow of labour across its borders. Ironically, immigration to Switzerland from EU countries has been declining since 1990.

[22] Thomas Dyllick, "Switzerland and 1992," *AEJ*, Vol. XVIII, #3 (September 1990) pp. 27-37.
[23] United Nations, *Statistical Yearbook: Thirty Ninth issue: 1992 Data Available as of 31 December 1993* (New York: 1994) p. 1011.

Table 2.4

Net development assistance to developing countries and multilateral organizations

Country	US$ billions	% of GDP
Australia	1.015	0.37
Austria	556	0.30
Belgium	865	0.39
Canada	2.515	0.46
Denmark	1.392	1.02
France	8.270	0.63
Germany (Allemagne)	7.583	0.39
Italy	4.22	0.34
Japan	11.151	0.30
Netherlands	2.753	0.86
Norway	1.273	1.16
Spain	1.518	0.27
Sweden	2.460	1.03
Switzerland	**1.139**	**0.46**
United Kingdom	3.217	0.31
United States	11.709	0.20

Source: United Nations, *Statistical Yearbook: Thirty Ninth Issues: 1992 Data Available as of 31 December 1993* (New York: 1994) p. 1011.

- Entry into the EU would mean changing many Swiss rules and regulations to conform to the European Union. Among those rules were ones governing information disclosure and banking secrecy. The average Swiss has a healthy distrust of Big Brother whether he sits in Moscow, Bern or Brussels. Membership in the EEA could have threatened Switzerland's cherished privacy.

- The EU is run by a central bureaucracy, whose accountability to the European Parliament was still not clear, and the allocation of political powers to the central body still undecided. Innate Swiss distrust of any centralized power will remain until people's control over the bureaucrats is well-established.

- The European Union's Common Agricultural Policy (CAP) opened a major controversy. Even though the CAP was one of the most generous agricultural support programmes in the world, it paled in comparison to Switzerland's policies. Swiss agricultural subsidies averaged 80 per cent of the domestic products' total value in 1991, compared to only 49 per cent in the EU.[24] As a result, the powerful Swiss farming lobby was forcefully against joining the EEA and EU.

---

[24] OECD, *Agricultural policies, markets and trade: Monitoring and outlook (1992).*

Economic implications of the 'No' vote for Switzerland: the negative side

Both Switzerland and the EU have clear economic interests in the free trade agreement. Approximately 57 per cent of Switzerland's exports go to, and 73 per cent of its imports come from, the European Community.[25] Switzerland is the second largest importer of EU products and the third largest exporter to the EU. It is clear that future laws passed by the EU will have substantial effects on Switzerland, but the 'No' vote precludes Switzerland from playing any active role in shaping these rules, many of which it will have to observe anyway. As a result, an important chance to influence both its own destiny and the liberalization of European trade passed by.

In addition to its self-disenfranchisement, Switzerland's 'No' decision will prevent it from participating in many joint research projects with the EU. Moreover, Swiss firms that are actively seeking EU public procurement contracts will experience difficulties handling the bureaucratic red tape associated with their applications. The EU has used the 'No' vote to deny Switzerland rights of cabotage (ie, the right to transport freight or passengers between destinations within the EU via Switzerland), and Swissair has been denied entry to the EU's single transport market. Swissair will be required to enter into bilateral negotiations with each EU nation if it wants to change either its routes or fares.[26]

Economic implications of the 'No' vote for Switzerland: the positive side

There is a positive side to the 'No' vote. The financial markets reacted with optimism to it. The value of the Swiss share index rose abruptly on the news of the vote. Part of the reason for the positive reaction was the belief that Switzerland would be better able to maintain its image as an island of financial stability on a turbulent European continent. European nations have been experiencing towering budget deficits, escalating taxes and armed internal conflicts. Many bond investors felt that Swiss entry into the EEA would be followed by its admission into the EU and the common currency agreement in 1999. They speculated that the financial union would cause Swiss bond prices to fall as Swiss interest rates rose to levels equal to or above those in Germany. It would also mean that because the Swiss franc would no longer be an independent currency, it would lose the ability to diversify risk in global portfolios. Many investors felt that rejection of EEA membership improved Switzerland's chances to maintain its financial autonomy, retain its strict bank secrecy laws, protect investors' privacy and continue to serve as a financial conduit for the rest of the world.[27]

The 'No' vote should not be taken in isolation or over-emphasized. It has not affected existing Swiss-EU treaties, such as the free trade agreement Switzerland has had with the EU since 1972,[28] but it does introduce obstacles for future agreements. The EU

---

[25] See Chapter 3 for a more complete discussion of Switzerland's international trade in goods and services.

[26] Swissair is remedying this by going into partnership (49.5 per cent stock holding) with the Belgian carrier, Sabena. The new company is the fourth largest airline in Europe after Lufthansa, British Airways and Air France.

[27] Ian Rodger, "Switzerland," *Financial Times Survey* (8 April 1994) p. 1.

[28] Switzerland has negotiated many bilateral treaties with the EU (140 as of 1990). Among the EFTA nations, it has become the most integrated with EU. See Thomas Dyllick, "Switzerland and 1992," *AEJ*, Vol. XVIII, #3 (September 1990) pp. 27-37.

might no longer negotiate with Switzerland bilaterally.[29] As a result, the 'No' vote would require Switzerland to get separate approvals from individual EU countries for each future agreement.

Swiss companies have responded to the vote by moving assertively into the EC, and, as a result, have increased substantially the net foreign direct investment outflows from Switzerland. A Swiss National Bank report has indicated that foreign direct investment (FDI) in Switzerland turned negative (by a net Sfr344 million) in 1993 for the first time since the figures were collected in 1984. It also noted that big Swiss companies have been adapting by shifting production and research facilities to the EU.[30] Many of the Swiss investments appeared to be moving toward Austria, the newest member of the EU and a potential doorway to the emerging Eastern European markets.

Swiss company response to the 'No' vote

The Swiss federal government was solidly in favour of joining the EEA and the 'No' vote was an embarrassment to these elected leaders. It brought into question whether the Swiss government could be considered a credible and reliable bargaining partner. A 1994 white paper on foreign policy in the 1990s reaffirmed the goal of becoming a member of the EU and pledged to change voluntarily part of Switzerland's legislation to conform to EU standards – the same standards it would have had to adopt had Switzerland become a member. Eurolex or Swisslex, as these reforms have been called, will entail major changes in the way business is done in the future. It will mean increasing competition by revising Switzerland's cartel laws and deregulating its industries; increasing labour flexibility, creating fairer rights for foreign workers, forming special training institutions, eliminating technical trade barriers between cantons and with EEA nations[31] and opening government procurement contracts to foreigners.[32] The government's goal is to minimize the distance between Swiss and EU rules in order to improve the chances for success in the next referendum.

Swiss government response to the 'No' vote

On 1 January 1995, Austria, Finland and Sweden joined the European Community casting Switzerland in the position of the country on the outside looking in. Many Swiss analysts wondered what would become of its relationship with the EU. Bilateral negotiations between Switzerland and the EU began in December 1994 focusing on six major areas: air and land travel, labour mobility, research, agricultural trade and tariffs, government procurement contracts, and product testing and certification (including trademarks, technical regulations and other legal barriers to trade). Progress has been hindered by the labour mobility issue.

Future relations between the EU and Switzerland

---

[29] Trevor Merriden, "The Economist Intelligence Unit's view of political and economic developments in Switzerland," *Business Guide to Switzerland: Guide to Investment, Trade and Tourism* No. 2, (April/May 1993) p. 36.

[30] Trevor Merriden, p. 36.

[31] The programme will try to create in Switzerland a single market where all trade barriers (eg, technical barriers to entry, discriminatory public contracts and the lack of mutual recognition of educational qualifications) are removed.

[32] Economic Intelligence Unit, "Policy Revitalization Program Moves Forward," (28 January 1994).

The Swiss have stood firm on the nation's right to preserve its pristine Alpine land-scape. In a February 1994 referendum, Swiss voters decided (52 per cent in favour) that from the year 2004, transit freight traffic would have to use rail lines rather than Alpine roads. An estimated 20 million tons of cargo pass through Switzerland each year and over 1,000 foreign trucks per day travel through the Gotthard Pass. This ban on lorry transit through the Alps helped to set back Swiss-EU negotiations. One point of concern was the highly discriminatory nature of the Swiss law, restricting only transit passing through Switzerland and not affecting traffic within Switzerland or traffic from Switzerland to for-eign destinations. Austria was concerned because the ban would divert north-south traffic to its roads. Moreover, the ban was another embarrassment to the government because it negated a Swiss-EU transportation treaty negotiated in 1992.[33]

The Swiss government has tried to make concessions to compensate for the ban. It has embarked on the NEAT (Neue Alpen-Transversale) programme to increase trans-border rail capacity. NEAT was approved by the Swiss voters in a September 1992 referen-dum and focussed on building two high-speed north-south transalpine tunnels through the Alps.[34] Its costs were estimated at Sfr15 billion, and, when it is completed, the tunnel under the Gotthard will rank among the longest twin-tunnel, single-track construction projects of the world. In terms of length and technical difficulty, the tunnel project will be more demanding than the Eurotunnel.[35] The hope is that when the time comes, rail travel will be financially more attractive and environmentally more sound than driving vehicles through the Swiss Alps. In 1995, over 80 per cent of existing traffic through the Alps was carried by rail.

The outlook

A referendum on membership in the EU is possible between 1996 and 1999.[36] In 1995, it appeared as though a slight majority of Swiss favoured such a union, but this referendum must be passed by both a majority of the people and a majority of the cantons. It is unlikely the latter requirement will be accomplished in the near future. There is too much resistance in the German- and Italian-speaking cantons. Moreover, the Swiss People's Party, representing Swiss rural populations and small businesses, holds one of the seven seats on the Swiss Federal Council and is adamantly opposed to Swiss entry.

Unless and until staying outside hurts financially, a positive vote cannot be expected. In the meantime, the debate will confirm whether Switzerland will open its domestic sec-tor to free market forces without pressure from the EU and whether the competitive external sector will be strong enough to support the subsidized domestic sectors. More importantly, the EU will define its nature and profile over the coming years and as a con-federation of European states under parliamentary control emerges, it should become a more acceptable option to the Swiss.

---

[33] The agreement imposed a 28-ton limit on trucks and a complete ban on night and weekend lorry traffic.
[34] One tunnel will be parallel to the Gotthard Tunnel and under the Gotthard Pass. The other one will be under the Lötschberg Tunnel and extending to the Simplon Tunnel. (See John Braun, "Ban it and bore it," *Financial Times Survey* (8 April 1994) p. IV.
[35] John Braun, "Rant and rail: The NEAT solution stays in place," *swissBusiness*, (May/June 1994) pp. 33-34.
[36] Joining the EEA is not as important since most of the major countries in the EEA have now joined the EU. Besides Switzerland, only Norway, Liechtenstein and Iceland remain outside the EU.

3

SWISS INDUSTRY, AGRICULTURE AND TRADE

For a country that could have specialized in many different areas, why has Switzerland focused on machinery, chemicals and watches? With the lack of an abundant natural resource base, the service and industrial sectors have been the backbone of the Swiss economy. Today, agriculture accounts for only 3 per cent of Switzerland's gross domestic product, the industrial and construction sectors constitute about a third and the remaining 62 per cent of its annual production is created in the services sector (see Figure 3.1).

Overview of the Swiss economy

Many of Switzerland's most competitive industries emerged from linkages to the textile industry, Switzerland's oldest major industry (see Figure 3.2). Dyestuffs grew from the need to colour fabrics. Chemicals, and later pharmaceuticals, emerged from the chemical expertise developed in producing dyestuffs. The machine industry, Switzerland's largest current employer, emerged from the service and supply needs of textile manufacturers, and metallurgy was a natural outgrowth of machinery manufacturing. Supporting the growth of all these areas were the railway network (built to transport the growing supply of industrial goods) and the financial system (providing capital and transaction settlement services).

1. Switzerland's major non-financial economic sectors

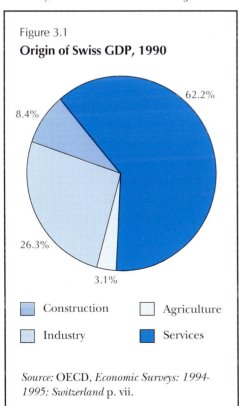

Figure 3.1
Origin of Swiss GDP, 1990

62.2%
8.4%
26.3%
3.1%

- ▨ Construction
- ▨ Agriculture
- ▨ Industry
- ▮ Services

Source: OECD, *Economic Surveys: 1994-1995: Switzerland* p. vii.

The machinery industry developed as a service agent providing spinning machines and spare parts to the much larger textile industry. Companies such as Escher-Wyss, Rieter, Rüti Machine Factory and Saurer all trace their origins and early expansion

Machinery, electronics and metals

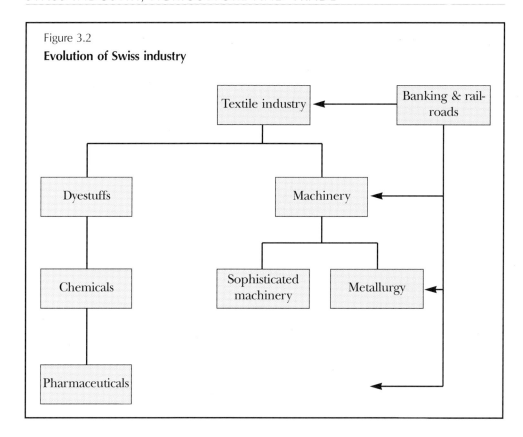

Figure 3.2

Evolution of Swiss industry

to the textile business. Over the first 60 years of the 20th century, textile production shifted to lower-cost nations, while the machinery industry stayed in Switzerland and grew. Today, it is composed of mainly small- and medium-sized companies that compete globally and cover the entire range of market segments. In fact, this industry has become Switzerland's largest industrial employer and exporter. In 1994, VDMA tables ranked Switzerland as the third largest producer of machine tools, scales and printing machinery; the fourth largest world-wide producer of textile machinery, precision instruments and compressors/vacuum pumps, and the fourth largest exporter of packaging machinery.[1]

Many Swiss machinery companies have earned international reputations in various segments of this market. Sulzer, Rieter and Saurer have established international positions for their textile machinery, as have Maegerle, Bobst, Bühler and von Roll for their electrostatic grinding equipment, cardboard packaging machinery and grain-milling machines. Switzerland is home to machine tool companies such as Feintool, and electrical discharge machining companies like Agie and Charmilles. SLM is a world competitor in the production of railway tracks and mountain transportation equipment, and Asea Brown Boveri has an established reputation in electrical equipment. Schindler (number two world-wide) sells elevators and escalators globally, and Kaiser produces rotating tools, as do Prematex, Gressel, Regofix, Dornaz, URMA and Schaeblin. There is enormous overlap among these competitors, and their location in Switzerland lends support to the

---

[1] VDMA, "Maschinen-Länder im Vergleich: Schweiz auf Rang 9," *Position Weltweit* 1994.

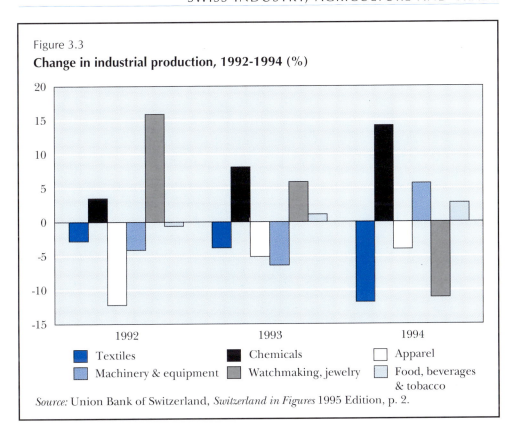

Figure 3.3

Change in industrial production, 1992-1994 (%)

Textiles — Chemicals — Apparel
Machinery & equipment — Watchmaking, jewelry — Food, beverages & tobacco

Source: Union Bank of Switzerland, *Switzerland in Figures* 1995 Edition, p. 2.

belief that national core competencies are best formed when world leaders are in close proximity competing head-to-head.

Just as Swiss companies have gained international recognition in the machinery industry, many others have had similar success in segments of the electronics industry. Landis and Gyr, Staefa Control and Saurer are among Europe's leading suppliers of heating, ventilation and air conditioning control. Rexton and Gfeller are important hearing-aid manufacturers. Sulzer is a world-class producer of pacemakers. Uster makes controls for textile machinery, and Huni manufactures process controls for the tanning industry. Sprecher and Schuh have established themselves as major participants in the low voltage switch-gear market. Switzerland is also an international competitor in the production of aluminium products (eg, wire, cable, cans, casings, tubing and foil) and fabricated metals (for construction such as reinforced steel, tubing, fittings and window frames).[2]

Figure 3.3 shows the decline in sales the machine industry suffered during the first part of the 1990s. In part, the slack performance was due to sluggish growth both at home and in many of the industrialized (customer) nations, such as the member nations of the European Union and Japan. The strength of the Swiss franc and high Swiss interest rates also contributed significantly to the sales slump. As well, many companies' hopes for future growth were pinned to a 'Yes' vote on joining the European Economic Area (EEA). The negative outcome was a bitter disappointment for these companies.

[2] Michael J. Enright and Rolf Weber, Studies in Swiss Competitive Advantage, (Harvard Business School, 9-794-048: 1993) p. 2-3.

33

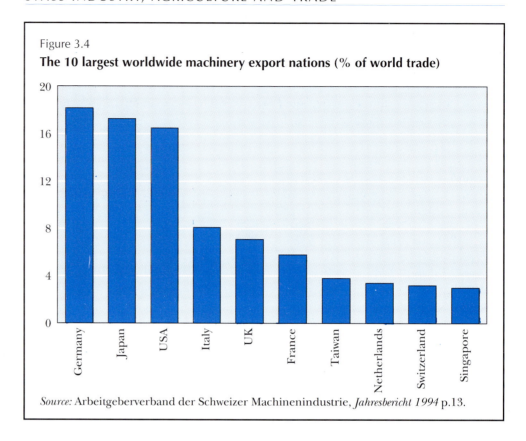

Figure 3.4

The 10 largest worldwide machinery export nations (% of world trade)

Source: Arbeitgeberverband der Schweizer Machinenindustrie, *Jahresbericht 1994* p.13.

The future for the machine industry can be characterized as one of guarded optimism. It thrives on quality research and development. Swiss companies have taken aggressive marketing strategies and succeeded in emerging markets such as South Korea, India, Malaysia, China and Brazil. This diversification strategy has expanded their customer base and stabilized sales.

Switzerland's recent 'No' vote to join the EEA might have reduced the chances for near-term recovery, but this negative may be offset or reversed by provisions in the Uruguay Round of GATT negotiations that portend reductions in world-wide tariffs, protection for intellectual property rights and improved access to international public contracts.

The Swiss machine industry is one of the world's top ten exporters (see Figure 3.4) and the machine, electronics and metal industries accounted for 43 per cent

Table 3.1

Major destinations for Swiss machinery, electronics and metal exports, 1994

Swiss exports to	% of exports
Germany	29
France	8
Italy	6
United Kingdom	5
Other EU nations	11
Total EU	59
EFTA Nations	7
USA	10
OPEC	3
Eastern Europe	3
Japan	2
Other	16
Total	**100**

Source: Arbeitgeberverband der Schweizer Machinenindustrie, *Jahresbericht 1994* p. 13.

of Switzerland's total exports in 1994.[3] Of these exports, nearly 60 per cent were destined for nations in the European Union. Only 10 per cent were sold in the US, and Japan's share was a diminutive 2 per cent (see Table 3.1). A rapidly increasing market for this export growth (especially for textile machinery) has been Asia, in general, and China, in particular.[4] Because of the relatively large labour forces in these nations, Swiss manufacturers have responded by building high quality machinery with and without advanced automation technology.

In the precision instruments area, Switzerland has displayed a clear international competitive advantage in areas where fine mechanics are combined with computers and electronics. Maillefer is an example of an international competitor in the field of micro wire producing machinery.

Swiss-based companies are among the world leaders in the production of chemicals, dyestuffs, agrochemicals, pharmaceuticals and plastics. Companies such as Roche, Ciba and Sandoz are multinational giants with significant international positions in many segments of these and other markets (eg, flavours and fragrances, vitamins and nutrition). In terms of market capitalization, Roche is ranked number one among Swiss-based companies, number two in Europe and number 10 worldwide.

Chemicals and pharmaceuticals

The chemical/pharmaceutical industry is one of Switzerland's largest industrial employers (70,185 employees in 1994), accounting for approximately 10 per cent of total Swiss industrial employment and hiring approximately 170,000 workers abroad.[5] Because of Switzerland's lack of natural resources and emphasis on research and development,

Table 3.2

Research & development expenditures in Switzerland by industry, 1992

	Domestic R&D (%)	Domestic & foreign R&D (%)	% of turnover
Machinery & metal	18.8	12.0	6
Electronics	22.3	31.8	8
Chemicals	41.3	42.8	15
Watches	1.3	0.7	4
Food	4.4	5.1	1
Paper	1.0	0.5	3
Research labs	5.6	4.2	14
Other	5.3	2.9	–
Total/average	**100.0**	**100.0**	**6**

Source: Schweizerische Gesellschaft für Chemische Industrie, *Zahlen und Fakten* (1995) p. 14, and Vorort and Bundesamt für Statistik.

---

[3] Arbeitgeberverband der Schweizer Maschinenindustrie, *Jahresbericht 1994* p. 12.
[4] In 1993, China became the second largest importer, behind the US, of Swiss textile machinery.
[5] Schweizerische Gesellschaft für Chemische Industrie, *Zahlen und Fakten* (1995) p.1, 5 & 10.

Table 3.3

Swiss chemical/pharmaceutical exports by product group (Sfr millions)

	1992	1993	1994
Chemical raw materials, ingredients & unformed synthetics			
Inorganic products	325.2	333.0	358.4
Organic products	2,312.2	2,304.9	2,571.1
Unformed synthetics	1,130.7	1,093.3	1,203.9
Total	*3,768.1*	*3,731.2*	*4,133.4*
Chemical end products including active substances			
Pharmaceutical products, vitamins, diagnostics	10,439.8	11,284.5	11,794.5
Plant protection and pest control	1,643.7	1,569.8	1,538.2
Chemical fertilizers	8.3	7.4	6.9
Colouring and pigments	1,931.5	2,140.3	2,104.0
Varnish and dyes	424.1	463.1	510.2
Ethereal oil, aromatic- and flavouring materials	711.9	757.4	850.3
Cosmetics and perfumes	641.5	763.1	825.9
Photochemical products	254.8	250.6	232.3
Auxiliary industrial ingredients	422.1	411.1	409.5
Other chemical end products	1,011.6	969.8	1,086.6
Total	*17,489.3*	*18,617.1*	*19,358.4*
Total of all exports	**21,257.4**	**22,348.3**	**23,491.8**

Source: Schweizerische Gesellschaft für Chemische Industrie, *Zahlen und Fakten* (1995) p. 19, and Vorort and Bundesamt für Statistik.

these industries focus on high value-added products rather than bulk chemicals. They account for over 40 per cent of all private Swiss research expenditures (see Table 3.2).

Approximately two-thirds of the industry's members are small- or medium-sized, each employing under 100 workers. In fact, only eight companies in this industry employ more than one thousand workers.[6]

Because of its emphasis on specialty products and the small home market, these industries are highly dependent on exports. Over 85 per cent of their production, on average, is sold abroad, most – almost 60 per cent – to nations that are members of the European Union (see Figure 3.5).[7] In 1994, Switzerland's chemical exports totalled Sfr23.4 billion and imports totalled Sfr12.5 billion, leaving a net trade surplus of nearly Sfr 11 billion (see Tables 3.3 and 3.4).

Switzerland imports most of its chemical and pharmaceutical needs from virtually the same nations to which it exports (see Figures 3.5 and 3.6). Imports from the European Union have significantly greater importance and imports from the US and Asia carry sig-

---

[6] Schweizerische Gesellschaft für Chemische Industrie, p. 3.
[7] Most of these exports are intra-corporate transfers.

Table 3.4

Swiss chemical/pharmaceutical imports by product group (Sfr millions)

	1992	*1993*	*1994*
Chemical raw materials, ingredients &			
unformed synthetics			
Inorganic products	432.2	406.5	420.3
Organic products	2,906.8	2,708.0	2,858.4
Unformed synthetics	1,499.4	1,444.2	1,568.8
Total	*4,838.4*	*4,558.7*	*4,847.5*
Chemical end products including			
active substances			
Pharmaceutical products, vitamins,			
diagnostics	2,970.0	3,589.1	3,795.0
Plant protection and pest control	243.9	293.6	288.5
Chemical fertilizer	100.7	90.3	81.1
Colouring and pigments	738.3	847.2	869.6
Varnish and dyes	271.2	271.5	278.6
Ethereal oil, aromatic- and flavouring			
materials	156.9	157.9	170.0
Cosmetics and perfumes	545.4	560.2	679.6
Photochemical Products	357.0	338.3	317.2
Commercial agents	361.5	338.5	343.6
Other chemical end products	869.1	808.4	869.6
Total	*6,614.0*	*7,295.0*	*7,692.8*
Total of all imports	**11,452.4**	**11,853.7**	**12,540.3**

Source: Schweizerische Gesellschaft für Chemische Industrie, *Zahlen und Fakten* (1995) p. 20. Also, Vorort and Bundesamt für Statistik.

nificantly less weight, another indication of Switzerland's close economic integration with the EU.

All three of Switzerland's major chemical/pharmaceutical companies have modernized and internationalized their corporate structures (eg, moving toward I.A.S. accounting standards and simplifying their share structures) and changed significantly the composition of their corporate activities. Roche, the sixth largest pharmaceutical company in the world (1994), is the world leader in the production of bulk vitamins, second in the world in the production of flavours and fragrances, among the leading 10 companies producing diagnostic machinery and a significant producer of over-the-counter pharmaceuticals. Sandoz is a world leader in dyestuffs, pigments, plastic adhesives and specialty chemicals for textiles.[8] Finally, Ciba has a large international presence in pharmaceuticals, health care, dyestuffs, plant protection and additives.[9]

---

[8] In the early 1990s, Sandoz decided to leave the industrial chemical business and focus on the drug and nutrition (eg, Ovomaltine, Isostar and Gerber baby foods) businesses. Sandoz' specialty chemicals for textiles business was sold and is now Clariant.

[9] In 1995, Ciba announced its intention to sell its subsidiary, Mettler-Toledo, the producer of commercial and industrial scales. The sale is consistent with Ciba's efforts to reduce its non-core activities.

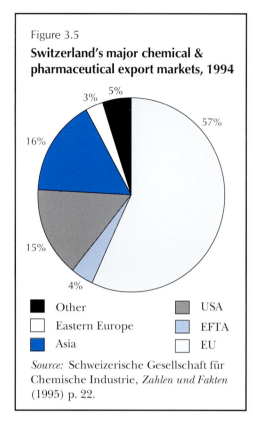

Figure 3.5

Switzerland's major chemical & pharmaceutical export markets, 1994

■ Other	■ USA
□ Eastern Europe	□ EFTA
■ Asia	□ EU

Source: Schweizerische Gesellschaft für Chemische Industrie, *Zahlen und Fakten* (1995) p. 22.

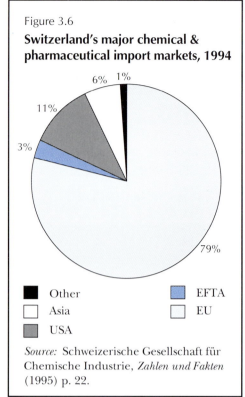

Figure 3.6

Switzerland's major chemical & pharmaceutical import markets, 1994

■ Other	□ EFTA
□ Asia	□ EU
■ USA	

Source: Schweizerische Gesellschaft für Chemische Industrie, *Zahlen und Fakten* (1995) p. 22.

These companies have always operated in changing global climates, but the winds of change seem especially strong in the 1990s. The chemical/pharmaceutical companies have opted to compete by stressing innovative, speciality products that start new product life cycles, rather than focusing on 'me-too' and bulk products that cannibalize existing markets. Since the early 1990s, this strategy has paid high dividends as new suppliers from nations in Eastern Europe and East Asia have flooded the markets with inexpensive bulk products, thereby lowering profit margins in these unsophisticated market segments.

Similarly, in the pharmaceutical industry, international efforts to curtail health care expenditures through bulk purchases, price controls and the use of generic drugs have led to considerable price compression for 'me-too' and bulk products. Fewer constraints have been placed on speciality products that are often more effective and carry lower "all-in" costs (product costs plus the cost of administering them to patients) than other products on the market.

Swiss companies have entered the biotechnology arena by making a string of acquisitions and building their own internal competencies. In 1990, Roche Holding acquired 60 per cent of the shares of US-based Genentech for US$2 billion and has the option until 1999 to take full control. In 1995, Ciba purchased 49.9 per cent of the shares in California-based Chiron for US$2.1 billion.[10] Acquisitions, loose affiliations and partnerships, as well as joint and collaborative agreements are signs of the future and will

---

[10] After 5 years, Ciba can raise its interest to 55 per cent.

become more commonplace as the chemical/pharmaceutical industry continues to consolidate its operations and as flexibility becomes ever more important.

In the early part of the twentieth century, Switzerland was the clear international leader in the production of watches. Immediately after World War II, Swiss companies controlled approximately 80 per cent of global watch production. This position was quickly eroded when US, Japanese and Hong Kong companies segmented the market and focussed on the low-to-medium priced segment of the market. By the late 1960s, Switzerland's world market share was down to 40 per cent, and the Swiss were left focussing almost exclusively on the slow-growing luxury watch segment while the medium-priced and inexpensive watch segments grew dramatically.[11] Among the leading Swiss producers of luxury watches were Audemars-Piguet, Girard-Perregaux, IWC, Jaeger-LeCoultre, Patek-Philippe, Piaget, Vacheron-Constantin and, of course, Rolex, the world's largest luxury watch producer.[12]

Watches

In the 1980s, the Swiss watch industry was able to reverse its declining market position in the low- and middle-priced watch segments when the Swiss Corporation for Microelectronic and Watchmaking Industries (SMH) began producing inexpensive and highly fashionable Swatch watches. SMH was the by-product of a merger between ASUAG and SSIH, two of Switzerland's largest watch holding companies. Today the company is the world's third largest producer of watches (in terms of units of output) and Switzerland's only large competitor in the international market for low-priced watches.[13] The company has aggressively diversified its products (ie, by means of plastic and more recently, metal watches) and has been named the official timekeeper for the 1996 Olympics in Atlanta, Georgia. Among its major brands are Omega, Longines, Rado, Tissot, Swatch and Hamilton.

Recently, SMH entered into a joint venture with Mercedes Benz to market by 1997 the SMART, an environmentally friendly, micro-compact car that will retail for less than US$12,500. This venture follows on the heels of an unsuccessful collaboration between SMH and Volkswagen to produce the Swatch-Mobil.

The Swiss Watch Federation reports that in 1995, Switzerland had the world's largest turnover (approximately 65 per cent) of all watches and timepiece movements.[14] At the same time, it was only the third largest producer of physical, time-related precision instruments. The discrepancy in rankings is explained by Switzerland's focus on the upper end of the watch market, leaving the rest to countries like Japan and Hong Kong. Because it focuses on luxury timepieces for which consumers are relatively price insensitive but very quality sensitive, Swiss watchmakers have not been as adversely affected as other Swiss producers by the rising value of the Swiss franc. In 1994, sales in both number and turnover increased in the face of a rapidly appreciating Swiss franc.

Watches are Switzerland's fourth largest export industry with foreign sales of approximately Sfr8 billion in 1994. Almost 90 per cent of these revenues come from fin-

[11] Urs Bumbacher, *The Swiss Watch Industry* (Harvard Business School, 9-792-046: 1992) p. 17.
[12] Urs Bumbacher, p. 17.
[13] Urs Bumbacher, p. 10.
[14] John Wicks, "Time is Money", *swissBusiness* (November/December 1994) p. 43-44.

ished timepieces. Exports to Asia and Oceania account for a growing share of Swiss watch exports. It is hoped that the intellectual property right agreements that were a part of the recent Uruguay Round of the GATT negotiations will help to stem the counterfeiting of Swiss watches in some developing nations and act to stimulate Swiss sales.

Textiles

The textile industry developed in Switzerland during the period from 1850 to 1880 as the nation's first major industry. Over time, Swiss textile production declined as other nations with lower costs were able to take market share, but from the textile trade emerged, either directly or indirectly, many of Switzerland's other major businesses.

Switzerland is still a significant exporter of textiles and apparel, accounting for just under 3 per cent of total world production. Swiss cottons, woollen and silken products along with embroidery, synthetic fibres, textile finishing, clothing and footwear are sold around the world. In 1994, Switzerland exported approximately 80 per cent of its textile production (a little over Sfr3 billion worth) and imported almost 90 per cent of the clothing sold domestically. Textile exports accounted for 5 per cent of Switzerland's total exports, with almost 85 per cent sold to either EU or EFTA nations.[15]

The Swiss textile market is relatively free from protectionist import barriers. Currently, there are no tariffs between the EU and Switzerland, but other countries (eg, the US and Far East) must pay customs duties.[16] Many participants were optimistic that Swiss entrance into the European Economic Area would boost sales and profitability. The 'No' vote in the December 1992 referendum quashed any near-term hopes they might have had. Furthermore, the decision by Austria, Sweden and Finland to join the European Union, could cause Swiss textile manufacturers to become even more isolated in the future. To increase sales, greater reliance on bilateral, international trading agreements may be required.

Over the first three years of the 1990s, the textile and clothing industry lost approximately 4,500 jobs, as firms closed, reduced capacity and shifted production to lower-cost foreign nations.[17] The industry has been in a period of intense price pressure due to the strong Swiss franc, growing cost pressure from labour abundant developing nations and stringent domestic environmental standards.

Viscosuisse, owned by the French company Rhône-Poulenc, is by far the largest Swiss textile company, and Noyfil, owned by the Italian group Radici, is the second largest. Albers & Company, Fisba and Möbelstoffweberei are also well-established Swiss companies in this industry. In the sports, leisure and casual wear market, Switzerland focuses on high-quality niche products with well-known names such as Calida, Hanro, Jockey and Triumph playing particularly important roles.

---

[15] Swiss textile manufacturers' efforts to sell their products in the European Union have been hampered by preferential tax agreements the EU has negotiated with some foreign nations (eg, Eastern European countries) that are not extended to Switzerland. Even though EU taxes against Switzerland do not rise in absolute terms, they rise relative to foreign competitors. See Ulrike Baldenweg-Bölle, "Textiles and Apparel" in Sectoral Trends in the Swiss Economy: Developments in 1994 and Outlook for 1995 pp. 10-11.

[16] See Paul Frei, The Sports, Leisure and Casual Wear Market in Switzerland (Zurich: American Consulate General, December 1993).

[17] Bundesamt für Statistik, *Statistisches Jahrbuch der Schweiz 1995* (Verlag Neue Zürcher Zeitung, 1994) p. 102.

Tourism employs about 360,000 people.[18] In 1993, it earned approximately Sfr.12.8 billion making it Switzerland's third largest export sector.[19] Hotels, the largest component of the industry, are strongly dependent on the employment of foreign workers, as are Swiss restaurants.

Many visitors are familiar with Switzerland's reputation for showcasing some of the loveliest regions in Europe. They expect spectacular mountains, rivers, waterfalls, valleys and lakes, but are typically surprised to find that the nation has such a diversity of climate and topography on such a small surface. Within three hours, one can travel from the rolling hills of the Jura to the flat central plains and into the southern Valais region where the Matterhorn rises 4,478 meters and Mount Rosa rises 4,634 meters above sea level. Farther to the east is the Ticino region with palm trees and a Mediterranean climate. A bit farther northeast one can visit the more rugged Engadine valley (St. Moritz) with its rough mountainous regions and the 65 square miles devoted to the Swiss National Park.

Despite Switzerland's beauty, Swiss tourism has experienced some serious difficulties during the early part of the 1990s. The number of overnight stays in Swiss hotels fell continuously in 1994 to the lowest level since 1979. The Swiss National Tourist Office's strategic plan entitled 'Switzerland Tourism 1995-1996' isolated many of the weaknesses that were at the heart of Switzerland's problem, such as high prices, unreliable weather, substandard hospitality and a lack of innovative vacation options. In addition, factors such as the stronger Swiss franc and stiffer competition from Austria, Italy and France added to the perceived problem.

One ray of sunlight for the tourism industry was the Swiss government's decision in June 1995 to reduce to 3 per cent the recently imposed 6.5 per cent value added tax (VAT) on hotels and self-catering accommodations. This concession was not extended to the network tourist offices all over Switzerland. Another positive factor was the government's decision to apply the value added tax only to domestic travel.

Tourism

Because many large Swiss companies earn more than 90 per cent of their sales in foreign markets, a thriving service industry has developed to accommodate Swiss exports. Trading companies such as André, Siber and Hegner, Desco von Schulthess, UHAG, UTC and Volkart are prominent in the industry. Société Générale de Surveillance and Inspectorate are leaders in inspection, trade monitoring and customs services.[20] Danzas (with 1994 turnover of Sfr.6.72 billion and 675 operations in 41 countries), Kühne & Nagel (with 1994 turnover of Sfr.5.16 billion and 450 offices in 80 countries) and Panalpina (with 1994 turnover of Sfr.4.0 billion and over 200 branches in 50 countries) are three of the world's largest freight forwarding companies.[21]

Trading companies

---

[18] Bundesamt für Statistik, p. 223.
[19] Bundesamt für Statistik, p. 233.
[20] Michael J. Enright and Rolf Weber, *Studies in Swiss Competitive Advantage* (Harvard Business School 9-794-048: 1993) p. 3.
[21] John Wicks, "A new look at niches: The old order changeth-very fast," *swissBusiness* (November/December 1994) p. 43. John Wicks, "Forwarding Agents: Adding Value," *swissBusiness*, (January/February 1994) pp. 43-48.

Foodstuffs

In 1993, there were almost 160 companies active in the Swiss foodstuffs industry employing some 70,700 individuals.[22] Some Swiss companies (eg, Nestlé, Kraft Jacobs-Suchard) are among the leaders in their global industries. Others (eg, ToniLait, Sandoz Nutrition, Hero and Lindt & Sprüngli) are, perhaps, less widely-known, but have sales in excess of Sfr1 billion.

Nestlé is the world's largest food producer and the second largest foodstuffs producer (behind Unilever) in Europe. Kraft Jacobs-Suchard, headquartered in Zürich, stands second behind Nestlé in Swiss food sales and is Europe's fifth largest food producer. Most of the industry's sales are to Germany, France, Italy and Austria, again highlighting the importance of western Europe as the foundation for Switzerland's on-going export strength.

Swiss producers have aggressively tried to increase export sales. Their efforts have been restrained by the rising Swiss franc and discriminatory regulations the European Union places on foreign imports. Tests and certification requirements are just two of the hurdles that many products have to clear before they can be sold in the EU.

Agriculture

Switzerland's topography does not lend itself to highly productive farming. In general, Swiss soil is stony and its growing season is relatively short. Over 70 per cent of Switzerland's land mass is mountainous (covered by the Alps, the Jura and 140 glaciers). Large-scale farming using the most technologically advanced machinery is not a feasible option in Switzerland. Potentially cultivable land areas are reduced further by lakes, woods, cities, towns, roads, railways and airports. For this reason, the airports of Basel and Geneva are mostly on French territory. The climate also fights against Swiss agricultural productivity. Approximately 75 per cent of Switzerland gets over 100 cm of rainfall per year – far too much for crops like corn.

Swiss agriculture is the *Sorgenkind* (problem child) of the Swiss economy. During the two world wars, Switzerland was cut off from international markets on which it had relied for food imports. Shortages prompted a move toward self-sufficiency, and today, some fifty years after World War II, the drive for self-sufficiency has still not ended. [23] In fact, the lobby supporting the uneconomic, environmentally damaging agricultural policy is so strong and the Swiss four-party consensus politics such an obstacle to fundamental reforms, that any attempt to change this ill-conceived patronage is condemned to fail.

The Swiss agricultural sector is one of the most heavily supported in the world, with yearly outright subsidies in the range of Sfr2 billion. The government calculates that if all forms of protection were made equivalent to outright subsidies, they would be equal to Sfr5 billion.[24] The OECD has estimated that farm support comprised 80 per cent of the

---

[22] Union Bank of Switzerland, "Food, Beverages & Tobacco", *Sectoral Trends in the Swiss Economy*, January 1995, p. 9 & Elizabeth Stocker-McLane, "Balancing the diet: Swiss companies stay in the world league", *swissBusiness* November/ December 1994, pp. 68 - 69.

[23] In 1992, Switzerland was 49 per cent self-sufficient in the plant protein area and 92 per cent self-sufficient in the animal protein area. (See, Bundesamt für Statistik, *Statistisches Jahrbuch der Schweiz: 1995* (Verlag Neue Zürcher Zeitung) p. 175.

[24] Economic Intelligence Unit Limited, *EIU Country Report* (June 1994).

Table 3.5

Twenty large, Swiss-based companies with highest turnover abroad, 1993

	Company	Turnover sold abroad (%)
1	Dow Europe	99.0
2	Kühne & Nagel	98.9
3	Richemont	98.5
4	Liebherr International	98.2
5	Nestlé	98.0
6	Ciba-Geigy	98.0
7	Roche Group	98.0
8	Jacobs-Suchard	98.0
9	Triumph-International	97.4
10	Sandoz	96.7
11	Merck	96.7
12	Georg Fischer	94.0
13	Landis & Gyr	92.4
14	Holderbank	91.0
15	Alusuisse-Lonza	89.0
16	Panalpina	87.0
17	Swissair Group	86.0
18	Sulzer	84.0
19	Schindler Holding	76.0
20	Elektrowatt	61.6

Source: Elizabeth Stocker McLane, "Where is Home?," *swissBusiness* (November/December 1994) pp. 34-35.

Swiss agricultural production value in 1990 and 1991, compared to 45 per cent in the OECD and 49 per cent in the EU.[25] For commodities such as milk, pork and wheat, Swiss prices in 1992 ranged from 50 per cent to 300 per cent above EU prices.

In fairness, subsidies are not paid solely to transfer income from the general public to farmers. They are also expended to maintain the undeveloped green areas of Switzerland and to preserve a dying way of life. Nevertheless, the cost of the Swiss agricultural policy to the Swiss consumer would not reach such grotesque dimensions if the farmers' lobby did not have such an undue influence on political decisions.

The government's strategy has been to attack the domestic farm problem on three levels, intending to: reduce excessive farming surpluses, curtail the negative impact farming has on the environment and promote larger farms so that economies of scale can be realized. Three referenda in March 1994 were held to implement this strategy. Ironically, and in spite of the recently negotiated Uruguay Round of GATT negotiations, the Swiss voters rejected the government's proposals on all three fronts.

The Swiss agricultural support system needs changing and virtually everyone in Switzerland knows it. Current policies are reducing general living standards of the Swiss public for the benefit of a select few. Regardless of the balloting in the referenda, many Swiss vote each day with their feet by crossing the border into France, Italy, Germany and Austria to purchase goods at lower prices. The savings can be considerable.

The recently concluded Uruguay Round of GATT negotiations has been ratified by the Swiss Parliament.[26] The agreement requires signatories to reduce production subsidies by 20 per cent, decrease the quantities of subsidized exports by 21 per cent and reduce tariffs by 36 per cent over a six year phase-in period. All non-tariff restrictions will be required to be converted into tariffs and then reduced by 36 per cent. The GATT agreement (now in the hands of the newly-formed World Trade Organization in Geneva) may be the lever the Swiss government needs to move its farming community from the current state to a more reasonable level of subsidies.

---

[25] OECD, *Agricultural policies, markets and trade: Monitoring and outlook* (1992).
[26] On July 1, 1995, Switzerland became a member of the World Trade Organization.

What is a typical Swiss company?

Switzerland has two broad types of companies. One type represents the thousands of small- and medium-sized companies that compete within Switzerland for Swiss consumers. The other type represents the huge multinational companies that compete at the highest levels on a world-wide scale. These latter companies sell relatively little within Switzerland (see Table 3.5), but often times have major domestic production and research facilities. It tends to be these multinational giants that come to mind when one thinks of typical Swiss companies.

Given the turnover profile of these large companies, it is not surprising that their sales performance reflects world-wide economic conditions more than they reflect economic conditions in Switzerland. Switzerland's decision not to join the European Economic Area had significantly less impact on them than did international delays in the Uruguay Round of GATT negotiations and the changing value of the Swiss franc.

2. Imports and exports

Relative to most other nations, Switzerland has an abundance of capital and a scarcity of both natural resources and labour. As a consequence, it is potentially a lucrative market for companies, domestic and foreign, selling products with state-of-the art technology and labour-saving capabilities. Historically, Switzerland has run deficits in its merchandise trade balance (see Figure 3.7). At the same time, services (eg, banking, insurance and freight forwarding) surpluses have more than compensated for the merchandise trade deficits. Switzerland's earnings from net foreign investments have helped to magnify these surpluses. The result has been consistent, healthy current account surpluses (see Figure 3.8) and the accumulation of investments in foreign nations. In 1992, Switzerland's net foreign assets equalled Sfr339.4 billion, making it one of the world's largest foreign asset holders when measured as a percent of GDP.[27]

Switzerland's major exports, imports and trading partners

Except for vehicles and agricultural goods, the categories of Swiss imports are almost exactly the same as its exports (see Figures 3.9 and 3.10). Moreover, these imports come from an almost identical list of nations as those to which Switzerland exports (see Figures 3.11 and 3.12). The major distinguishing factor between its imports and exports is the level of value-added. Switzerland focuses on exporting sophisticated and specialized high value-added products and importing commodities, unfinished materials and low-value chain products.

The European Union is Switzerland's major trading partner. In 1994, 57 per cent of the nation's exports went to, and 73 per cent of its imports came from, the EU's member nations (see Figures 3.11 and 3.12). The US is the third most important trading partner, and Japan accounts for only 3 per cent to 4 per cent of Switzerland's total trade. Over the past decade, Switzerland's sales to China have increased substantially.

---

[27] IMF Survey: Swiss Economy Faces Unaccustomed Challenges (April 18 1994) p. 126. Prior to 1983, the Swiss National Bank did not publish quarterly estimates of the Swiss international capital transactions. Consequently, trend analyses of the Swiss balance of payments are limited by this lack of information.

Figure 3.7

Nominal & real exports & imports of goods and services, 1984-1994 (Sfr billions)

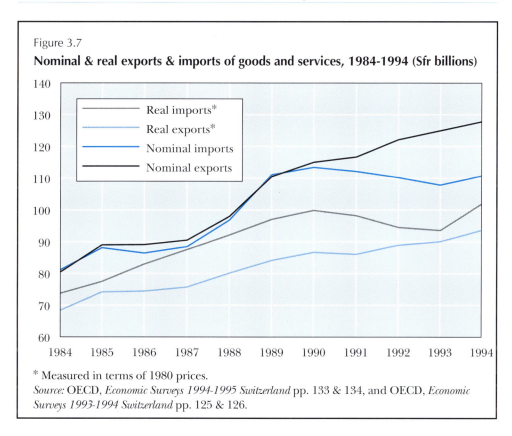

* Measured in terms of 1980 prices.
Source: OECD, *Economic Surveys 1994-1995 Switzerland* pp. 133 & 134, and OECD, *Economic Surveys 1993-1994 Switzerland* pp. 125 & 126.

Figure 3.8

Current account to GDP ratio, 1984-1994 (%)

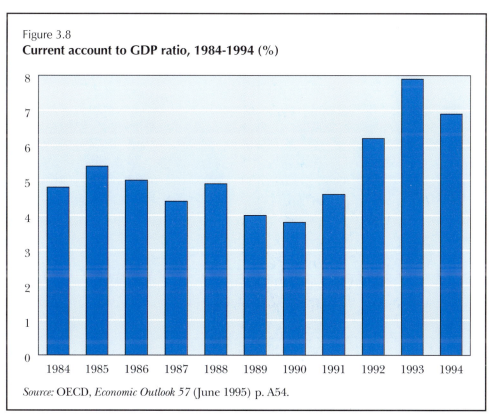

Source: OECD, *Economic Outlook 57* (June 1995) p. A54.

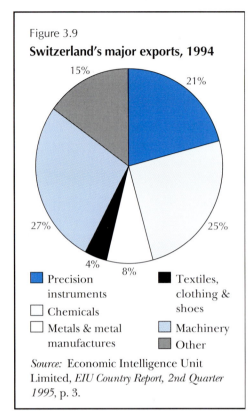

Figure 3.9

Switzerland's major exports, 1994

- Precision instruments
- Chemicals
- Metals & metal manufactures
- Textiles, clothing & shoes
- Machinery
- Other

Source: Economic Intelligence Unit Limited, *EIU Country Report, 2nd Quarter 1995*, p. 3.

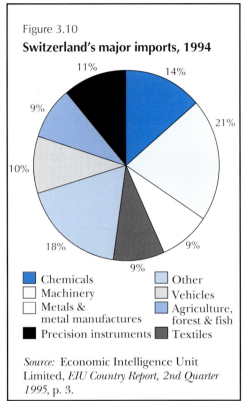

Figure 3.10

Switzerland's major imports, 1994

- Chemicals
- Machinery
- Metals & metal manufactures
- Precision instruments
- Other
- Vehicles
- Agriculture, forest & fish
- Textiles

Source: Economic Intelligence Unit Limited, *EIU Country Report, 2nd Quarter 1995*, p. 3.

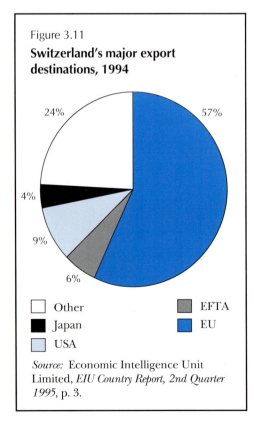

Figure 3.11

Switzerland's major export destinations, 1994

- Other
- Japan
- USA
- EFTA
- EU

Source: Economic Intelligence Unit Limited, *EIU Country Report, 2nd Quarter 1995*, p. 3.

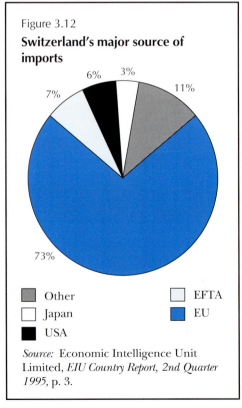

Figure 3.12

Switzerland's major source of imports

- Other
- Japan
- USA
- EFTA
- EU

Source: Economic Intelligence Unit Limited, *EIU Country Report, 2nd Quarter 1995*, p. 3.

Exports are a significant portion of Switzerland's GDP, and some of its inherent risks can be guaranteed by the Swiss Office for Export Risk Guarantees (ERG).[28] ERG is a self-supporting government institution, financed by export risk premiums. These premiums are based on the nominal value of the guaranteed exports (ie, invoice value plus interest less down payments), and are assessed on a sliding scale, influenced by such factors as the term of the guarantee, commercial risk, extent of coverage, control of risks and number of non-Swiss suppliers. Because Switzerland does not subsidize exports, ERG has to balance its accounts and recuperate possible losses over a period of time.[29] For intermittent shortfalls, the federal government has to advance the necessary funds.

Export risk guarantees

Founded in 1934, the ERG's function is to promote Swiss exports by offering protection to businesses for risks beyond either their control or the control of their foreign customers. Among the covered risks are:

- political risk (eg, wars and revolutions),
- transfer- and debt-rescheduling risk (eg, due to the buyer's inability to pay as a result of government restrictions on international capital flows),
- credit risk on foreign businesses that are majority-owned by a foreign government (eg, public utilities), and
- production risks (the risk of not being able to deliver an individually-produced item because of political events or measures taken by foreign states).

In general, the risks that are not covered by ERG are ones that can be insured privately or are a part of normal business.[30] ERG coverage is only granted to Swiss exporters who are registered in Switzerland. Exporters may qualify even if more than 50 per cent of their products' value is added abroad (up to a maximum 70 per cent), but premiums are raised with the percent of foreign content. Guarantees are not limited to goods. Bid and performance bonds, know-how agreements and licenses are among the services covered. Moreover, both short-term and long-term credit guarantees can be provided, with maximum coverage of 95 per cent for capital and interest.[31]

ERG handles applications and submits them to a commission comprised of eight individuals, who are elected by the Federal Council for four year terms. Four of the members are from different departments of the federal government and four are from industry and labour unions.

The approval process comes before different federal departments depending on the size of the guarantee. Guarantees up to Sfr1 million are brought before the Federal Office for Foreign Economic Affairs; guarantees between Sfr1 million and Sfr2 million

---

[28] ERG guarantees are governed by the laws and regulations of the Swiss Federal Law (Bundesgesetz, September 26, 1958), the decree of the Swiss Federal Council (Verordnung, January 15, 1969) and the decree of the Federal Department of Public Economy (March 15, 1985).

[29] Export subsidies are against OECD rules. As a result, Switzerland has made this a self-financing institution.

[30] ERG's policy to cover only sovereign credit risk and to issue only guarantees denominated in Swiss francs is under review. In the future, it will be possible to cover the del credere risk (ie, commercial risk) of prime private banks and to insure credits denominated in US dollars as well.

[31] Typically, long-term guarantees require down-payments of at least 15 per cent.

are forwarded to the Federal Department of Public Economy, and guarantees over Sfr2 million are approved by the Federal Department of Public Economy with the advice and consent of the Federal Department of Finance.

In an effort to simplify the administration of these guarantees, a few industrial associations have been appointed to manage the global guarantees for the industry they represent. The specific associations are:

- Chemical industry: Swiss Society for the Chemical Industry SGCI, Zürich,
- Textile industry: Chamber of Commerce and Industry, St. Gallen, and
- Watch industry: Federation of the Swiss Watch Industry, Biel.

Switzerland: an island of high prices in Europe

On an *ad valorem* basis, Swiss tariffs average under 3 per cent. Yet, according to OECD purchasing power parity calculations, Switzerland's consumer price level is 40 per cent above the average of all OECD countries and its investment goods are 30 per cent more expensive.[32] With tariffs as low as they are, why do these international price discrepancies persist? Most of the answer can be traced to five sources:

- *Non-tradable goods and services:* Non-tradable private services account for almost 40 per cent of the Swiss private sector GDP. If construction were included, non-tradable goods and services would account for nearly 50 per cent of the Swiss private sector GDP. International arbitrage does not directly affect such prices permitting international price discrepancies to persist.
- *Non-tariff barriers:* During the 1960s and 1970s, non-tariff trade barriers (eg, quotas and technical restrictions) rose substantially. Between 1966 and 1986, the portion of imported goods covered by such regulations rose from 19 per cent to 50 per cent (mainly food and textiles).[33] Such trade impediments prevent arbitrage and price equalization.
- *Exclusive wholesale networks:* Approximately 85 per cent of all Swiss imports are handled by wholesale traders who use exclusive distribution networks, thereby reducing the possibility for either parallel imports or direct foreign competition.
- *Agricultural supports:* Many of the existing tariffs and government subsidies support the agricultural sector. Even if the purpose of these subsidies was to improve the environment, curtail land development and maintain a vanishing way of life, the effect has been to keep domestic prices above international levels.
- *Business associations:* Many importers and their foreign affiliates are members of the same business associations. Such affiliations can lead to non-competitive market agreements.

---

[32] See OECD, *Economic Surveys: Switzerland: 1991/1992* p. 75.
[33] S. Laird and A. Yeats, "Non-Tariff Barriers of Developed Countries 1966 - 1986," *Finance & Development* vol. 26, Iss. 1, March 1989, pp. 12 - 13.

4

SWISS BANKS AND OTHER FINANCIAL INSTITUTIONS

Banks are as much a part of Switzerland's international image as the Alps, chocolates and watches. For centuries, their stability, competence and discretion have attracted billions of Swiss francs of foreign financial capital to centres such as Zürich, Geneva, Basel, and Lugano. These early financial institutions were instrumental in facilitating economic growth in both Switzerland and Europe, but the pre-industrial banks were created more for the purpose of exporting financial capital than lending to entrepreneurs.

Since the 16th century, Switzerland has had a savings surplus due to the nation's relative lack of demand for investment funds. To effectively manage the international allocation of savings, private banks were created. In the 17th century, Geneva's private banks financed much of the capital needs of the French court, and beginning in around 1730, regular capital exports started for which financial institutions were required.

The structure of Switzerland's banking system, as it exists today, was not created until the mid-19th century – mainly between 1850 and 1880 – peaking in 1889, when the number of banks in Switzerland totalled 449.

Consolidation followed in the first half of the 20th century, leading to the emergence of the Big Banks: Credit Suisse, Union Bank of Switzerland and Swiss Bank Corporation. The first federal banking law was decreed in 1934. Previously, there were some cantonal regulations, but controls and interventions by the state were still kept to a minimum. The law left sufficient room under the universal banking concept for adjustments to market needs. Since the 1970s, regulations and controls have become tighter, and Swiss banks are now among the most closely supervised banks in the world.

Overview of banking and the Swiss economy

Today, banking is Switzerland's most important service industry. Between 1960 and 1994, the industry's assets grew at a compound annual rate of 9.3 per cent (see Figure 4.1), nearly twice as fast as the Swiss economy as a whole. Furthermore, over the 1980s and early 1990s, bank revenues grew considerably faster than other important Swiss industries, such as chemicals, metals and machinery, and watches (see Table 4.1).

Due to its ability to compete at the top ranks of the global financial markets, the banking/finance industry has become one of Switzerland's most important sources of foreign exchange. In 1994 – an exceptionally successful banking year – banking contributed

1. Swiss banks in the broader Swiss economy

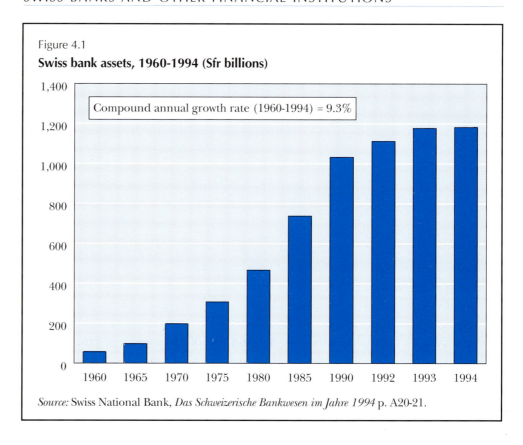

Figure 4.1

Swiss bank assets, 1960-1994 (Sfr billions)

Compound annual growth rate (1960-1994) = 9.3%

Source: Swiss National Bank, *Das Schweizerische Bankwesen im Jahre 1994* p. A20-21.

Table 4.1

Compound annual sales/revenue growth for various Swiss industries, 1980-1992

Industry	Compound annual growth rate (%)
Banking	9.8
Chemicals	5.7
Metals & machinery	4.4
Watches	6.3

Source: Bundesamt für Statistik, *Taschenstatistik der Schweiz 1994*, Bern/Schweiz (1994) p. 13.

Sfr6.6 billion[1] to the invisibles surplus of the nation's balance of payments – by far the largest surplus of all the service sectors.[2]

In 1992, the banking industry accounted for approximately 6.5 per cent[3] of Swiss GDP, and in 1994, it employed 121,271 people, roughly 3.6 per cent of the nation's total workforce.[4] The discrepancy between the relatively low proportion of individuals employed in banking and the industry's large share of GDP is accounted for by the high level of bank employee productivity. In 1991, the gross value-added per bank employee was Sfr245,000, sizably above the Swiss industrial average (Sfr97,000) and over 70 per cent ahead of the second largest contributor, the chemical industry (Sfr142,000).[5]

---

[1] Swiss National Bank, *Die Schweizerische Zahlungsbilanz 1994* p. 19.
[2] Tourism had the second largest surplus (Sfr2.4 billion).
[3] Swiss National Bank, Monatsbericht June 1995 p. 129.
[4] Swiss National Bank, *Das Schweizerische Bankwesen im Jahre 1994* p. 48.
[5] Swiss Bankers Association, *The Swiss Banking Sector: Development, Structure and International Position* (1994 Edition) p. 7.

Switzerland is one of the most intensively banked countries in the world. In 1994, it had a total of 3,922 domestic banking establishments for a population of 7,037,800 people, representing one bank office per 1,794 inhabitants. Competition for these offices has been fierce and prevailing concerns about efficiency and profitability are being carefully analyzed to determine whether, how and where to cut back.

The scope and efficiency of Swiss banking are especially evident when the industry is compared and contrasted to other developed nations. Figure 4.2 shows the 10-year average of selected financial statistics for Switzerland, Germany, France, the US and Japan.

The figures reveal that Switzerland's banking system plays a relatively large role in the domestic economy. Bank assets relative to GDP in Germany, France and Japan are less than half the relative size of Switzerland and the US banking sector's ratio is less than one-fiftieth Switzerland's relative size.

Furthermore, even though Swiss banks earn a sizable portion of their revenues from the interest spread, they derive almost half of their income from off-balance sheet sources such as trading commissions, trading income and portfolio management fees. Since the early 1980s, Swiss banks' on-balance sheet business has lost ground to off-balance sheet activities. In large part, this exceptionally high level of off-balance sheet activity relative to other nations is due to the Swiss system of universal banking, a focus on portfolio management and also to a general banking trend away from lending toward securitization.

2. Swiss banks relative to other nations

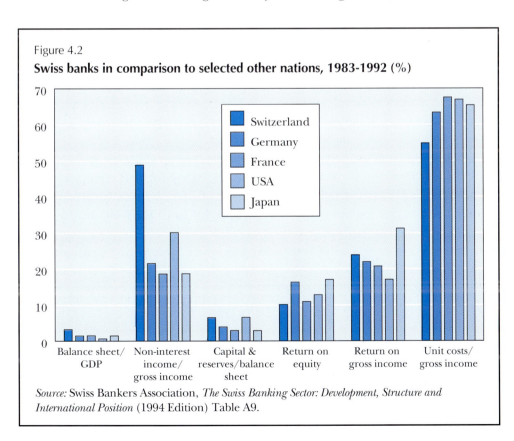

Figure 4.2

Swiss banks in comparison to selected other nations, 1983-1992 (%)

Source: Swiss Bankers Association, *The Swiss Banking Sector: Development, Structure and International Position* (1994 Edition) Table A9.

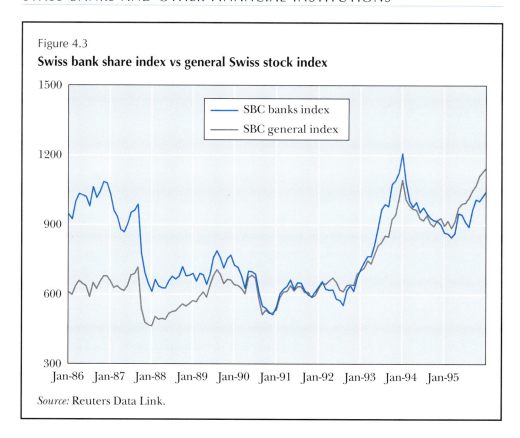

Figure 4.3

Swiss bank share index vs general Swiss stock index

Source: Reuters Data Link.

Figure 4.2 also shows that Swiss banks were among the safest in the world when measured in terms of capital and reserves relative to total assets.[6] Nevertheless, this safety came at the price of comparatively lower returns on equity. Over the 10-year period between 1983 and 1992, Swiss banks registered the lowest average return on equity of all the major nations considered. Swiss banks' performance improved when measured in terms of return on gross income, in large part, because of effective bank actions to lower costs (ie, staff and office expenses) relative to income.

In comparison to the performance of other Swiss companies, Swiss banks have lost ground since the mid-1980s. As Figure 4.3 shows, the Swiss bank index was considerably above the general Swiss stock index in 1986, but the two indices gradually converged and in 1991, they met. For most of the period between 1991 and 1995, banks held a narrow lead, but in 1995 this advantage was lost.

From the investors' point of view, the total return (ie, price plus dividends) on Swiss bank stocks has been disappointing over the 1986-1995 period. Table 4.2 shows the financial performance of the Big Banks along with some other representative Swiss bank shares. Over the 10 years, the average (non-weighted) total return amounted to less than the interest earned on a savings account. Among the Big Banks, Union Bank of Switzerland showed the highest 10-year yield with 4.6 per cent. Swiss Bank Corporation

---

[6] Safety is also evident when measured in terms of low variation of return. See Niklaus Blattner, "The Swiss Financial Centre Revisited," D.E. Fair and R. Raymond (Eds.), *The Competitiveness of Financial Institutions and Centres in Europe* (Kluwer Academic Publishers, 1994).

Table 4.2

Total return for representative exchange-listed Swiss banks, 1986-1995

Name	Type of instrument	Total return (%)*
Union Bank of Switzerland	B	4.6
CS Holding	R	2.5
Bär Holding	B	2.3
Gotthard Bank	B	2.1
Swiss Bank Corporation	B	0.0
VP Bank, Vaduz	P	-0.5
Rothschild	B	-2.2

* Total return = Dividends plus price appreciation/depreciation;
B = bearer share; R = registered share; P = Participation Certificate

Source: Calculated based on published figures.

showed no net yield, and other banks performed even worse. These low yields can be traced to greater portfolio riskiness as evidenced by the billions of Swiss francs set aside as provisions and losses on mortgages during the early 1990s.

For centuries, Switzerland's financial system has had close ties to the international community, but as Figure 4.4 shows, over the past four decades, its globalization efforts have intensified. Between 1950 and 1994, the proportion of Swiss bank assets devoted to international customers increased from 8.9 per cent to 36.5 per cent.

The location of Switzerland's international assets has also changed over time, but the overwhelming majority has been invested in developed nations. The debt crisis in the 1980s caused Swiss banks to reduce their exposure to Latin America, and recent turmoil in Eastern and Central Europe has had a sobering effect on Swiss investments there. Figure 4.5 shows the structure of Swiss banks' foreign assets in 1994 and their relatively low participation rate in developing nations.

Over the course of the 20th century, the net foreign investments of Swiss banks have grown and reached US$66 billion at the end of 1994 (see Tables 4.3 and 4.4). Relative to other nations, this income earning asset base is second only to Japan in size (see Table 4.5).

Swiss banks act as financial turntables by attracting funds from external (ie, foreign) sources and investing them abroad. Of the total bank liabilities to foreigners in December 1994, the non-bank sector was the source of 63 per cent (ie, US$214.8 billion), but the destination of only 18 per cent (ie, US$ 70.8 billion) of all Swiss bank foreign assets.

Of the total liabilities owed by Swiss banks to foreigners in December 1994, 78 per cent (US$264.4 billion) were denominated in foreign currencies and almost the same portion (76 per cent, or US$309 billion) of Swiss bank assets was invested in foreign currency form.

3. Internationalization of Swiss banks

Figure 4.4

Swiss banks' foreign and domestic bank asset composition, 1950-1994 (%)

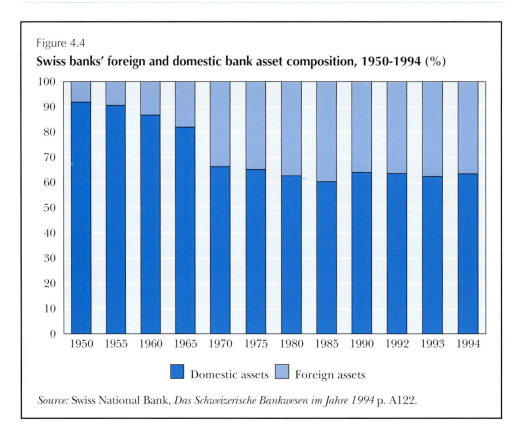

Source: Swiss National Bank, *Das Schweizerische Bankwesen im Jahre 1994* p. A122.

Figure 4.5

Swiss banks' foreign assets by region, 1994 (Sfr billions)

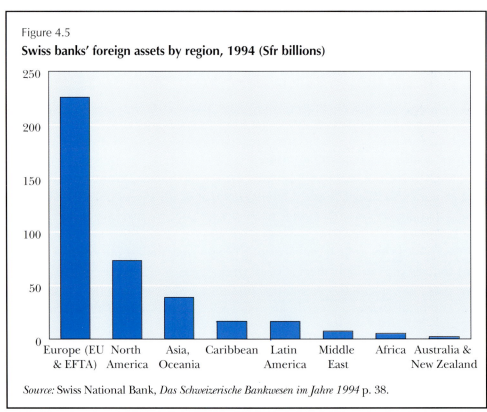

Source: Swiss National Bank, *Das Schweizerische Bankwesen im Jahre 1994* p. 38.

Table 4.3

External positions of Swiss banks, December 1994 (US$ billions)

(In all currencies vis-à-vis banks and nonbanks)

	Assets	*Liabilities*	*Net*
Nonbanks	70.8	214.8	-144.0
Banks	333.5	123.5	+210.0
Total	404.3	338.3	+66.0

Source: Bank for International Settlements, *International Banking and Financial Market Developments* (Basel, May 1995) Appendix pp. 2 & 3.

Table 4.4

External positions of Swiss banks in domestic and foreign currency, December 1994 (US$ billions)

	Assets	*Liabilities*	*Net*
Domestic currency	**95.3**	**73.9**	**+21.4**
Nonbanks	28.7	36.3	-7.6
Banks	66.6	37.6	+29.0
Foreign currency	**309.0**	**264.4**	**+44.6**
Nonbanks	42.1	178.5	-136.4
Banks	266.9	85.9	+181.0
Total	**404.3**	**338.3**	**+66.0**

Source: Bank for International Settlements, *International Banking and Financial Market Developments* (Basel, May 1995) Appendix pp. 4, 5, 6, & 7.

Table 4.5

Banks' cross border assets and liabilities, December 1994 (US$ billions)

Rank	*Country of residence*	*Assets* Stock: End 1994	*Liabilities* Stock: End 1994	*Net* Assets
1	Japan	1,007.6	723.7	+283.9
2	**Switzerland**	**404.3**	**338.3**	**+66.0**
3	Germany	469.2	411.9	+57.3
4	Luxembourg	390.7	347.3	+43.4
5	Spain	110.6	103.2	+7.4
6	Netherlands	176.6	169.5	+7.1
7	Belgium	230.8	234.4	-3.6
8	Austria	65.2	73.7	-8.5
9	France	526.8	550.6	-23.8
10	United Kingdom	1,199.8	1,278.1	-78.3
11	Italy	136.6	230.2	-93.6
12	US	531.8	820.7	-288.9
13	All other countries	174.5	217.1	-42.6

Source: Bank for International Settlements, *International Banking and Financial Market Developments* (Basel, May 1995) p. 16.

4. Swiss banking structure: an overview

Rivalry in Swiss banking and banking conventions

Switzerland's banking structure in the 1990s has gone through profound changes due to economic, political and technological forces such as deregulation, integration, internationalization, computerization, the elimination of many cartel agreements and enactment of legislative reforms. To survive and prosper, banks have had to adapt in dramatic ways.

Though dominated by the Big Banks – Credit Suisse, Union Bank of Switzerland and Swiss Bank Corporation – smaller financial institutions provide businesses with a wide array of potential financing partners and options. Most companies have more than one banking relationship and use these multiple affiliations to extract the best terms. These "best terms" are provided in the form of slight variations in the range and quality of financial services, efficiency, safety and reputation, but price competition is becoming increasingly important.

In the past, the Swiss banking system had a tradition of strong mutual agreements that eliminated or substantially reduced price competition. In a small country like Switzerland, such formal and informal mutual agreements were an outgrowth of interconnected family businesses, joint military service, professional organizations, social club memberships and university education that homogenized and personalized potential business competitors. Bank conventions (see Table 4.6) permitted many otherwise inefficient financial institutions to survive, but they became out of place in the globalized, modern-day competitive banking environment.

Swiss bank conventions were cited as anti-competitive in a 1989 report by the Swiss Cartel Commission, and since then, many have been abolished (see Table 4.6). Because most of these conventions were developed under the auspices of the Swiss Banking Association, it has been working to reduce or eliminate many of the remaining anachronistic practices.

Swiss universal banking

Swiss banks operate under the Banking Law of 1934, which regulates management quality, organizational structure, bank liquidity and capital adequacy. As confining as it is in some areas, this law has no stipulations regarding the type of activities in which banks may participate. Unlike the US and Japan, Swiss law does not distinguish between commercial and investment banking activities. As a result, there are no clearly defined lines of functional responsibility among Swiss financial institutions. Technically, all of Switzerland's financial institutions enjoy universal banking privileges and can, therefore, participate in virtually every financial line of business in any location within the country.

Even though there are no legal barriers preventing it, universal banking is practiced only by a small portion of the Swiss banks, mainly the Big Banks and the larger cantonal banks. The remaining institutions specialize, more or less, on lending or portfolio management activity, usually in narrow regional locations.

Over time, the industry has segmented itself into pockets with varying degrees of competition. This segmentation process has been evolutionary in nature and not judicially or legislatively imposed. Different lines of Swiss financial activity are not, at present, equally competitive, but virtually all of these markets are contestable. High profits in one area or declining profits in others will spirit the movement of institutions into and out of different lines of business.

Table 4.6

Banking conventions

Convention		Status
I	Protection of bills of exchange business	Current
II	Payment of interest on current accounts	Expired Feb. 1, 1993
III	Customer acquisition and promotion activities (This is now a "recommendation".)	Revised Jan. 1, 1994
IV	Uniform charges for safekeeping fees	Expired Jan. 28, 1993
V	Charging of stamp tax duties to customers	Current
VI	Conditions for cash payments, performance of travel services, issuing letters of credit and money orders by post	Expired Jan. 1, 1991
VII	Expenses for and value dating of transfer and cash payments	Expired Jan. 1, 1992
VIII	Limitations on the refund of commissions to sub-agents for new issue business	Expired August 31, 1989
IX	Collection fees and retrocession fees payable in Swiss francs relating to coupons and redeemable stock business	Current
X	Collection of commissions on coupons and redeemable bonds in foreign currency (in cases where there is no paying agent in Switzerland)	Expired Jan 1, 1977
XI	Minimum conditions for documentary credit business	Expired Jan. 1, 1991
XII	Conditions for acceptance credits	Expired Oct. 1, 1983
XIII	Simplification of the paying of bills and checks	Current
XIV	Production, issue and use of Swiss checks	Current
XV	Production, issue and use of Eurocheque cards	Current
XVI	Procedures relating to inquiries from the SEC for information in investigation of cases of misuse of insider information	Expired Jan 1, 1989
XVII	Domestic new issue business	Expired Mar. 1, 1990
XVIII	Reimbursement of savings accounts and salary accounts in cases of forced liquidation of a bank; (This is now called an "agreement".)	Revised July 1, 1993
XIX	Note business for foreign borrowers	Current

Source: Schweizerische Bankiervereinigung.

5. Swiss banking structure

The Swiss National Bank divides the domestic banking industry into eight major institutional categories: Big Banks, cantonal banks, regional and savings banks, mutual credit associations and Raiffeisen banks, other banks, foreign banks, private banks and finance companies. Table 4.7 and Figure 4.6 show that between 1989 and 1994 the number of reporting banks dropped by 137. The largest attrition occurred in the number of regional and savings banks and finance companies. These declining sectors have been affected significantly by growing domestic and foreign competition, the need for sufficient size to benefit from economies of scale[7] and changes in bank legislation.

Only foreign banks have increased their ranks over the intervening period and this increase was due in large part to regulatory changes made in 1990 that brought finance companies under the closer scrutiny of the Swiss National Bank. As a result of increased supervision, many foreign-owned finance companies changed their legal status to banks.

Between 1950 and 1994, the importance of the Big Banks has grown. They moved from a market share of a little over 27 per cent of all bank assets to their current position at almost 51 per cent. Through both mergers and internal expansion (ie, growth by means of branch networks and single location extensions) they have secured a lock on the heart of Switzerland's banking activity (see Figure 4.7). Nevertheless, smaller institutions have been able to create niches and survive in spite of their size. Regional banks have tried to capitalize on their vast numbers and close relations with customers. Cantonal banks have offered customers deposit safety and widespread recognition as mortgage lenders. Foreign banks have thrived on their trading expertise, capital market knowledge and ingenuity in meeting international customers' trade financing and asset management needs. Finally, private banks have competed by means of their confidentiality, investment management skills and international reputations.

Table 4.7

Number of banks and finance companies, 1984-1994

	1984	1985	1986	1987	1988	1989	1990	1991	1992	1993	1994
Cantonal banks	29	29	29	29	29	29	29	28	28	28	27
Big Banks	5	5	5	5	5	5	4	4	4	4	4
Regional & savings banks	217	216	215	214	213	210	204	189	174	155	135
Mutual credit assn. & Raiffeisen banks	2	2	2	2	2	2	2	2	2	2	1
Other banks (not foreign)	82	85	88	91	89	91	92	92	93	87	86
Foreign banks	119	120	125	128	133	135	142	146	148	156	153
Finance companies	103	112	119	130	133	137	130	112	101	79	71
Private banks	24	24	24	23	22	22	22	19	19	18	17

Source: Swiss National Bank, *Das Schweizerische Bankwesen im Jahre 1994* p. 22 & Swiss National Bank, *Das Schweizerische Bankwesen im Jahre 1993* p 22.

[7] Information technology and the requirement for uniform system architectures have been especially important new costs for banks seeking to remain competitive.

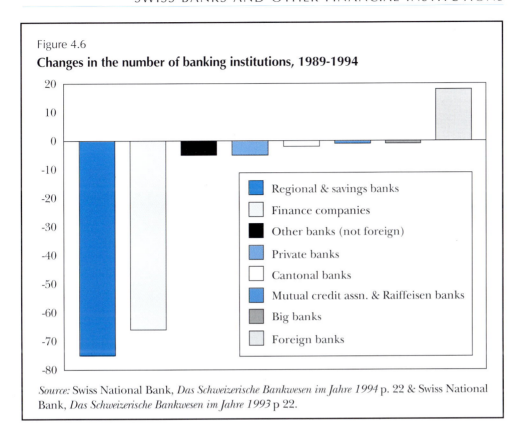

Figure 4.6

Changes in the number of banking institutions, 1989-1994

Legend:
- Regional & savings banks
- Finance companies
- Other banks (not foreign)
- Private banks
- Cantonal banks
- Mutual credit assn. & Raiffeisen banks
- Big banks
- Foreign banks

Source: Swiss National Bank, *Das Schweizerische Bankwesen im Jahre 1994* p. 22 & Swiss National Bank, *Das Schweizerische Bankwesen im Jahre 1993* p 22.

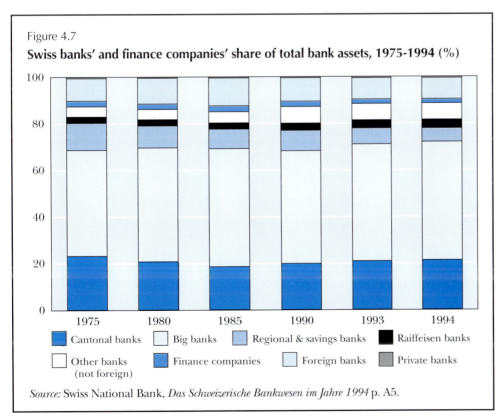

Figure 4.7

Swiss banks' and finance companies' share of total bank assets, 1975-1994 (%)

Legend:
- Cantonal banks
- Big banks
- Regional & savings banks
- Raiffeisen banks
- Other banks (not foreign)
- Finance companies
- Foreign banks
- Private banks

Source: Swiss National Bank, *Das Schweizerische Bankwesen im Jahre 1994* p. A5.

Internationalization of Swiss banks' balance sheets

On average, Swiss banks have high international profiles, but as Table 4.8 and Figure 4.8 show this level of global involvement is not homogeneous among the various forms of legal institutions. Moreover, even though finance companies and foreign banks devote a larger proportion of their balance sheets to international business, due to the relatively small size of their footings, almost two-thirds of all foreign bank business is done by the Big Banks. A few of the larger cantonal banks are now entering the international market with inspired efforts, but the overwhelming portion of their operations is still cantonal contained.

Table 4.8

International composition of Swiss banking institutions' assets, 1994

Financial institution	*Total Swiss bank assets (%)*	*International assets as % of bank assets*
Big Banks	50.8	48.2
Cantonal banks	21.2	4.5
Regional & savings banks	5.8	1.1
Mutual credit assn.	3.7	0
Other banks (not foreign)	7.0	40.8
Foreign banks	9.1	70.0
Private banks	0.6	27.3
Finance companies	1.8	88.5

Source: Schweizerische Nationalbank, *Das Schweizerische Bankwesen im Jahre 1994* pp. A5 & 33.

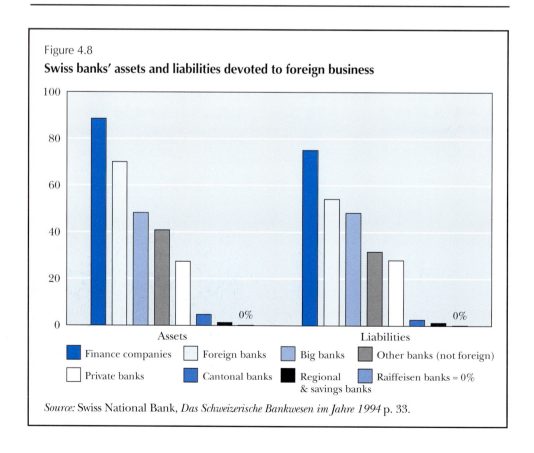

Figure 4.8

Swiss banks' assets and liabilities devoted to foreign business

Source: Swiss National Bank, *Das Schweizerische Bankwesen im Jahre 1994* p. 33.

Table 4.9

Swiss bank and finance companies' foreign affiliates

Financial institution	1988	1994
Cantonal banks	0	0
Big Banks	113	124
Regional & savings banks	0	0
Raiffeisen banks	0	0
Other banks (not foreign)	22	55
Commercial banks	15	26
Investment banks	7	29
Consumer credit banks	0	0
Other banks	0	0
Finance companies	5	4
Foreign banks	57	77
Private banks	0	1
Total	**197**	**261**

Source: Swiss National Bank, *Das Schweizerische Bankwesen im Jahre 1992* p. A 244-246 and Swiss National Bank, *Das Schweizerische Bankwesen im Jahre 1994* p. A 200-202.

Figure 4.9

Asset composition of the Big Banks, 1994

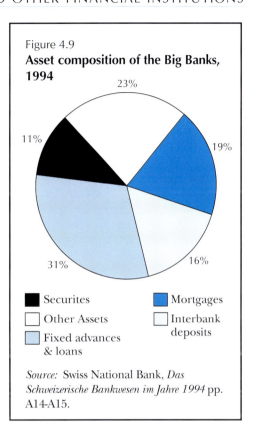

- Securites
- Other Assets
- Fixed advances & loans
- Mortgages
- Interbank deposits

Source: Swiss National Bank, *Das Schweizerische Bankwesen im Jahre 1994* pp. A14-A15.

Between 1988 and 1994, foreign banks and foreign finance companies reduced their participation in Switzerland from 235 to 205 institutions.[8] Over the same period, Swiss financial institutions increased their branch offices abroad from 197 to 261 (see Table 4.9). Most of this international activity was conducted by the Big Banks, other banks and the foreign banks. Cantonal banks, regional and savings banks, Raiffeisen banks and private banks remained predominately domestic institutions with virtually no foreign affiliates.

The Big Banks

Credit Suisse, Union Bank of Switzerland and Swiss Bank Corporation are the three Swiss Big Banks. Founded in 1856, Credit Suisse is the oldest of the three financial institutions. Only recently, it took the effective market leadership position after acquiring Bank Leu and Swiss Volksbank.[9]

Even though the Big Banks dominate the Swiss banking industry and have significantly increased their international presence, Table 4.10 shows that they are not among the largest financial institutions in the world in terms of assets. Nevertheless, they are regarded to be, as Table 4.11 reveals, among the safest in the world. In general, the Big

---

[8] Swiss National Bank, *Das Schweizerische Bankwesen im Jahre 1994* p. 22.
[9] CS Holding acquired a majority ownership of Bank Leu in 1989 and increased it to almost 100 per cent in 1994. Bank Leu and Volksbank will remain separate subsidiaries, but their activities will be focused.

Table 4.10

Top 35 banks in the world by assets: 1995

Rank	Bank	Country	Assets (US$ billions)
1	Fuji Bank	Japan	534.1
2	Dai-Ichi Kangyo Bank	Japan	531.2
3	Sumitomo Bank	Japan	527.7
4	Sanwa Bank	Japan	521.1
5	Sakura Bank	Japan	519.7
6	Mitsubishi Bank	Japan	456.4
7	Industrial Bank of Japan	Japan	411.7
8	Deutsche Bank Group	Germany	370.0
9	Crédit Lyonnais	France	347.5
10	Industrial & Commercial Bank of China	China	337.5
11	Caisse Nationale de Crédit Agricole	France	328.2
12	Tokai Bank	Japan	326.1
13	HSBC Holdings	UK	314.9
14	Long Term Credit Bank of Japan	Japan	312.6
15	ABN-AMRO Holding	Netherlands	290.8
16	Société Générale	France	278.0
17	Asahi Bank	Japan	275.5
18	Bank of Tokyo	Japan	271.8
19	Banque Nationale de Paris	France	271.6
20	Dresdner Bank	Germany	258.4
21	Barclays	UK	253.8
22	Citicorp	US	250.5
23	Bank of China	China	245.7
24	Natwest	UK	245.1
25	Westdeutsche Landesbank Girozentrale	Germany	244.4
26	Groupe Paribas	France	242.2
27	Bank of America	US	215.5
28	Bayerische Vereinsbank	Germany	205.4
29	Caisse d'Epargne et de Prévoyance	France	187.4
30	People's Construction Bank of China	China	183.6
31	Agricultural Bank of China	China	182.0
32	**Union Bank of Switzerland**	**Switzerland**	**179.7**
33	Daiwa Bank	Japan	178.1
34	Bayerische Hypotheken und Wechsel-Bank	Germany	177.8
35	**Credit Suisse Holding**	**Switzerland**	**176.6**

Note: This table does not account for Credit Suisse Holding acquisition of Volksbank

Source: Charles Piggott, "The Euromoney Bank Atlas: The world's most important banks," *Euromoney Magazine* (June 1995) pp. 188-190.

Banks are well-capitalized, and because of the estimated hidden reserves, they have accumulated over the years, their actual equity is considered to be larger than that reported. Figure 4.9 shows that the Big Banks' balance sheets are weighted toward fixed advances and loans. Moreover, in spite of their commercial and international profiles, they do a substantial volume of business in mortgage lending.[10]

---

[10] UBS is the largest mortgage lender in Switzerland.

Table 4.11

The 12 safest* banks in the world, 1994 (Top 4 Ranks)

#	Rank	Bank	Country
1	1	Deutsche Bank	Germany
2	**1**	**Union Bank of Switzerland**	**Switzerland**
3	1	Bayerische Landesbank	Germany
4	1	J.P. Morgan	US
5	1	Rabobank Nederland	Netherlands
6	1	Südwestdeutsche Landesbank	Germany
7	1	Landesbank Hessen-Thüringen	Germany
8	1	Landeskreditbank Baden-Württemburg	Germany
9	**2**	**Swiss Bank Corporation**	**Switzerland**
10	**3**	**Credit Suisse**	**Switzerland**
11	4	Kreditanstalt für Wiederbau	Germany
12	4	Crédit Local de France	France

*Source: Ellen Memmelaar, "The World's Safest Banks," *Global Finance* (September 1994) pp. 98-110.

The range of financial services provided by the Big Banks is extensive and provides an insight into why they are called universal banks. Among their product offerings are deposits, commercial and consumer loans, trade and project financing, mortgages, money market instruments, foreign exchange, factoring, forfeiting and discounting. They also provide off-balance sheet transactions such as portfolio management, credit lines, stock issues, brokerage services, bond and note underwriting, leasing, security custody services, fiduciary accounts, precious metals trading, documentary credits, guarantees and forward exchange contracts. This array of financial services has created strong financial synergies (eg, links to asset administration, trading, placing and underwriting) and has given these financial institutions the opportunity to reduce the volatility of their earnings through diversification.

Only about half (51.8 per cent) of the Big Banks' assets in 1994 were claims on Swiss residents – making their international assets relatively large by international standards. Over the early-to-mid 1990s, the growth of their international operations helped to support sales and profitability. They were able to draw on a large domestic deposit base that enabled them to support domestic and foreign loans at a relatively low cost. In fact, the Big Banks attracted for the first time in 1994 more non-bank customer deposits than the cantonal banks.

During the 1990s, changing conditions in both the domestic and international markets have forced the Big Banks to reevaluate their strategies and to become much more aggressive in their competitive behaviour. In the domestic market, increased pressure to perform has been stimulated by three major factors: financial liberalization (eg, the abolition of fixed commissions and fixed syndicates), an extended recession (from the first quarter 1991 until the second quarter 1993) with slow growth thereafter and, increasing competition from niche players (eg, BZ Bank). At the international level, this pressure was the result of intensified competition from US, European and Japanese banks, as well as the Big Banks' move toward international accounting standards, leading to more open disclosure of financial information and restricting their use of hidden reserves.

Domestic acquisitions and banking industry consolidation

To survive and grow, the Big Banks were forced to become more efficient. In the stagnating domestic market, this meant rationalizing branch offices, raising operating efficiency and putting more emphasis on "shareholder value" while continuing to offer a full line of financial services.

Switzerland's recession and slow growth in recent years (along with an avalanche of bad property lending) intensified the consolidation of the domestic banking industry that had been going on for over a decade. Many banks (especially regional banks) failed and were acquired by the Big Banks. For the most part, these acquisitions were relatively small, but there were notable exceptions, such as CS Holding's acquisition of Swiss Volksbank (1993), Bank Leu (1994) and Neue Aargauer Bank, a large regional bank (1994).[11]

Domestic competition from niche players

Competition increased as niche players, such as BZ Bank, BK Vision and Bank am Bellevue, gained financial clout and put a high emphasis on creating "shareholder value". BZ Group is especially interesting. Founded in 1985, this Zürich-based, equities and options boutique has pioneered covered warrants and active block trading of large cap Swiss equities. In recent years, it has also entered the portfolio management market. BZ Group's most recent investment fund, Stillhalter Vision, was started in 1994 and has trailblazed covered equity warrant offerings on the Swiss capital markets. Foreign investors have found these warrants to be useful vehicles for circumventing restrictions that some Swiss companies put on foreign ownership of Swiss registered shares. By purchasing the fund's covered warrants, foreign investors expected to profit from the diminishing differential between the prices of Swiss bearer and registered shares.[12]

Changing international market focus

During the 1990s, the Big Banks have considerably increased their presence in Southeast Asia through a network of subsidiaries, branches and representative offices. Though their organizational structures differ, the common denominator among them is the desire to tap this rapidly growing and enormous segment of the international market. Their participation has been mainly in the areas of private customers, corporate banking, trusts, treasury financing and trade credits.

Focus on derivatives, investment banking activities and other international dimensions

To succeed internationally, the Big Banks (and virtually all global players) have devel-

---

[11] A trend in Switzerland is for acquired banks to keep their corporate identities. As a result, Swiss Volksbank, Bank Leu, Neue Aargauer Bank, and Solothurner Bank have all kept their corporate names. SBC's purchase of US-based Brinson Partners was also made with the understanding that it would operate out of the Chicago office and under its own name.

[12] Due to restrictions imposed by some companies on the purchase of their registered shares, non-registered bearer shares tended to be higher priced.

oped significant positions in London, Tokyo and New York. SBC, CS Holding and UBS have also moved deliberately and strongly into the derivatives (and other off-balance sheet) business and strengthened their capital bases (eg, with American Depository Receipts). The derivatives market seems to be a perfect fit for the Big Banks, that are geographically well-diversified and have high credit ratings making them desired counterparties for derivative trades.

Swiss Bank Corporation has been one of the most aggressive in the derivative market, but only since the early 1990s. In 1986 (prior to the "Big Bang"), it acquired the London stockbroker, Savory Milln, but entered the 1990s as an "also ran" in the international investment banking and international derivative markets. Its position changed dramatically and suddenly in 1992 with the acquisition of O'Connor Associates, a Chicago-based options and futures specialist. The purchase catapulted SBC into a top-ranking international position. Subsequently, its acquisition of the US fund management group, Brinson Partners Inc., gave the bank a solid position in the US money management business. In 1995, SBC further enhanced its international position in the investment banking area (especially in the equities and mergers and acquisitions areas) when it purchased S.G. Warburg, the largest UK merchant bank.[13]

Credit Suisse entered the 1990s with one of the strongest international positions of the Swiss banks. In 1988, it merged its international investment bank with the US firm First Boston to form Credit Suisse First Boston. In the derivatives area, CS Holding linked Credit Suisse and CS First Boston in a joint venture, Credit Suisse Financial Products, to engineer and sell derivatives.

Union Bank of Switzerland made a significant stride in the investment banking business when it purchased in 1986 (prior to the "Big Bang") Phillips & Drew, London (now, UBS Ltd.), a British stock broker and fund manager. In contrast to SBC and CS Holding where derivative market skills and positions were largely purchased, UBS has developed its derivatives capabilities internally.

At the end of 1994, Switzerland had 27 cantonal banks for its 26 cantons and half cantons. The canton Vaud was the only canton with two such banks, but market pressures were forcing these institutions to merge.[14] Founded in the second half of the 18th century by means of cantonal legislation, these financial institutions have been closely tied to the growth and development of the cantons that created them. Most cantonal banks are quasi-public financial institutions that are owned entirely or in part by the cantons.[15] Their size varies considerably, some having assets in the tens of billions of Swiss francs. To

Cantonal banks

---

[13] This acquisition complements SBC's strength in the fixed income, treasury and derivatives markets. The acquisition did not include Warburg's 75 per cent holding of the highly profitable Mercury Asset Management group (MAM).

[14] The Banque Cantonale Vaudoise and Credit Foncier Vaudois have agreed to merge (December 31, 1995) creating a bank with assets of over Sfr32 billion. The Solothurner Kantonalbank was privatized in 1994 and taken over by Swiss Bank Corporation.

[15] Traditionally, they have been owned by the cantons. Lately, these financial institutions have issued participation certificates in an effort to supplement their capital bases without sacrificing control. With the recent passage of the Swiss Company Law, this source of funds should grow increasingly more difficult to tap.

Table 4.12

Top 10 Swiss banks by equity and balance sheet size, 1994 (Sfr billions)

Rank	Bank	Type	Capital	Reserves	Balance sheet
1	Union Bank of Switzerland	Big Bank	2.58	14.13	235.66
2	Swiss Bank Corporation	Big Bank	3.85	8.84	192.86
3	Credit Suisse	Big Bank	2.15	8.77	155.39
4	Zürcher Kantonalbank	Cantonal	1.93	0.41	54.50
5	Swiss Volksbank	Big Bank	0.85	1.13	38.08
6	Banque Cantonale Vaudoise	Cantonal	0.27	0.61	19.28
7	Berner Kantonalbank	Cantonal	0.65	0.30	18.73
8	St Gallische Kantonalbank	Cantonal	0.47	0.93	16.27
9	Luzerner Kantonalbank	Cantonal	0.50	0.19	15.75
10	Credit Foncier Vaudois	Cantonal	0.15	0.34	12.93

Source: Swiss National Bank, *Das Schweizerische Bankwesen im Jahre 1994* pp. B3-B5.

gain perspective into the relative size of the cantonal banks, Table 4.12 ranks the top 10 Swiss banks in terms of assets and equity.

The cantonal banks escape Swiss banking laws in a number of important areas. Since they do not need a federal banking license, they are not bound by the rules concerning reserves and civil liabilities of bank policy makers. Their activities are not governed by the Federal Bank Commission, and they cannot be dissolved by bankruptcy proceedings (only the canton can dissolve them).[16]

In part, the mandates under which cantonal banks were created have undermined their ability to compete against the Big Banks. Though profitability has always been considered to be a goal, they were established to accomplish equally important social and political objectives for the cantons. Among these objectives have been the promotion of home ownership, encouragement of thrift and support for cantonal economic growth. After they outgrew the original objective for which they were founded, cantonal banks often became the victims of political party objectives or the missions of individual politicians.

Unlike the major Swiss banks, they are restricted, depending on their by-laws, from pursuing alternative profit-making activities. Historically, the cantonal banks have been able to compete with the Big Banks and other banks because they pay no taxes and offer deposits that are backed fully by the cantons. In the 1990s, following the mismanagement calamities and abuses of such banks as the Berner Kantonalbank and the Solothurner Kantonalbank, the concept of the state-run bank has been under attack, and at present, the *status quo* of cantonal banks is being questioned. As politicians tend to be on the boards of these banks, questions are also being raised about the required competences needed to guide a bank, and who should pay for mistakes.

The cantonal banks are under pressure to merge or to become more efficient. Privatization is also being advanced as a possible option. An indication of that pressure came as far back as 1985, when they formed the Swiss Cantobank (today: Swissca Securities

---

[16] OECD, *Economic Survey 1994-1995: Switzerland* p. 102.

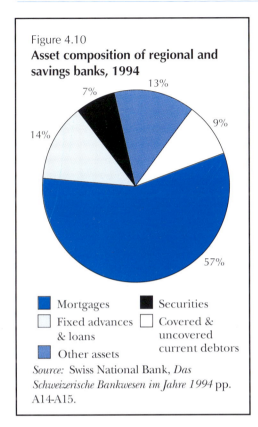

Figure 4.10

Asset composition of regional and savings banks, 1994

- Mortgages
- Fixed advances & loans
- Other assets
- Securities
- Covered & uncovered current debtors

Source: Swiss National Bank, *Das Schweizerische Bankwesen im Jahre 1994* pp. A14-A15.

Ltd.), a commercial bank through which they hoped to gain greater access to foreign markets.[17] In 1993, they formed a common company, Swissca Holding, for the purpose of combining their financial and human resources for asset and unit trust management. Moreover, the Association of Swiss Cantonal Banks, formed in 1907, has recently become more active in helping its members solve practical problems.

The cantonal banks have relatively few foreign assets. They are largely domestic mortgage lenders and the source of their funding comes mostly from local Swiss depositors. Except for the largest cantonal banks, they restrict their activities to domestic borrowers.

Regional and savings banks are in the same basic line of business as cantonal banks, but typically restrict their business to smaller regions or selected territories within Switzerland. They earn most of their net revenues from the spread between deposit and lending rates – staying away from many of the off-balance sheet fee-generating activities of the major banks. Nevertheless, there has been a trend for these financial institutions to move toward offering more universal banking services.

Regional and savings banks

Regional and savings banks are among the most obvious victims of the new Swiss banking environment. Because of their small size and domestic orientation, operating costs per transaction are considerably higher than larger financial institutions. Historically, they have financed their activities with deposits of local customers and have lent to support local home purchases (see Figure 4.10).

The sizes of the regional and savings banks vary widely. Figure 4.11 shows the distribution in 1994 ranged from small banks with assets of Sfr4 million to the largest banks with assets in excess of Sfr5 billion. Because they often provide no competitive cost advantages or deliver any speciality services, their numbers have been dwindling. Figure 4.6 reveals that 75 regional and savings banks vanished between 1989 and 1994.

The Swiss Federal Banking Commission has urged the Swiss regional banks to restructure themselves. The Commission suggests that they are too small to take advantage of competitive economies of scale, offer too wide an array of services and are excessively reliant on a specific region. Many have been acquired by the Big Banks.

Following the example of the mutual savings banks (see following section), 98 of these institutions formed RBA Holding in 1994 to provide collective support and

---

[17] Cantobank was established as an ordinary commercial bank in order to avoid many of the restrictions placed on cantonal banks.

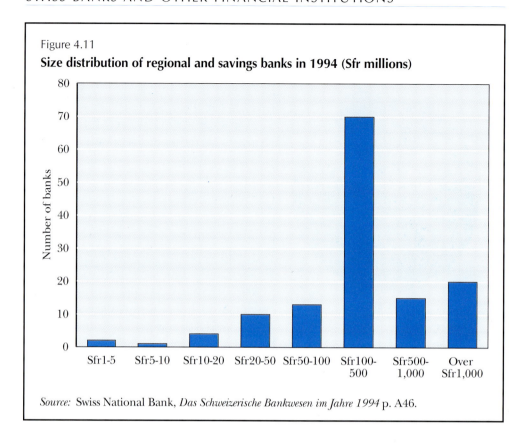

Figure 4.11

Size distribution of regional and savings banks in 1994 (Sfr millions)

Source: Swiss National Bank, *Das Schweizerische Bankwesen im Jahre 1994* p. A46.

economies of scale in auditing, financial management services, inter-bank operations and back office business. These responsibilities are carried out by the three RBA Holding subsidiaries: RBA-Finance, RBA-Service and RBA-Central Bank.

Mutual credit associations and Raiffeisen banks

In contrast to cantonal banks and regional and savings banks, mutual credit associations and Raiffeisen banks[18] have had remarkable success in maintaining their position at about 3.5 per cent of total Swiss bank assets (see Figure 4.7). These institutions take deposits from and make collateralized loans (mainly mortgages) to members.[19] Typically, they operate in small regional areas (mountain regions, rural communities and country areas) where it is generally unprofitable for the larger banks to operate, and they keep their costs low by often running operations with part-time staff. As cooperatives, they maintain their own legal identities, and until the end of 1995, members stood mutually liable for amounts up to forty times their participation of Sfr200. Starting in 1996, members will be allowed higher participations in cooperatives, but their maximum liability will stay at Sfr8,000 per member.

To reduce costs, distribute risks and have access to funds, the mutual banks have banded together to form two associations, the Swiss Federation of Raiffeisenkassen and

[18] Raiffeisen banks were founded in Switzerland during the beginning of the twentieth century. They were named after F.W. Raiffeisen (1818-1888), who proposed an alternative to capitalism through a socialist or cooperative model in which capital served labour. He founded rural cooperatives in Germany.
[19] These financial institutions reinvest 100 per cent of their profits (ie, no profits are distributed).

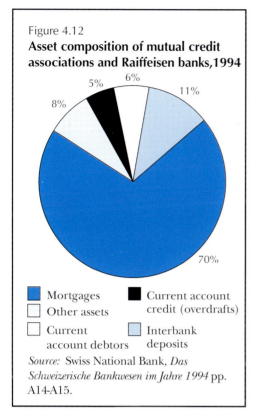

Figure 4.12

Asset composition of mutual credit associations and Raiffeisen banks,1994

- ■ Mortgages
- □ Other assets
- □ Current account debtors
- ■ Current account credit (overdrafts)
- ▨ Interbank deposits

Source: Swiss National Bank, *Das Schweizerische Bankwesen im Jahre 1994* pp. A14-A15.

the Fédération Vaudoise des Caisses de Credit Mutuel.[20] Their job is to centralize many of the administrative tasks, such as liquidity management and accounting, that would otherwise be undertaken by each credit association. They also provide research, marketing and advice on matters relating to business management, information technology, investment counselling, personnel and law.

In this way, the group has been able to take advantage of economies of scale denied any individual member. In an effort to focus on the home mortgage market, they agreed in 1994 to engage Bank Vontobel, a private bank, to manage their five mutual funds.

Other banks (not including foreign banks)

The 'other banks' category of Swiss financial institutions includes commercial trade banks, stock exchange banks, investment management specialists, small credit institutes, consumer credit banks and banks not otherwise classified under any other heading. There is substantial dissimilarity among these financial institutions in both size (see Figure 4.13) and activity. About two-thirds of their assets are devoted to fixed advances, loans, mortgages and bank deposits (see Figure 4.14).

Foreign banks

Foreign banks are defined as banks that are either incorporated under Swiss law with over 50 per cent of their ownership in the hands of persons and/or companies domiciled outside Switzerland or are established as branches of foreign banks. Under Swiss banking law, they have substantially the same rights and obligations as Swiss banks. Swiss law permits foreign banks to practice in Switzerland only if the banks' home countries offer reciprocal privileges to Swiss banks. Moreover, foreign banks must have names that do not suggest Swiss ownership and are required to make a commitment to the Swiss National Bank to observe Switzerland's credit and monetary policies. In 1994, they employed 15,715 Swiss residents.

These banks tend to be larger than regional banks or Raiffeisen banks (see Figure 4.15) and their assets are heavily concentrated in bank deposits, fixed advances and loans (see Figure 4.16).

---

[20] Since 1994, the Swiss National Bank has combined the statistics for the members of the Fédération Vaudoise des Caisses de Credit Mutuel with the Raiffeisen Banks. It is for this reason that Swiss National Bank figures show only one association after the "Mutual Banks and Raiffeisen Banks" category.

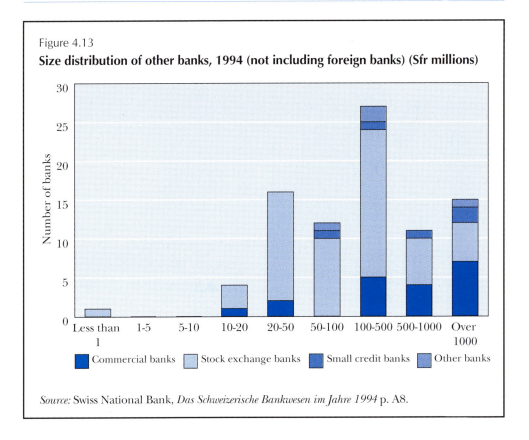

Figure 4.13

Size distribution of other banks, 1994 (not including foreign banks) (Sfr millions)

Legend: Commercial banks · Stock exchange banks · Small credit banks · Other banks

Source: Swiss National Bank, *Das Schweizerische Bankwesen im Jahre 1994* p. A8.

Most foreign banks' business is done with non-Swiss residents. Like the major Swiss banks, foreign banks have followed their domestic customers into nations, like Switzerland, as business expanded internationally. Most of them were established when Switzerland became a major international capital market in the 1960s. Before World War II, there were only a few foreign banks in Switzerland, mainly from neighbouring countries.

During the 1970s, excessive worldwide liquidity created intense competition among the international lenders, creating thin spreads and making balance sheet-based business less attractive. Increasingly, institutions sought to supplement interest-based income with off-balance sheet revenues. A glance at Swiss banks' income statements induced many international banks to enter the Swiss markets. In many cases, activities that could be conducted in

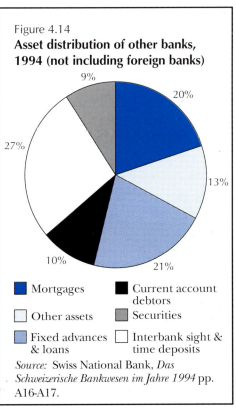

Figure 4.14

Asset distribution of other banks, 1994 (not including foreign banks)

Legend: Mortgages · Current account debtors · Other assets · Securities · Fixed advances & loans · Interbank sight & time deposits

Source: Swiss National Bank, *Das Schweizerische Bankwesen im Jahre 1994* pp. A16-A17.

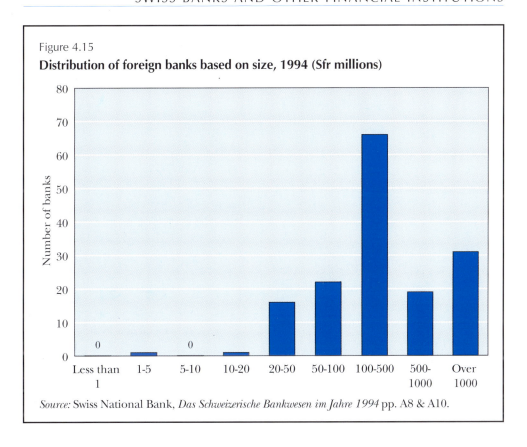

Figure 4.15
Distribution of foreign banks based on size, 1994 (Sfr millions)

Source: Swiss National Bank, *Das Schweizerische Bankwesen im Jahre 1994* pp. A8 & A10.

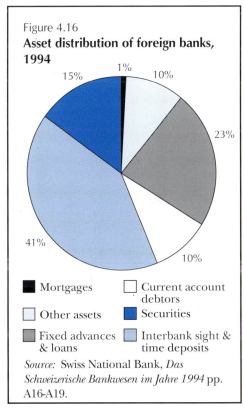

Figure 4.16
Asset distribution of foreign banks, 1994

- Mortgages
- Other assets
- Fixed advances & loans
- Current account debtors
- Securities
- Interbank sight & time deposits

Source: Swiss National Bank, *Das Schweizerische Bankwesen im Jahre 1994* pp. A16-A19.

the Swiss markets were restricted in their home countries. For these reasons, Japanese brokerage houses and banks were particularly prominent among the newcomers.

The most important activity of foreign banks in Switzerland, except for a few institutions that are very strong in international trade finance, is portfolio management, a fee-generating activity that is typically not reflected in the balance sheet. Fiduciary accounts exemplify the level of foreign banks' participation in this area. In 1994, foreign banks controlled Sfr128.1 billion (58 per cent) of Switzerland's total Sfr222.2 billion fiduciary deposits. This contrasts with balance sheet-based business, where all foreign banks accounted for only 9.5 per cent of the consolidated balance sheet total of the Swiss banking system.

Many foreign banks are also involved in underwriting which, until 1970, was a quasi-monopoly of the Big Banks. A large number of them has entered this lucrative business. Most visible numerically have been Japanese brokers and Japanese banks that are not allowed to pursue this business in Japan due to the American-inherited division between commercial and investment banks. They began by bringing Japanese clients to the Swiss franc capital market, but increasingly have participated as underwriters.

Finance companies

In 1994, there were 71 finance companies in Switzerland. As Figure 4.17 shows, their assets were dominated by interbank deposits. Two general types of finance companies exist in Switzerland: bank-like finance companies and commercial or industrial finance companies. In both categories, these financial institutions are regulated by the Swiss Banking Law only if they publicly solicit deposits from third parties

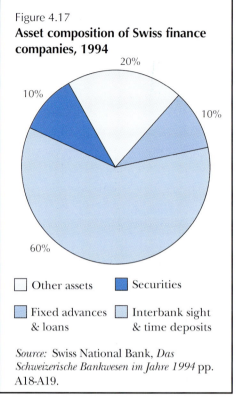

Figure 4.17
Asset composition of Swiss finance companies, 1994

- ☐ Other assets
- ■ Securities
- ☐ Fixed advances & loans
- ☐ Interbank sight & time deposits

Source: Swiss National Bank, *Das Schweizerische Bankwesen im Jahre 1994* pp. A18-A19.

to finance an undefined number of unrelated persons, finance such transactions from a number of banks or acquire, on a firm commitment or a commission basis, securities or other rights for the purpose of offering them publicly on the primary market.[21] Finance companies are not regulated by the Swiss banking law but are controlled by the Swiss Code of Obligations,[22] and will also be regulated, to a certain degree, by the new Swiss Stock Exchange Law.

Some quasi-bank finance companies owned by banks tend to concentrate on providing medium-term financing, often for customers to whom (or purposes for which) their owner bank might not wish to extend credit. Most finance companies in Switzerland do not solicit funds from the public but are only finance vehicles for large groups of companies, and therefore are not subject to the same provisions of the Banking Law.

Since 1 January 1990, the Swiss Banking Commission has expanded its definition of finance companies that are regulated by Swiss banking law. The changes were enacted to regulate the flow of foreign finance companies coming to Switzerland to set up operations. Many foreign banks found that entry into the Swiss markets was much easier as "bank like" finance companies than as regular banks. The finance company structure was employed largely to circumvent the restrictive Swiss banking regulations and/or to evade laws in their own countries prohibiting them from acquiring foreign bank status.

---

[21] See Article 2a of the Swiss Banking Law. Article 3 and 3a define what "soliciting deposits" and "the public" mean.

[22] Bank-like finance companies that do not accept deposits are required to follow Articles 7 and 8 of the Swiss Banking Law regarding articles of association, scope of operations, and supervision.

Private banks are organized as sole proprietorships, partnerships or limited partnerships. As a result, owners are personally liable for the institutions' debts. Most of them are located in Geneva, Basel and Zürich. Their numbers have dwindled from 200 at the beginning of the century to 17 in 1994. This attrition has been due to a number of causes, such as a vital partner dying, stock exchange crashes and/or the severe restraints that low capitalization has put on their activities. As a group, private banks are misrepresented in the official statistics, showing assets of only Sfr6.8 billion (approximately 0.6 per cent of total Swiss bank assets in 1994) of which 27 per cent were foreign. Based on these statistics, this sector would appear to be scarcely worth mentioning, but in this case appearances are wrong.

Private banks

    These financial institutions are the oldest Swiss banks and specialize in the administration and management of portfolios. They conduct all types of security activities such as trading, underwriting, and placement. So long as they do not advertise for deposits, they are not required to publish their balance sheets. As a result, there is no firm estimate of the client numbers or volume of business done by the private banks.

Table 4.13

List of private Swiss bankers, 1994

	Founded	*City*	*Private bank*
1	1841	Basel	Bank Sarasin & Cie*
2	1920	Basel	Baumann & Cie
3	1886	Basel	E Gutzwiller & Cie
4	1787	Basel	La Roche & Cie
5	1844	Geneva	Bordier & Cie
6	1796	Geneva	Darier, Hentsch & Cie
7	1845	Geneva	Gonet & Cie
8	1798	Geneva	Lombard, Odier & Cie
9	1819	Geneva	Mirabaud & Cie
10	1869	Geneva	Mourgue d'Algue et Cie
11	1805	Geneva	Pictet & Cie
12	1882	Lausanne	Hentsch, Chollet & Cie
13	1780	Lausanne	Landolt, Lonfat & Cie
14	1875	Luzern	Falck & Cie
15	1741	St. Gallen	Wegelin & Co, Inhaber Eugster & Co
16	1968	Zürich	Hottinger & Cie
17	1750	Zürich	Rahn & Bodmer

* Bank Sarasin is a Kommanditgesellschaft, a combination of a partnership and a corporation. The partners have the majority of the voting power (62.5 per cent), but only 25 per cent of the capital.

Source: Swiss National Bank, *Das Schweizerische Bankwesen im Jahre 1994* p. B35.

Mortgage funding institutes

Switzerland has two major mortgage funding institutes headquartered in Zürich: the Central Mortgage Bond Institute of the Swiss Cantonal Banks (Pfandbriefzentrale der schweizerischen Kantonalbanken) and the Mortgage Bond Bank of the Swiss Mortgage Institutes (Pfandbriefbank schweizerischer Hypothekarinstitute). Both institutions issue public bonds and use the proceeds to refinance members' mortgage loans.

6. Deposit insurance scheme

Almost all cantonal banks benefit from a general or depositors' guarantee from their respective cantons. Such security has been one of the major competitive advantages these banks have had over other financial institutions.

In spite of such protections, certain political groups considered the Swiss system of deposit protection to be insufficient and inefficient. In response to their requests, the Swiss Bankers' Association introduced, in 1984 and revised in 1993, a non-compulsory Deposit Insurance Scheme for all its member banks. Under it, savings deposits enjoy preferential treatment in bankruptcy cases with owners of any bank deposit liability covered up to Sfr30,000. Funding for this insurance scheme is not made from a dedicated asset pool, but rather is on call from members on an as-needed basis.[23]

7. Swiss banks' off-balance sheet activities

In addition to credit facilities, Swiss banks offer their domestic and foreign customers off-balance sheet services such as asset management (including trust business), underwriting services, brokerage, foreign exchange and gold trading. In 1994, almost half of the Swiss banks' net revenues were derived from off-balance sheet activities. As a result of these services, the impact of Swiss banks on the financial market is significantly larger than their balance sheet totals would imply.

Fiduciary deposits

Fiduciary deposits are funds placed with banks in Switzerland and invested in the name of the bank for the account and risk of the depositor. Since 1950, they have grown at a compound annual rate of 18.5 per cent (see Figure 4.18), raising their relative balance sheet importance from 0.5 per cent in 1950 to 22 per cent in 1994 (see Figure 4.19).

Because banks act as agents, these deposits (assets and liabilities) do not enter into their balance sheets. Approximately 90 per cent of the funds are invested offshore in the Euro-interbank market (mostly, in the UK, Belgium, Luxembourg, the Netherlands and France),[24] and about two-thirds (21 per cent from Switzerland and 41 per cent from other European nations) of the funds are from European depositors.

As Figure 4.20 shows, most fiduciary accounts are invested in US dollars, Swiss francs and Deutschmarks. Moreover, there is a near perfect match between the currency structure of banks' off-balance sheet fiduciary liabilities and assets (ie, dollar fiduciary deposits are invested mainly in dollar assets).

---

[23] The Swiss bankruptcy legislation is currently under revision.
[24] Big Banks became major players in the inter-bank market because of the lack of a short-term capital market of any size in Switzerland. See Chapter 5.

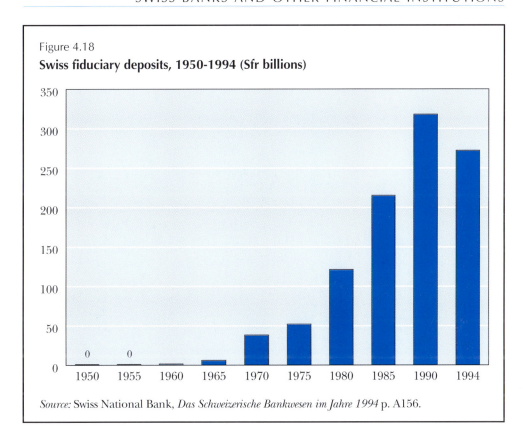

Figure 4.18

Swiss fiduciary deposits, 1950-1994 (Sfr billions)

Source: Swiss National Bank, *Das Schweizerische Bankwesen im Jahre 1994* p. A156.

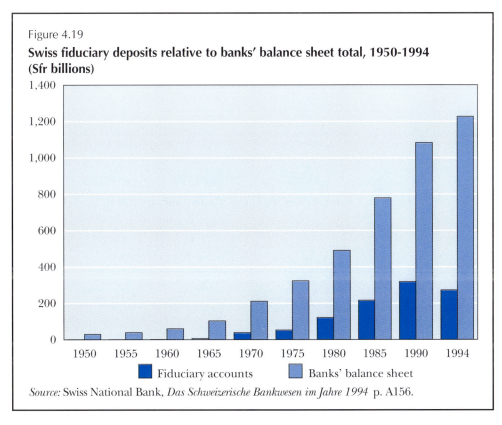

Figure 4.19

Swiss fiduciary deposits relative to banks' balance sheet total, 1950-1994 (Sfr billions)

Fiduciary accounts   Banks' balance sheet

Source: Swiss National Bank, *Das Schweizerische Bankwesen im Jahre 1994* p. A156.

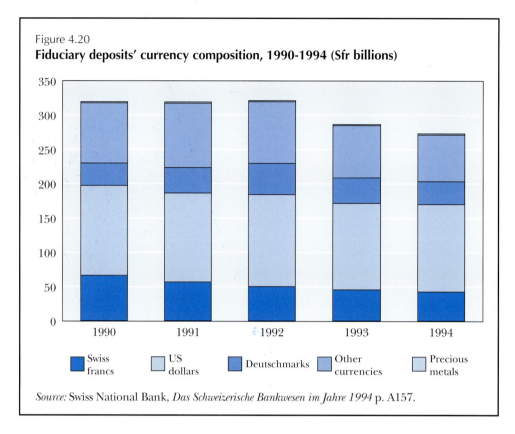

Figure 4.20

Fiduciary deposits' currency composition, 1990-1994 (Sfr billions)

Legend: Swiss francs | US dollars | Deutschmarks | Other currencies | Precious metals

Source: Swiss National Bank, *Das Schweizerische Bankwesen im Jahre 1994* p. A157.

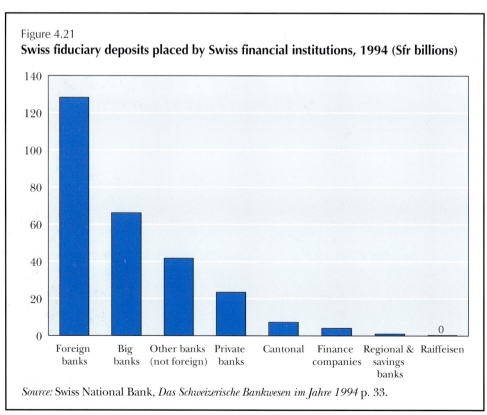

Figure 4.21

Swiss fiduciary deposits placed by Swiss financial institutions, 1994 (Sfr billions)

Source: Swiss National Bank, *Das Schweizerische Bankwesen im Jahre 1994* p. 33.

Together, foreign banks and the Big Banks account for most fiduciary deposits (see Figure 4.21). These deposits are favoured by both Swiss and non-Swiss residents because they offer anonymity, but are especially attractive to foreigners because they are free of the 35 per cent Swiss withholding tax (if invested outside Switzerland). To date, offshore fiduciary accounts have not been subject to Swiss withholding tax because they are invested in the name of a bank, but at the client's risk. All objective arguments, as well as the Swiss tax law system, which does not recognize the extra-territoriality concept, speak against taxing them, but certain political forces aware of the empty fiscal coffers favour it.

Fiduciary accounts were at the centre of Swiss public debate in the early 1980s because they were one of the few remaining investments in which the fiscal authorities did not yet directly participate. The debate continues in the 1990s.

Unlike US and UK asset managers, who have tended to focus their efforts on institutional investors, Swiss banks and investment specialists have focused on private customers (ie, wealthy individuals) who require relatively high levels of customer service. The Swiss investment philosophy is typically conservative with preservation of capital carrying a high priority. Precise statistics are not reported, so there is no accurate record of Switzerland's assets under management. A popularly quoted study has estimated their size at Sfr2.1 trillion, with Sfr819 billion held on behalf of foreign private clients, Sfr220 billion due to foreign institutional investors, Sfr515 billion owned by Swiss private individuals and the remaining Sfr546 billion coming from Swiss institutional investors.[25]

The Big Banks have a competitive advantage in this area because of their network of branches, direct access to both domestic and international exchanges, underwriting strength, and international reputation for safety. Private banks have competitive strength due to their tradition, experience with personalized service and discretion.[26]

Asset administration/ management

Trade in gold can be physical (eg, coins, ingots and medals) or non-physical (eg, futures contracts). The physical gold market is divided into a primary and secondary exchange. The primary market caters to the manufacturing industry and the secondary market to investors. Zürich and London are the world's most important primary markets, while the Middle East and Asia dominate the secondary market.

Since 1968, the Zürich gold pool has played a prominent role in the global physical gold market, but its relative international position has varied widely. Switzerland's entry into this market began in 1968 when the UK temporarily closed its gold window due to the US dollar crisis. The Zürich market remained open and grew quickly to take a near

Gold trading

---

[25] B. Gehrig, "Ausländische Privatkundschaft spielt eine dominierde Rolle," *Finanz und Wirtschaft* No. 76, September 25, 1993. Other estimates put the figure closer to Sfr1-1.5 trillion. See, L. Schuster, "Die Rolle der Schweizer Banken im internationalen Finanzwesen", *Oesterreich. Bankarchiv*, No. 7, 1987. Also, see L. Koenig, "Can the UBS Colonels Win the Overseas Battle?", *Euromoney* July 1989, and Vontobel, "Schweizer Börsen in internationalen Wettbewerb," NZZ, Jan 27, 1990.

[26] Recently, private banks have shifted some of their marketing focus toward the growing institutional investor market.

70 per cent world market share. Domestic market growth was stopped abruptly over the 1980 to 1986 period when the Swiss government imposed a tax on these transactions. By 1987, Zürich's world position had fallen to 40 per cent. This decline was caused also by the conscious efforts of gold producers from areas such as South Africa and the former Soviet Union to diversify their distribution channels.[27]

Bank note trading

The Swiss banks (mainly the Big Banks) are among the world's largest traders of bank notes, but their wholesale and retail market positions have been seriously eroded over the last 20 years. Due to competition from England's deposit banks, Germany's universal banks, French banks, Austrian banks and US money centre banks, the Swiss have gone from having an approximate 50 per cent market share in the 1970s to well under 20 per cent in the 1990s.[28]

The key to profits in the bank note market is good inventory control. Successful banks understand how to optimize the number, amount and variety of non-interest earning notes they hold. Foreign exchange risk, transportation costs and seasonal variations in demand are also important considerations. Because of its location in the centre of Europe and relatively low interest rates (ie, low opportunity costs), Swiss banks have traditionally had a competitive advantage in this market. The sources of these notes are hotels, restaurants, companies, tourists, wealthy individuals and foreign workers who cross the Swiss border each day.

Underwriting

The Swiss banks have underwriting and placement power in all of the major domestic, foreign[29] and Euro-[30] markets. Because of low Swiss interest rates, liberal capital export policies, efficiency in underwriting, and large placing power, Switzerland is now second only to the US in placement activity (see Table 4.14).

The Eurobond market is fiercely competitive with narrow margins and high volumes.[31] In general, the level of competition has become so intense that these financial instruments are profitable only if attached to a cross-currency swap. Credit Suisse has gained a leading position in this market through its subsidiary, CS First Boston. UBS has concentrated on equity-related business, and SBC has a strong hold on the Euro-commercial paper market. With the acquisition of S.G. Warburg, SBC has further improved its position in the equity- and Eurobond markets.

---

[27] See Urs Brumbacher, *The Swiss Banking Industry*, Harvard Business Case #9-792-076, 2 June 1992. If the Big Banks' operations in other countries were included, the percent of market share would be larger.

[28] Brumbacher, p.7.

[29] The foreign bond market involves the issuance of Swiss franc bonds in Switzerland by foreign companies or institutions.

[30] Eurobonds are bonds that are marketed globally in countries other than the country of the currency in which they are denominated (eg, dollar bonds marketed outside the US) and are distributed by multinational syndicates.

[31] Switzerland's high withholding taxes on domestic Swiss bond issues created the incentive to develop a market in Swiss franc securities issued in foreign nations (ie, the Euro-Swiss Franc market). Through this market, investors are able to purchase (short- and medium term) Swiss franc-denominated assets and avoid the high Swiss withholding taxes. Because the Swiss National Bank has not sanctioned Swiss franc bond issues abroad, there is no significant Swiss franc eurobond market.

Table 4.14

Top 20 underwriters of Euro and global bonds

Rank	Name	Amount (US$ millions)
1	Merrill Lynch	31,533
2	**CS First Boston/ Credit Suisse**	**21,657**
3	Goldman Sachs	21,075
4	**Swiss Bank Corporation**	**17,309**
5	Nomura Securities	15,998
6	Lehman Brothers	15,391
7	J.P. Morgan	13,540
8	Morgan Stanley	13,284
9	Deutsche Bank	12,723
10	**Union Bank of Switzerland**	**12,676**
11	Daiwa Securities	12,359
12	Nikko Securities	9,455
13	Salomon	8,894
14	Banque Paribas	8,879
15	ABN Amro	8,388
16	Industrial Bank of Japan	7,292
17	Société Générale	6,210
18	Barclays de Zoete Wedd	6,066
19	HSBC Group	5,069
20	SG Warburg	4,035

Source: Euromoney Bondware. Clive Horwood, "Top 20 bookrunners of Euro and global bonds," *Euromoney Magazine* (December 1994) p. 33.

The Swiss markets are commonly used to raise funds for private companies, public authorities and supranational organizations such as the World Bank. Because the commissions from these debt or equity transactions are recorded off-balance sheet, their service fees have contributed to Swiss banks' profitability without changing their balance sheet ratios.

Switzerland has two parallel systems for clearing checks and transferring funds. One is operated by the Swiss National Bank and the other by the Swiss Postal Telephone and Telegraph (PTT). In 1994, there were 1.55 million postal checking accounts through which 566.7 million domestic and international transactions worth Sfr2.6 trillion were handled by Switzerland's 39,039 post offices.[32]

Since most companies, organizations, professionals and households have postal checking accounts, the availability of a parallel payment system has relieved Swiss banks from handling a large number of small payment transactions. Merchant invoices typically include postal payments forms, and most banks maintain accounts at the post office for some of their customer transactions. Deposits at the PTT once earned no interest and cost the PTT only the transactions expense to clear checks and deal with customers. Since 1987, the PTT has offered 2 per cent interest on individual accounts up to Sfr10,000. Business accounts earn 1/4 per cent interest.[33]

Unlike banks, the PTT is regulated by neither the Swiss Banking Act nor the Federal Banking Commission. Moreover, it has no access to either national or international capital markets. Nevertheless, it has moved increasingly into competition with Swiss banks. Making use of its widespread post office network, the PTT introduced in 1988 a variety of products to facilitate customer payments and investments. It was the first institution in Switzerland to offer a debit card – called the Postcard and containing an elec-

8. Swiss Postal Telephone and Telegraph (PTT)

---

[32] PTT, *Annual Report* 1994 pp. 13, 25, 36 & 37.

[33] In 1993, the average interest paid on PTT liabilities was 1.2 per cent. (See OECD, *Economic Survey 1994-1995: Switzerland* p. 120, footnote 86).

tronic chip – that allowed expense-free cash withdrawals throughout Switzerland and in 24 other countries through thousands of foreign post offices.

Increasingly, the PTT has moved Switzerland toward a cashless payment system that permits customers at train stations, stores with EFT-POS terminals, gas stations and other retail outlets to complete transactions without paying cash or requiring the assistance of bank personnel. To aid customers' cash management needs, the PTT now offers both private businesses, and customers, software that permits payment tracking through the clearing system, Telegiro PTT. In October 1992, it began offering, on a commission basis, federal money market paper (Bundesfestgelder) with 1-, 2- and 3-year maturities.

The Swiss PTT is a government department. In 1997, it hopes partially to privatize operations by creating a government holding company of which the telecommunications portion would go public. It is anticipated that 51 per cent of the stock will be owned by the state and 49 per cent will be in the hands of the private sector. The move toward privatization is to free the PTT for international postal and telecommunication ventures that are currently prohibited or require prior government approval.[34] Privatization is expected to precede the deregulation of the European Union's telecommunications industry in 1998.

9. Swiss numbered accounts

The importance of numbered accounts to the Swiss banking system is more myth than reality. All Swiss bank accounts have identification numbers, but only a small portion are numbered accounts. What distinguishes the famous, Swiss numbered accounts from normal accounts is the limited number of people in the bank who can link the account number to the depositor's name. To get one, depositors must be established customers and justify their needs to a senior bank official. Typically, the accounts are reserved for individuals with names that could be easily recognized (politicians, film stars, artists and writers) and attract the attention of bank employees.

Numbered accounts have disadvantages. They cannot be used for commercial transactions and transfers are very difficult. Special problems may also arise over the power of attorney. For legal reasons, anonymous accounts do not exist in Switzerland.[35] At least one bank official must have access to an account holder's name, and under Swiss law, these accounts receive no special treatment. The secrecy of these accounts is protected as strongly as other accounts, and banks depend on verification by the depositor that the money has been legally acquired.[36]

---

[34] In 1992, the Swiss PTT formed Unisource with Dutch and Swedish counterparts for the purpose of tapping the growing international telecommunications business. Since its birth, the new company has been joined by Spain's Telefonica and the European arm of AT&T.

[35] The only time an account can be maintained without anyone in a bank knowing the depositor is if the depositor is a special Swiss agent. If a customer is represented by a Swiss lawyer, notary or member of a Swiss trust or auditing company, the agent does not - so far - have to identify the name of the principal to the bank.

[36] Robert Louis Stauter, "Swiss Bank Secrecy Laws and the US Internal Revenue Service: Are the Swiss to Blame for Tax Dollars that the US Internal Revenue Service Cannot Collect when US Citizens "Hide" their Money in Swiss Banks?", *Case Western Reserve Journal of International Law* Vol. 20 (Summer 1988) pp. 623-641.

In Switzerland, depositors must identify themselves in the same way regardless of whether their accounts are numbered or not. Unless power of attorney is given, depositors must visit the bank in person. The only reason the numbered accounts cost more than regular accounts is due to the extra back office expense the bank must incur to maintain them.

On 1 February 1995, the revised Swiss Federal Law on Banks and Savings Banks as well as the Swiss Banking Ordinance came into force. The major changes brought about by the new law and ordinance were in the areas of cantonal supervision, "foreign controlling interests", international reciprocity, the international transmission of information between bank supervisory authorities and capital requirements.

10. Revisions in the Swiss bank law and bank ordinance

Regarding cantonal bank supervision, cantons may now transfer the supervision of their cantonal banks to the Swiss Banking Commission. To qualify, the cantonal banks must meet the requirements of the Swiss Bank Law concerning licensing, by-laws, partnership agreements and internal regulations.[37]

The new Bank Law narrowed the definition of a "foreign controlling interest". A bank is considered to have a "foreign controlling interest" if "foreigners with qualified investments directly or indirectly hold more than 50 percent of its voting rights or otherwise exert a controlling influence".[38] Previously, foreign controlling interests required direct or indirect interests that exceeded 50 percent of the company's capital stock or voting rights or otherwise exerted a controlling influence. A "foreigner" is any natural person without Swiss citizenship or residence permit or a legal entity with registered office outside Switzerland or that is controlled by persons who qualify as foreigners.

Regarding international banking reciprocity, under Swiss Bank Law, any bank, branch, branch office or agency of a foreign or foreign controlled bank must receive Swiss authorization and meet special conditions to receive a license. Such authorization is contingent on the "special conditions" (e.g, reciprocity by the countries where the foreign founders or controlling interests are resident and the choice of a name that indicates the bank is not Swiss-controlled).[39] The new law empowers the Federal Government with the option to declare these "special conditions" inapplicable as a result of international treaties (eg, GATT) it has negotiated.

A new section has been inserted into the Banking Law that establishes a legal basis for international cooperation and the exchange of information among bank supervisory authorities.[40] To qualify, the foreign authorities must use the information only for the direct supervision of banks or other financial intermediaries; they are bound by their own secrecy rules. Recipients of such information may not forward the information to other supervisory authorities without the prior approval of the Swiss Banking Commission or on the basis of a blanket approval contained in a state treaty.[41] The transmittal of infor-

---

[37] More specifically, they must meet the requirements of Bank Act Article 3a para. 2.

[38] Swiss Federal Law on Banks and Savings Banks, Article 3bis, para. 3, November 8, 1934 (revised 1994).

[39] Swiss Federal Law on Banks and Savings Banks, Article 3bis, November 8, 1934 (revised 1994).

[40] The new section is Swiss Federal Law on Banks and Savings Banks, Article 23sexies, November 8, 1934 (revised 1994).

[41] The Banking Commission decides after consulting with the Federal Office for Police Matters.

mation from the first recipient to penal prosecuting authorities is not permitted whenever legal assistance in penal matters would be excluded.

Under the Implementing Ordinance to the Swiss Banking Law, bank capital requirements were changed. The Ordinance directs banks to follow the Bank for International Settlements approach to calculating capital requirements. The new requirements are based on the risk weighting system.[42] The new capital requirements cover more completely both on- and off-balance activities.[43]

---

[42] Different capital requirements are defined for categories such as claims by counterparty, non-counterparty related assets, contingent liabilities, irrevocable commitments, forward contracts, purchased options, netting, lending and repo transactions with securities, precious metals and commodities, issuer-related default risk positions involving securities and, finally, market risk positions.

[43] The ordinance identifies four types of risk weighted positions; namely, balance sheet assets, off balance sheet transactions expressed in their credit equivalents, net long positions (issuer related default risk positions) and open positions (market risk positions) in foreign exchange, precious metals and commodities.

5

SWISS BANKING SECRECY AND RELATED SWISS LAWS

The Swiss banking and legal system have deserved reputations for protecting the confidentiality of depositors. Both in law and in practice, the Swiss have made the disclosure of confidential banking information a civil, criminal and banking offense punishable by fines and/or jail terms.[1]

Prior to 1934, there were no statutes regulating the Swiss banking industry. Banking secrecy was implied from personal rights that protected all individuals, and from agency laws that treated banks as agents of customers with fiduciary responsibilities to act as their representatives.[2] The first statutory protection of Swiss citizens' privacy rights was approved in Article 28 of the Swiss Civil Code in December 1907 (and revised in 1983). These civil protections were based on the contract between the bank and its customer on one side and the right of every individual to maintain his/her secrecy on the other. Such rights to privacy applied (and still apply) not only to civil rights but to a person's economic background as well.

The Swiss Banking Secrecy Act was passed in 1934 to provide specific measures of protection for bank depositors. It was the Swiss response to a critical list of concerns, including the lack of confidence in international banking systems after the Great Depression, the failure of a significant Geneva bank and the efforts of German Nazi agents to confiscate the assets of Jewish depositors. Though many nations have similar or even more restrictive laws, the Swiss have a record of strict enforcement that has lent credibility to the formal statute.

---

[1] Many finance companies that are not covered by Swiss banking laws must still abide by virtually the same rules as banks because of the civil and criminal statutes.

[2] Robert Louis Stauter, "Swiss Bank Secrecy Laws and the US Internal Revenue Service: Are the Swiss to Blame for Tax Dollars that the US Internal Revenue Service Cannot Collect when US Citizens "Hide" their Money in Swiss Banks?," *Case Western Reserve Journal of International Law* Vol. 20, Summer 1988: pp. 623-641. Ruchford, "The Effect of Swiss Banking secrecy on Insider Trading, 7 B.C.," *International and Comp. L. Review* (1984) pp. 547-548.

Table 5.1

Swiss laws covering banking secrecy

Law	Article	Regulation
Code of Obligations[3]	398	• The agent is obligated, in general, to use the same care as the employee under an employment contract. • He is liable towards the principal for the faithful and careful performance of the mandate. • He shall personally perform his obligations unless he is duly authorized or compelled by the circumstances, to entrust a third person with their performance, or if the right of substitution is considered permitted customarily.
Swiss Civil Code	28	Any person whose privacy is violated without legal justification or personal consent can seek protection from a judge.
Banking Law	47	1. Whoever divulges a secret entrusted to him or of which he has become aware in his capacity as officer, employee, mandatory, liquidator or commissioner of a bank, as representative of the Banking Commission, officer or employee of a recognized auditing company and whoever tries to induce others to violate professional secrecy, shall be punished by imprisonment for not more than six months or by a fine of not more than Sfr50,000. 2. If the act has been committed by negligence, then the penalty shall be a fine not exceeding Sfr30,000. 3. The violation of professional secrecy remains punishable even after termination of the official or employment relationship or the exercise of the profession. 4. Federal cantonal regulations concerning the obligation to testify and to furnish information to a government shall apply.

[3] Translation from: Swiss-American Chamber of Commerce, *Swiss Code of Obligations, Vol. 1, Contract Law Articles 1-551 English Translation of the Official Text* Third Edition, 1995.

Article 47 of the Swiss Banking Act protects basically the same scope of information as both Article 28 of the Civil Code and the various contractual (implied or explicit) rights of a person, but goes one step beyond by attaching an additional sanction, imprisonment or a fine, to secrecy infringements.[4] It also states that certain actions might infringe upon provisions of Swiss law, in general, and the Swiss Criminal Code, in particular.[5]

Specifically, the Article prohibits a bank employee, agent, representative or receiver in his/her function to disclose a secret entrusted to the bank. It broadens the penalties to bankers who fail to protect the information. Violators are to be punished by prison terms not to exceed six months or by a fine not exceeding Sfr50,000. If the violation is due to negligence, the fine is not to exceed Sfr30,000. Violations remain punishable even after the termination of the official or employment relationship or the exercise of the profession.

2. Exceptions to Swiss banking secrecy

Criminal proceedings, bankruptcy and debt collection

Embezzlement (Article 140 of the Swiss Criminal Code), fraud (Article 148), inducing speculation (Article 158), mismanagement (Article 159) and fraudulent bankruptcy (Article 163) are offenses that have long been punishable under Swiss law and are not covered by the protections of Swiss banking secrecy.

Finally, banking secrecy was not intended for protection against certain public law limitations, including debt collection and bankruptcy proceedings. In bankruptcy attachment cases, banks are required to declare the relevant assets only when the Swiss distraint order is in hand, or when a Swiss bankruptcy declaration is presented. Bankruptcies abroad are ruled by bilateral treaties.

Taxes

Swiss banking protections do not extend to taxpayers who falsify documents in order to mislead the Swiss tax authorities (the Federal or Cantonal Tax Administration). Falsification of records constitutes fraud under Swiss law and waives the depositors' rights of privacy. However, the right of the account holder to banking secrecy is maintained in cases of tax infringements as violations of procedural duties (*Verletzung von Verfahrenspflichten*) and tax evasion (*Steuerhinterziehung*) and non-declaration (*Steuerhinterziehung*) of taxable income. With regard to withholding taxes, stamp duties and custom duties, an account holder's right to banking secrecy is not maintained.

The European Convention on Mutual Assistance in Criminal Matters (April 20, 1959 and amended in March 1978) was signed by members of the Council of Europe. Its purpose was to harmonize its members approach in assisting in criminal investigations.

---

[4] Under Civil Law only simple damages can be recovered. There are no punitive damages imposed on the discloser.

[5] Articles 159, 162 and 273 of the Criminal Code could be applicable, but, due to their general nature, bank and capital market customers are unlikely to base their claims on them. If a bank inappropriately released information, it could create a criminal liability under the Swiss Criminal Code. Specifically, Article 273 of the Criminal Code makes it a crime to release client information to a foreign party, and Article 162 makes it a crime to disclose information when a contractual obligation existed to protect such information. Finally, Article 159 forbids the release of any information that would materially harm a client's financial position.

Since 1978, the convention has been used to obtain information on tax violators. But Switzerland provides information only if the crime under review is a criminal act under Swiss law. In most cases observed, the Swiss Banking Secrecy rule has prevailed.

Family law and estate law

In family and estate law proceedings, Swiss banking secrecy provisions do not protect individuals having the legal obligation to manage the property of another. Asset disclosure must be made upon legitimate request. In the event of death and inheritance, banks have an obligation to report to the heirs, but not to the authorities.

Civil proceedings

In Switzerland, the enforcement of the banking secrecy rules in civil procedures (as well as in criminal procedures) is a matter of the cantonal legislation. Some cantons such as Basel-Stadt, Ticino (Tessin) or Solothurn, require a witness or defendant to disclose information to the court even if such information is protected by bank secrecy. In other cantons, such as Zürich, Zug or Schwyz, the judge has to decide on a case-by-case basis whether the interest of one party to maintain bank secrecy outweighs the other party's interest in disclosing the respective information. In a number of other cantons such as Genève, Bern and Aargau, bank secrecy prevails over the evidence rules of the cantonal legislation, and therefore, information protected by bank secrecy is not to be disclosed in court.

Disclosures to foreign authorities

Disclosures to foreign authorities are prohibited by Swiss Criminal law unless there are provisions under a special treaty. When such a treaty exists, disclosure is made of only the information that would have been given to the Swiss authorities.

3. Legislation and international treaties that limit banking secrecy

Over the past 20 years, the "humanitarian" and civil rights aspects that gave rise to the Banking Secrecy Act have been forgotten or down-played, and its possible misuse by criminals and tax-evaders stressed. Within Switzerland, some voices have gone so far as to request that residents of developing countries not be permitted to open an account in Switzerland so as to prevent capital flight from those nations. To reduce possible abuses and address legitimate foreign concerns, the Swiss government has negotiated a number of significant international treaties (especially with the US) covering organized criminal activities and white collar crimes (eg, insider trading and money laundering) that are also punishable by the Swiss Criminal Code.

Serious crimes, criminal investigations and organized crime

Enacted to combat organized crime, the US-Swiss Mutual Assistance Treaty (1973) requires that Swiss banks disclose otherwise secret information when the US government is investigating serious crimes as defined by the Treaty. The requesters must prove that reasonable, but unsuccessful, efforts were made to obtain the requested information.

In 1994, the Swiss Parliament passed legislation in order to fight organized crime. The law enables Swiss authorities to improve cooperation with international policing

Table 5.2

Swiss criminal code: insider trading (Article 161)

Provisions

A member of the board of directors, the management or the auditors or an agent of a stock company controlling or being controlled by a stock company, a member of a governmental body or a public official, an assistant of the aforementioned persons, who procures a pecuniary benefit for himself or for another by exploiting or conveying to another his knowledge of confidential information which, if and when publicized, can be expected to materially influence the price of shares, of other securities or of options traded on a Swiss stock exchange, is liable to imprisonment or fine.

The recipient of the information obtained from an insider as defined under paragraph 1 above who procures a pecuniary benefit for himself or for another by exploiting this information is liable to imprisonment of up to one year or to a fine.

Confidential information within the meaning of paragraphs 1 and 2 above includes an impending issue of rights of participation, a merger or a similar event of comparable significance.

In case of a merger of two stock companies, paragraphs 1 to 3 apply to both companies.

Paragraphs 1 to 4 apply accordingly in the event that the exploitation of confidential information relates to participation certificates, other securities, debentures or options of a cooperative society or a foreign corporation.

efforts without violating Swiss banking secrecy laws. Like the money laundering and insider trading regulations, this piece of legislation releases bank employees, who suspect organized crime activity under certain defined conditions, from the provisions of the Banking Secrecy Act. These employees have the "right to report" their suspicions to the Swiss authorities, but "not the obligation" to do so.

Accepting illegally obtained funds

The Agreement on the Observance of Care in Accepting Funds and Practice of Banking Secrecy (signed in 1977 and updated 1 July 1982) was written by the Swiss Bankers' Association and the Swiss National Bank to prevent the use of Swiss banks for illegally acquired funds.[6] This agreement includes controls as well as punishments for offenses of up to Sfr10 million. It requires banks to:

- Ascertain the identity of clients who wish to open an account or rent a safe;
- Refuse to accept funds that appear to have been acquired under acts that, according to Swiss law, are punishable or call for extradition; and
- Refrain from aiding and abetting capital flight, tax evasion, etc.

Insider trading

Insider trading, in general, occurs when an individual, as an insider of a public company, derives pecuniary rewards for himself or for others from confidential facts that could materially affect the market value of a company's stock. The misuse of insider informa-

---

[6] This Agreement is a private understanding between banks and their association. It serves as a minimum standard for the care that banks should apply.

tion has been heavily pursued by authorities (especially in the US by the Securities and Exchange Commission) beyond their jurisdictions.

Nonetheless, for years, it was virtually impossible for foreign authorities to obtain from Swiss banks the information needed to convict perpetrators. Part of the problem was that, until 1988, this specific activity was not a *per se* violation of Swiss law. Therefore, insider trading activity did not meet the Swiss "reciprocal punishability"[7] criterion for information disclosure and was not covered by the provisions of the International Mutual Assistance agreements.[8] As a result, Swiss banking secrecy laws prohibited disclosures of bank-related information on these transactions.

On 1 September 1982, the US and Switzerland established a non-binding agreement to cooperate on matters dealing with insider trading.[9] It remained in force until the Swiss law on insider transactions was passed in 1988. For this Memorandum to apply, the information sought has to have been used for activities recognized in Switzerland as punishable. By criminalizing insider trading, Switzerland aligned itself with virtually all OECD countries that have legislatively tried to stop these activities.

Money laundering

Swiss banking secrecy laws have long been blamed for protecting the laundering of illegitimate sources of international funds. Because there were sufficiently strong reasons to keep existing laws in place to protect the private sphere of citizens, the Swiss government took time finding ways to eliminate any undesirable by-products of this rule. Near the end of the 1980s, Switzerland took energetic action curtailing the alleged flow of illegal funds through its banking system.

In 1988, the Federal Banking Commission required banks to disclose the beneficial owners of bank deposits when such owners are under criminal charges, and in 1990, the Swiss Criminal Code was amended to treat money laundering (Article 305bis) and the improper care of financial transactions (Article 305ter).[10] The Code was subsequently revised on 1 April 1992.

Due to these rules, bank employees can be punished if they knowingly accept, safeguard, invest or transfer assets that derive their existence from criminal activities.[11]

---

[7] The "reciprocal punishability" principle requires an act to be unlawful in both Switzerland and the prosecuting foreign nation before disclosure requests would be entertained.

[8] In a case involving Santa Fe International's takeover by Kuwait Petroleum Corporation, the Swiss Supreme Court rejected a foreign request for information on the grounds that insider trading was not illegal in Switzerland and therefore disclosure violated the double prosecution (reciprocal punishment) requirement. See, Swiss Supreme Court Reporter Vol. 109, Part Ib, 47.

[9] The Memorandum of Understanding is not a treaty and has not been approved by either the US Senate, or Swiss parliament.

[10] Switzerland's criminalization of money laundering follows directly from a 1988 United Nations Convention Against Illicit Traffic in Narcotic Drugs and Psychotropic Substances in Vienna. The Convention mandates that signatories criminalize activities connected with money laundering. Such laws, combined with the increased cooperation of international regulatory authorities, have increased the chances that criminals will be caught.

[11] See Rule No. 126, Articles 305bis and 305ter. Article 305bis imposes a prison sentence on anyone who knowingly facilitates the prevention of inquiry into the source of or the discovery and seizure of assets which he knows or must assume are of criminal origin. It also defines serious cases where the prison sentence is supplemented by a fine of up to Sfr1 million. Article 305ter imposes imprisonment up to one year, detention or a fine when due care is not taken to identify the true commercial beneficiary of assets.

Punishment of offenders is imprisonment for up to three years or a fine. For "serious" offences, sentences as long as five years and/or a fine up to Sfr1 million may be imposed.[12]

Banks must exercise due diligence in discovering the true beneficial owners of the assets (accounts, passbooks, securities accounts, fiduciary transactions and safe-deposit boxes) and refrain from actively assisting either capital flight or tax evasion activities.[13] When they suspect money laundering, they have three major courses of action: investigate more deeply either the client relationship or the transactions, sever the relationship with their client, or report their suspicions to the proper authorities. Once discovered, banks are expected to cooperate with domestic authorities in tracing these transactions.[14]

The reporting requirements in the Swiss Criminal Code seem at odds with Swiss banking secrecy laws that protect customer confidentiality. Banks have an obligation both to safeguard customers' privacy and conduct efficient and timely transactions. Banking is a business that is highly dependent on customer satisfaction. Reporting suspicions concerning customer transactions could result in blocked funds, seized assets and unexecuted transactions. If the suspicions are later judged to be unfounded, customers could (and probably would) sever all future relationships with the bank. Banks must be attentive to the provisions of the Swiss Criminal Code. At the same time, they have a responsibility to their shareholders to maximize net worth by keeping good customers and attracting new business. The line between one and the other can be very thin in many cases.

In 1994, Switzerland passed legislation narrowing the criteria for reporting cash transactions, but broadening the existing regulations to include non-bank institutions handling cheque cashing, money orders, traveller's cheques and wire transfers. In January 1995, the Swiss Bankers' Association recommended that the money laundering provisions regulating banks and brokers be extended under a new Financial Services Law to regulate non-bank employed asset and portfolio managers as well as finance companies. Industry associations representing these newly covered groups still argue that their self-regulatory measures are sufficient without the added need for formal government laws.

Under the amended Article 305 of the Criminal Code, bank employees have the right to report these transactions to the Swiss authorities without violating banking

---

[12] A serious offense occurs if the offender is: a member of a criminal organization, a member of an organized money laundering scheme or earned substantial gains.

[13] The lack of due diligence in this area is punishable under the Swiss Criminal Code (Article 305[ter]). Negligent acceptance of assets was not a crime, but indicated a flaw in bank management (ie, internal operations) and was therefore a breach of the Swiss Banking Law. For instance, banks are required to investigate when a customer deposits bank notes or precious metals valued at more than Sfr100,000. To help banks identify and institute good operating practices, recommendations were made by the Bank for International Settlements (December 12, 1988 of the Basel Committee for Banking Supervision), the European Economic Community (June 10, 1991 Guidelines of the European Economic Community) and Switzerland's 1990 Financial Action Task Force on Money Laundering. See: KPMG Fides Peat, "Unofficial Translation: Guidelines for the Combating and Prevention of Money Laundering," *FBC Circular 91/3* (May 1, 1991) pp. 1-8.

[14] One major problem with the Guidelines is that they deal exclusively with "transactions" and not idle balances. In a recent case, Union Bank of Switzerland was criticized for not having discovered the US$150 million account of a suspected Colombian drug dealer. The account was dormant from 1970 to 1995 and was discovered only when the wife of the suspected drug dealer attempted to purchase Swiss real estate with assets from the account. See, Ian Rodger, "Swiss clean up rules on dirty money", *The Financial Times* April 23, 1994.

secrecy laws but not the obligation to report them. It is highly likely that future court challenges and legislative reforms will continue to shape these provisions.

Automation has given government authorities the ability to track illicit transactions far more effectively than in the past. In US$100 notes, cash is three times heavier than equivalent-value cocaine. Consequently, transporting and safeguarding cash after drugs are sold has become as cumbersome a job as handling the drugs themselves.[15]

The willingness of Switzerland to adapt its banking secrecy regulations and prosecute money laundering is symptomatic of a general change in the way Switzerland has reformed its capital markets. For years, analysts and political observers linked Swiss banking success to an ability to capture cheap funds that were escaping political turmoil, economic disasters, confiscatory taxes and criminal prosecution throughout the world. By adapting its secrecy provisions, a clear signal was sent. The Swiss intend to compete internationally on the basis of technological sophistication, low costs and quality service. Though protections of individual privacy rights will still be enforced, the Swiss will simultaneously continue to crack down on financial abuses.

4. Banking secrecy and Switzerland

Banking secrecy and Swiss citizens

Swiss laws were created primarily for citizens of Switzerland, and not to attract foreign money – unlike tax shelters and offshore banking centres. But in Switzerland the same laws apply also to foreigners, and the Swiss are reluctant to become the fiscal agents of other governments. The question of whether Swiss banking secrecy is conducive to, or enables avoidance of income taxes, can be answered by a simple proposition – well over 99 per cent of all tax evaders around the world operate without a Swiss bank account. Abolishing Swiss banking secrecy, or numbered accounts, would not substantially reduce tax avoidance.

Banking secrecy and the Swiss government

Certain idealistic Swiss organizations have, in the past, argued that a cause-effect relationship exists between Swiss banking secrecy and fund exports from developing countries. Yet, there are strong indications that Switzerland is a lower tier alternative for funds from developing countries because of the lack of traditional colonial ties, proximity, cultural affinity and common language. Places such as Miami, New York, Paris, Amsterdam, Hong Kong and Singapore probably administer most funds from such countries, very often acting as bankers for these same countries by transferring funds back in the form of large loans.

The Swiss capital market is one of the two, if not the most important, capital market for organizations that support developing countries or help refugees. International

---

[15] For drug dealers trying to escape detection, electronic fund transfers reduce the cost to safeguard and transport currency, but substantially raise the probability of being caught. Increased levels of international cooperation have also increased the odds of detection. Regulatory authorities have decided that if they cannot stop drugs from entering their nations, they can stop ill-gotten gains from flowing to agents who produce and distribute them. Their strategy has been to increase the cost of drug transactions to dealers and thereby lower profitability. Increased monitoring, along with bad publicity, have been enough to dissuade many banks from undertaking such transactions. It became a bad business from a bottom line point of view.

development banks such as the World Bank, the Inter-American Development Bank, the Asian Development Bank, the European Investment Bank, and the Council of Europe's Fund for Refugees are regular borrowers on the Swiss capital market.

Internationally allocating funds is a basic function of the Swiss capital market. Since Switzerland in its own right is a net capital exporter, any capital entrusted by foreigners to Swiss banks, will, on balance, be re-exported. On a net basis, Switzerland is not the beneficiary of funds entrusted to its banks, but only the administrator.

SWISS INSURANCE AND INSTITUTIONAL INVESTMENT MARKETS

Among the major financial institutions capturing savings, the private insurance sector, including the private pension funds, is the most important single source of funds for the Swiss capital market. In 1993, the capital investments of these institutions amounted to Sfr242.4 billion.[1]

Overview of Swiss insurance companies and the Swiss capital market

Switzerland is a small part of the total world insurance market, comprising just a little over 1 per cent, but insurance plays a relatively important role in the Swiss economy. Among all nations, Switzerland ranked second only to Japan in terms of insurance per capita and third behind Japan and Great Britain in the proportion of its GDP devoted to insurance (see Table 6.1).

1. Insurance and the Swiss economy

Table 6.1

Insurance: international comparisons of its importance,1993
(Ranked by premiums per capita)

Rank	Country	Per capita insurance (US$)	Insurance expenditure/GDP	Market size (US$ millions)	World share (%)
1	Japan	4,395	12.64	430,553	42.61
2	**Switzerland**	**3,097**	**9.26**	**12,817**	**1.27**
3	USA	2,192	8.90	235,621	23.32
4	United Kingdom	1,914	11.73	71,263	7.05
5	Netherlands	1,741	8.62	13,731	1.36
6	France	1,647	7.58	57,252	5.67
7	Luxembourg	1,556	5.89	168	0.02
8	Germany	1,430	6.74	45,898	4.54
9	Denmark	1,366	5.26	3,630	0.36
10	Norway	1,295	5.40	2,215	0.22

Source: Schweizer Rück, *Sigma: Assekuranz Global 1993: Beschleunigung des Prämienwachstums* (May 1995) Tables III, IV & V, pp. 26-29.

---

[1] Schweizerischer Versicherungsverband, *Zahlen und Fakten* (1995) p. 8.

Table 6.2

Largest life insurance companies in the World, 1993

Rank	Company	Country	1993 Premiums (US$ millions)
1	Nippon Life	Japan	53,662.5
2	Dai-Ichi Mutual Life	Japan	37,384.2
3	Sumitomo Life	Japan	33,498.5
4	Meiji Mutual Life	Japan	23,968.5
5	Prudential of America	USA	23,968.5
6	Metropolitan Life	USA	19,411.5
7	Asahi Mutual Life	Japan	17,811.5
8	Mitsui Mutual Life	Japan	15,417.5
9	Yasuda Mutual Life	Japan	15,179.4
10	Prudential	Britain	12,926.9
27	**Swiss Life**	**Switzerland**	**6,304.5**

Source: "The 50 Largest Life Insurance Companies," *Fortune Global Service* (August 1994) p. 188.

Table 6.3

Largest non-life insurance companies in the World, 1994 (Ranked by premium size)

Rank	Company	Country	1994 Premiums (US$ millions)
1	Alliance Holding	Germany	40,415.2
2	State Farm Group	US	38,850.1
3	American International Group	US	22,385.7
4	**Zürich Insurance**	**Switzerland**	**21,740.8**
5	CIGNA	US	18,392.0
6	Tokio Marine & Fire	Japan	17,547.4
7	Aetna Life & Casualty	US	17,524.7
8	Yasuda Fire & Marine Insurance	Japan	12,818.8
9	Mitsui Marine & Fire Insurance	Japan	9,302.5
10	Royal Insurance Holdings	UK	8,458.7

Source: "500 World's Largest Corporations," *Fortune Magazine* (August 7, 1995) pp. F1-F10.

In spite of the relatively small size of its domestic market, Swiss insurance companies rank among the leaders in the world (see Tables 6.2, 6.3 and 6.4). In contrast to the typical Swiss multinational company that conducts over 95 per cent of its business abroad, Swiss insurance companies conduct a large part (but not the majority) of their business in Switzerland.

Swiss insurance market structure

The Swiss insurance industry is divided into three major segments: life, non-life (ie, property and casualty) and reinsurance. In general, competition in the life and non-life seg-

94

Table 6.4

Largest reinsurers in the world, 1993 (Ranked by premium size)

Rank	Company	Country	1993 premiums (US$ billions)
1	Munich Re	Germany	9.21
2	**Swiss Re**	**Switzerland**	**7.59**
3	Employers Re	US	3.34
4	Assicurazoni Generali	Italy	2.88
5	Hannover Re	Germany	2.80
6	Cologne Re	Germany	2.66
7	General Re	US	2.52
8	Frankona Group	US	1.83
9	Gerling Global Re	Germany	1.76
10	SCOR S.A.	US	1.74
17	**Winterthur Swiss Insurance Co.**	**Switzerland**	**0.88**

Source: Stacy Shapiro, "World's largest reinsurers," *Business Insurance* (August 29, 1994) p. 3.

ments tend to be nationally- or regionally-oriented. Participants in these markets have relatively few opportunities to benefit from economies of scale and their distribution systems (mainly through agents) tend to be labour intensive.[2] In contrast, competition in the reinsurance industry is international in scope. It enjoys wide opportunities for economies of scale and since their customers are generally other insurance companies, price competition across country borders is intense.[3]

In 1993, the Swiss insurance industry earned approximately Sfr65 billion in gross premiums, of which 41 per cent, 40 per cent and 19 per cent were for non-life, life and

Table 6.5

Domestic and foreign premiums of Swiss insurance companies, 1993

Type of insurance	Premiums	Total Swiss insurance market (%)
Life insurance	25,723	40
Non-life	26,865	41
Reinsurance	12,533	19
Total	65,121	100

Source: Bundesamt für Privatversicherungswesen, *Die Privaten Versicherungseinrichtungen in der Schweiz: 1993* p. 9.

reinsurance coverage (see Table 6.5). Tables 6.6, 6.7 and 6.8 show the top ten companies in each market segment and the variability in their size, ranging from multinational giants with premiums of nearly Sfr8 billion to companies earning just over Sfr51 million. Even though a relatively large number of Swiss insurance companies are active in the market, this industry is highly concentrated. In 1993, the three largest life insurance companies (Swiss

---

[2] John B. Goodman, "International Insurance: A Risky Business?," in Samuel L. Hayes, III, ed., *Financial Services: Perspectives and Challenges* (Boston: Harvard Business School Press, 1993) pp. 93-130.

[3] Randall Geehan, "Economies of Scale in Insurance: Implications for Regulation," in Bernard Wasow and Raymond D. Hill, eds., *The Insurance Industry in Economic Development* (New York: New York University Press, 1986) p. 148.

Table 6.6

The 10 largest life insurance companies in Switzerland, 1993 (Ranked by gross premiums)

Rank	Company	Gross premiums (Sfr '000s)
1	Swiss Life	4,785,874
2	Winterthur Leben	3,446,768
3	Zürich Leben	2,213,756
4	Basler Leben	1,749,757
5	Patria Leben	1,260,769
6	Elvia Leben	804,933
7	La Suisse Leben	669,085
8	Genevoise	575,412
9	PAX Lebensversicherung	524,575
10	CS Life	423,247

Source: Bundesamt für Privatversicherungswesen, *Die Privaten Versicherungseinrichtungen in der Schweiz: 1993* p. 54.

Table 6.7

The 10 largest non-life insurance companies and co-operative societies in Switzerland, 1993 (Ranked by premiums)

Rank	Company	Premiums (Sfr '000s)
1	Zürich	7,773,743
2	Winterthur	4,155,197
3	Basler	1,526,363
4	Schweizerische Mobilar	1,304,168
5	Helvetia	1,138,867
6	Elvia	1,122,087
7	Berner Allgemeine	497,012
8	Schweizerische National	484,329
9	Alpina	483,884
10	Vaudoise	479,008

Source: Bundesamt für Privatversicherungswesen, *Die Privaten Versicherungseinrichtungen in der Schweiz: 1993* p. 120.

Life, Winterthur and Zürich Insurance) accounted for 54 per cent of the Swiss market, the three largest non-life insurance companies (Zürich, Winterthur and Basler) comprised 61 per cent of their segment, and the three largest reinsurers (Schweizer Rück, Union Rück and Veritas Rück) accounted for 77 per cent of their market.

Competition in the Swiss insurance industry

The Swiss insurance industry is in a state of transition. Traditionally, business was done in an environment characterized by a high level of government regulation, cartel-like price agreements, a lack of efficiency-enhancing innovation and very little foreign competition. The beginning of the transition period began in 1988 when the Swiss government initiated a cartel inquiry into the non-life insurance industry. The product of these efforts set in motion a liberalization movement in the Swiss insurance industry.

Table 6.8

The 10 largest Swiss reinsurance companies, 1993 (Ranked by gross premiums)

Rank	Company	Gross premiums (Sfr '000s)
1	Schweizer Rück	6,719,079
2	Union Rück	1,125,284
3	Veritas Rück	803,457
4	Vitodurum Rück	465,533
5	Europäische Rück	461,684
6	Nouvelle Réassurance	440,223
7	Guardian Rück	225,071
8	Globale Rück	203,175
9	General Rück	201,666
10	Commercial Union Réassurance	51,076

Source: Bundesamt für Privatversicherungswesen, *Die Privaten Versicherungseinrichtungen in der Schweiz: 1993* p. 186.

The initiative gained renewed strength after a popular Swiss referendum rejected Swiss membership in the European Economic Area in December 1992. The vote effectively put the nation's membership application to the European Union on hold. Disappointed by the vote, the Swiss government enacted legislation that forced Swiss insurance companies to compete as if Switzerland had joined the European Union, and the EU has moved quickly to deregulate all segments of its insurance industry.[4]

Deregulation has forced Swiss insurance companies to become more sensitive to reducing costs, rationalizing their sales organizations, pruning bad policies and introducing new products. This shift in the competitive environment has come at a time when Swiss insurance companies are already under considerable pressure. Premium growth has become sluggish and increased competition has caused commissions to fall. Among the most aggressive new competitors are foreign insurance companies and banks.

The Swiss insurance industry is asymmetric in its level of internationalization (see Table 6.9). Swiss companies have established significant positions in many foreign nations, but the level of foreign participation in Switzerland is relatively low. Of the Sfr86.2 billion earned in Swiss insurance premiums during 1992, Sfr56 billion (65 per cent) were from foreign sources, and, at the end of 1993, of the 136,254 world-wide jobs provided by Swiss insurance companies, 64.5 per cent were provided outside of Switzerland.

Competition within the Swiss market is quite different, but changing rapidly. In 1992, there were only 24 foreign firms (all non-life) in Switzerland with a market share of

Level of internationalization

Table 6.9

Swiss insurance segments and international distribution, 1994

Segments	Domestic & foreign insurance companies in Switzerland			Premiums of Swiss insurance companies (including affiliates) by source (Sfr billions)			
	Swiss	*Foreign*	*Total*	*Swiss*	*EC*	*Other*	*Total*
Life insurance	30	0	30	19.9	12.6	1.3	33.8
Non-life	70	25	95	13.4	22.0	11.8	47.2
Reinsurance	21	0	21	1.1	14.3	7.2	22.6
Total	121	25	146	34.4	48.9	20.3	103.6
Per cent	83	17	100	33	47	20	100

Source: Informationsstelle des Schweizerischen Versicherungsverbandes, *Die Schweizer Privat Versicherungen: Zahlen und Fakten* (1995) p.9. Schweizerischer Versicherungsverband, Jahresbericht 94-95 p. 81.

---

[4] After 17 years, Switzerland and the EC negotiated a freedom of establishment agreement that took effect in January 1993. Now Swiss companies can compete with EU companies and EU companies (if they meet Swiss capital requirements) can offer services in Switzerland. There has been no such agreement in the life insurance area. Swiss life-insurance companies will not be able to take advantage of the single license provisions and will be required to satisfy the solvency requirement of each country in which they transact business.

2 per cent. Since then, the level of international participation has increased significantly. The liberalization of the Swiss domestic market is the major factor that has caused the surge in foreign competition.

In 1994, there were numerous foreign purchases of Swiss insurance companies. German penetration was most visible. The German insurance company, Allianz, bought a majority share of Elvia, the fifth largest Swiss direct insurer, from Swiss Re and a 31 per cent share of Berner Insurance Group.[5] In 1995, Alliance increased its share in Elvia to nearly 100 per cent through a public offering. Alte Leipziger and Münchner Rück of Germany acquired participations in Helvetia and the Italian insurer, Assicurazoni Generali, bought a majority of Fortuna (a small Swiss company active in life insurance) and Schweizer Union. By the end of 1995, foreign participation is expected to reach 10 per cent of the Swiss market.

Competition with banks

Increasingly, banks and insurance companies are becoming vigorous competitors and forming strategic alliances.[6] That is not surprising given the similarity of their functions. Banks and insurance companies are financial intermediaries that issue liabilities (policies or deposits) and invest the proceeds. They compete in the labour markets for virtually the same qualified investment managers and vie for customers who are interested in adjusting their risk levels.

Insurance companies are specialists at shifting risk from individual customers to a diversified pool of assets. Their debt instruments are contingent liabilities, and their investments mirror the term structure of their liabilities (eg, relatively long-term for life insurance companies and short-term for property and casualty companies).

Banks commonly offer forward exchange contracts, forward interest rate transactions, swaps and options to modify both customers' and their own risk levels. Insurance, another tool of risk management, is developing its own set of instruments – instruments that will compete with bank products. In the competition between banks and insurance companies, Swiss banks have found that their extensive branch networks and frequent contact with potential insurance customers have allowed them to make inroads into the life insurance segment of the industry.[7]

Cooperative agreements are also growing in number and popularity as strategic initiatives. In 1994, Credit Suisse Holding and Swiss Re announced an agreement to cooperate in ways that will expand Swiss Re's geographic range and product offerings. The agreement expands Swiss Re's activities in the financial reinsurance business (currently about 10 per cent of Swiss Re's business),[8] creates an investment fund to promote new insurance companies in Asia (perhaps combining investment banking and insurance) and gives Swiss Re 20 per cent control over Credit Suisse Financial Products (CSFP), a

---

[5] Berner Insurance Group is one of Switzerland's leading 10 insurers. Allianz already owned Allianz Continentale Allgemeine and Allianz Continentale Lebensversicherung in Switzerland.

[6] Joseph Marbacher, "Combining Banking and Insurance Services: Some Implications for Marketing Strategies," in M.M. Kostecki, ed., *Marketing Strategies for Services: Globalization Client-Oriented Deregulation* (Oxford: Pergamon Press, 1994) pp. 125-136.

[7] Similar inroads are being made by banks in other nations such as Spain, France and the Netherlands.

[8] Financial reinsurance deals with investing customer funds to provide a guaranteed reserve against insurable risks such as natural disasters.

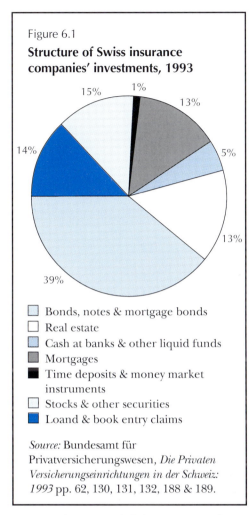

Figure 6.1

Structure of Swiss insurance companies' investments, 1993

- ☐ Bonds, notes & mortgage bonds
- ☐ Real estate
- ☐ Cash at banks & other liquid funds
- ☐ Mortgages
- ■ Time deposits & money market instruments
- ☐ Stocks & other securities
- ■ Loand & book entry claims

Source: Bundesamt für Privatversicherungswesen, *Die Privaten Versicherungseinrichtungen in der Schweiz: 1993* pp. 62, 130, 131, 132, 188 & 189.

London-based financial derivatives specialist. The participation in CSFP was undertaken in order to develop new financial derivatives for the reinsurance industry (eg, catastrophe futures contracts).

During 1994, Swiss Bank Corporation entered into a strategic alliance with Zürich Insurance. The association was negotiated so the companies could cross sell each other's services and develop joint products. In June 1995, the two companies announced the extension of their partnership to non-life insurance and a broader range of banking products. Zürich Insurance has also beefed up its asset management activities for both institutional and private customers. Its creation of Zürich Investment Management and its purchase of the Zürich private bank, Rud Blass & Cie., indicate the intention to compete for both institutional and private customers.[9]

Figure 6.1 and Table 6.10 show the security composition of life-, non-life- and reinsurance companies, as well as cooperative societies.[10] The investments of life insurance companies are mainly long-term and conservative in nature. They include bonds, mortgages, loans, and book entry claims. This safety consciousness is reflected in the investment yield of between 5 per cent and 6 per cent prevailing over the past 60 years. Non-life insurance companies, reinsurance companies and cooperative societies invest heavily in government securities and mortgage bonds.

Asset structure of insurance companies

Foreign borrowers have not found the private Swiss insurance sector to be a significant source of funds. Swiss insurance companies have tight investment prescriptions which usually favour Swiss government bonds and other safe Swiss securities. Together with the social security system, including the private pension funds, the private insurance sector finances the deficits of the federal, cantonal and municipal governments, which amounted to roughly Sfr151.7 billion of accumulated debt in 1993.[11]

---

[9] Axel P. Lehmann, "Deregulation of Insurance and Market Organization: A Case Study of Zurich Insurance Group," in M.M. Kostecki, ed., *Marketing Strategies for Services: Globalization Client-Oriented Deregulation* (Oxford: Pergamon Press, 1994) pp. 137-154.

[10] Cooperative societies are generally combined with non-life insurance companies, but since their investment profiles differ, they are separated here. Among the largest cooperative societies, by far the largest is Schweizerische Mobilar. Other cooperatives include firms such as Schweizerische Hagel and V V S T.

[11] Bundesamt für Statistik, *Eidgenössische Finanzverwaltung*, November 1995 (Figures obtained by telephone from Bundesamt für Statistik).

Table 6.10

Investments of Swiss life, non-life, reinsurance and cooperative insurance companies: 1993 (Sfr billions)

	Life	*Non-life*	*Cooperative*	*Reinsurance*	*Total*
Stocks, other securities & participations	16.3	13.5	0.4	4.7	34.9
Bonds, notes & mortgage bonds	58.6	19.2	1.8	12.7	92.3
Mortgages	27.2	3.4	0.3	0.4	31.3
Real estate	20.8	7.4	0.6	1.6	30.4
Time deposits & money market instruments	1.7	0	0	0	1.7
Loans & book entry claims	25.6	5.4	0.2	0.8	32.0
Cash at banks, other liquid funds & other assets	10.0	2.5	0.1	1.0	13.6
Total	**160.2**	**51.4**	**3.4**	**21.2**	**236.2**

Source: Bundesamt für Privatversicherungswesen, *Die Privaten Versicherungseinrichtungen in der Schweiz: 1993* pp. 62, 130, 131, 132, 133, 188 & 189.

2. The influence of Swiss pension funds and social security system on Swiss capital markets

Like other developed nations, Switzerland has a population that is ageing, and this demographic change has important implications for both domestic and international capital markets. Many members of the post-World War II baby boom generation have only 15-20 work years remaining before they retire. Because of their numbers, the volume of accumulated savings, investment and pension liabilities will grow to unprecedented levels. By the year 2000, Swiss pension fund assets are expected to exceed the nation's GDP.

Between 1985 and 2025, the proportion of the Swiss population receiving pensions is expected to rise from 14 per cent to 21 per cent.[12] Financing their retirement needs and determining the role government will play in supporting them are issues that relate directly to Switzerland's interest rates, economic growth and income distribution. To the extent that these needs are financed by the Swiss government, inter-generational conflicts could arise. The federal social security programme contemporaneously taxes the current work force to provide for current pensioners. Any surpluses or deficits that arise are unintended and not a conscious policy of asset accumulation. Given the fact that there are insufficient assets to support future pension liabilities, the arithmetic is disconcerting. Currently, three Swiss workers support each Swiss pensioner, but, in 2025, less than half that number will be in the work force to support pensioners.

Occupational pension programmes and personal savings are two alternative sources of financing for future retirement needs. The extent to which they are used raises important issues concerning the proper composition of investment assets (eg, bonds versus

---

[12] Stefan Hepp, *The Occupational Pension Schemes in Switzerland – An Emerging Institutional Investment Force* Dissertation Nr. 1149, Verlag Paul Haupt, (Bern/Stuttgart, 1990) p. 1.

equities, versus real estate, versus commodities), their geographic distribution, currency diversification, level of risk and duration. Most nations severely restrict the portfolio decisions of pension portfolio managers – erring on the side of safety over return. But this safety comes with a significant cost. A mere 1 per cent lower return compounded over 45 years of one's working life has significant implications for future living standards. An example is illuminating.

Suppose an individual retired in 1987 after working 42 years. His base salary in 1946 was Sfr10,000 and, over the years, he earned annual pay raises that averaged 5 per cent. If he contributed 12.5 per cent of his salary each year toward retirement and his pension fund earned 4.5 per cent, he would be able to retire with a pension equal to roughly Sfr1,900 per month, 30 per cent of his final year's monthly pay. Had the pension fund earned 5.5 per cent rather than 4.5 per cent, his monthly pension would have increased to Sfr2,800, 40 per cent his final year's monthly pay.[13]

The Swiss social security system is based on three financing pillars: the state-run, basic benefit plan extended to all residents (AHV/IV)[14], the mandatory occupation pension

Swiss social security: the three pillars

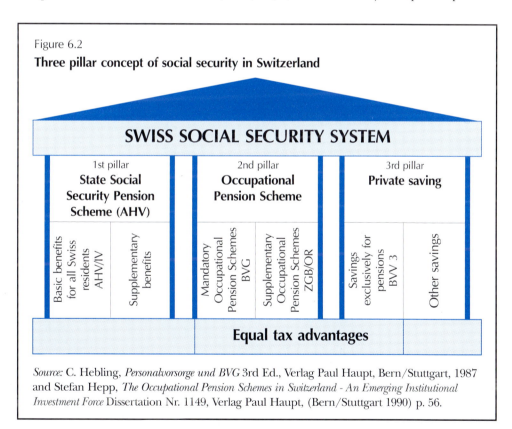

Figure 6.2

Three pillar concept of social security in Switzerland

Source: C. Hebling, *Personalvorsorge und BVG* 3rd Ed., Verlag Paul Haupt, Bern/Stuttgart, 1987 and Stefan Hepp, *The Occupational Pension Schemes in Switzerland - An Emerging Institutional Investment Force* Dissertation Nr. 1149, Verlag Paul Haupt, (Bern/Stuttgart 1990) p. 56.

---

[13] Hepp, p. 249.

[14] The two federal, social security schemes are the Alters- und Hinterlassenversicherung, AHV, (ie, old age and survivors insurance) and Invalidenversicherung, IV, (ie, disability insurance). They are administered separately, but paid jointly via automatic payroll deductions. They are usually referred to jointly as AHV/IV. AHV and IV began in 1946 and 1960, respectively.

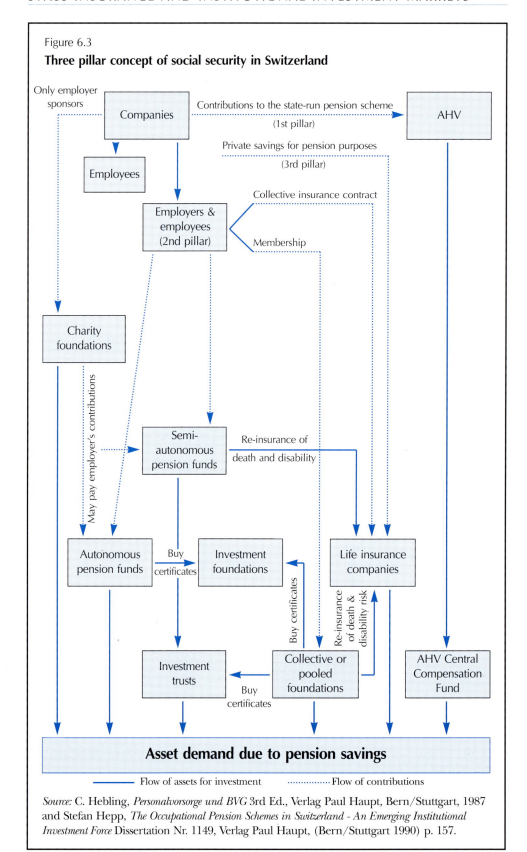

Figure 6.3

Three pillar concept of social security in Switzerland

Flow of assets for investment .... Flow of contributions

Source: C. Hebling, *Personalvorsorge und BVG* 3rd Ed., Verlag Paul Haupt, Bern/Stuttgart, 1987 and Stefan Hepp, *The Occupational Pension Schemes in Switzerland - An Emerging Institutional Investment Force* Dissertation Nr. 1149, Verlag Paul Haupt, (Bern/Stuttgart 1990) p. 157.

Table 6.11

The 10 largest Swiss, individual pension fund companies, 1993 (ranked by total premiums)

Rank	Name	Individual premiums (Sfr '000s)	Group Premiums (Sfr '000s)	Total (Sfr '000s)
1	Swiss Life	225,170	2,168,057	2,393,227
2	Winterthur Leben	146,385	1,083,904	1,230,289
3	Zürich Leben	62,044	699,554	761,598
4	Basler Leben	59,782	615,686	675,468
5	Providentia	4,636	385,499	390,135
6	Patria Leben	57,484	308,512	365,996
7	La Suisse Vie	61,054	219,497	280,551
8	Elvia Vie	42,255	192,418	234,673
9	PAX	23,465	137,176	160,641
10	Vaudoise	45,829	107,563	153,392

Source: Bundesamt für Privatversicherungswesen, *Die Privaten Versicherungseinrichtungen in der Schweiz: 1993* pp. 46 & 47.

scheme (BVG)[15] and private saving (see Figure 6.2). These financing schemes are highly interdependent. Changes in any one could very well lead to offsetting adjustments in the others. For instance, as of 1995, AHV/IV benefits were not fully indexed. Over time, its benefits were expected to fall relative to income, thereby putting greater emphasis on occupational pensions and savings as the means of supporting retirement living standards.

To channel savings from these three retirement financing sources to investment assets, a labyrinth of financial intermediaries has evolved in Switzerland (see Figure 6.3). For large companies with significant pension assets, in-house pension management is possible, but for most companies, pooling arrangements must be made. At the end of 1992, there were over 3.4 million members of nearly 13,700 Swiss pension plans. Most of these pension plans relied on the financial skills of investment trusts, collective or pooled foundations and Swiss life insurance companies to manage their retirement savings. Table 6.11 shows the leading Swiss insurance companies for pension administration in 1993.

Mandatory state run pension and disability insurance (AHV/IV)

The Swiss social security scheme (AHV/IV) guarantees a minimum level of benefits to pensioners and is considered to be the first line of defence against poverty or undue social hardship. This minimum level is fixed by the government and is not based on either the salary levels prior to retirement or years of contribution. Above the minimum level, benefits are adjusted in accordance with pre-retirement income, but they are capped far below levels sufficient for all but the lowest income earners to maintain their standards of living. As a result, occupational pensions and private savings play an important role in making up the difference in the Swiss retirement equation.

---

[15] BVG is the German abbreviation for Berufs Vorsorge Gesetz (ie, occupational pension law).

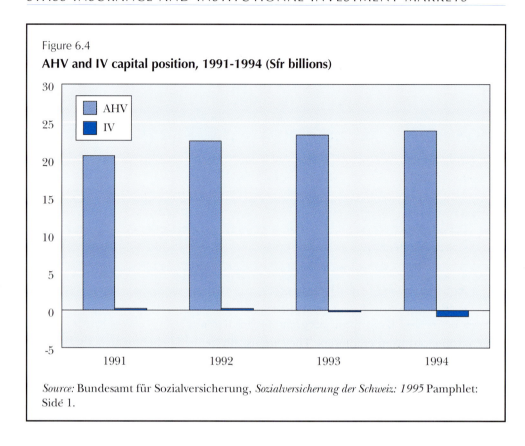

Figure 6.4

AHV and IV capital position, 1991-1994 (Sfr billions)

Source: Bundesamt für Sozialversicherung, *Sozialversicherung der Schweiz: 1995* Pamphlet: Side 1.

Theoretically, under the AHV/IV pension scheme, current benefits are supposed to be financed by current contributions with zero annual surpluses or deficits. In practice, the timing and flow of contributions and pay-outs have not matched exactly, creating an investment pool to be administered (see Figure 6.4). Swiss law requires all surpluses from the state-run social insurance schemes to be placed in and invested by the Swiss Central Compensation Fund. The Swiss Central Compensation Fund is required to invest these state-run pension funds in Swiss-based fixed-income assets. As a practical matter, virtually all of them are invested in federal, cantonal and municipal bonds.

Over the post-World War II period until 1995, the average return on funds invested by the Swiss Central Compensation Fund was slightly above 4 per cent per annum. This low rate of return was due largely to the restrictions placed on the range of allowable investments. As a result, the return was insufficient to finance benefit liabilities, but the deficiency (until 1985) was filled by surpluses that arose from Swiss workers changing jobs. Prior to 1985, pension-vesting rules decreased workers' benefits when they changed employment. Since 1985, the pension vesting rules have been modified for the benefit of Swiss workers.[16]

In 1994, AHV had a surplus capital position totalling Sfr23.8 billion, and IV was in debt by approximately Sfr0.81 billion (see Figure 6.4). Most analyses forecast a declining surplus and significant deficits after the first decade of the 21st century. The rate at which

---

[16] Since January 1, 1995, Swiss pension have become fully portable without financial loss. (See OECD, Economic Survey 1994-1995: Switzerland p. 65.)

the current surplus declines will depend on factors such as increases in benefits, the growth of real wages, inflation rates, returns on invested capital and the net size of the work force. Immigration levels, female participation rates, longevity, fertility rates and average retirement age will also play significant roles.

A simple example is revealing. Over the period until 2025, if retirement benefits are unchanged, the retirement age remains at 65 for men and 62 for women, average inflation rate is 3 per cent, real wage growth is 2.2 per cent and the rate of return on investment is 4.5 per cent, the AHV surplus will grow until 2012 and peak at Sfr42 billion. Thereafter, it will fall, approaching zero in 2022 and register a Sfr25 billion deficit in 2025.[17] Under these assumptions, the net annual flow of funds from AHV to the capital markets will average approximately Sfr0.7 billion until 2012 and then will decline by approximately Sfr5 billion per year. If conditions are less favourable, the deficit could occur earlier and be significantly greater.[18]

Occupational pensions (Berufsvorsorge – BV)

In 1985, the Swiss Parliament made occupational pension plans mandatory for virtually all Swiss businesses. BV pension programmes are financed by direct payroll deductions and contributions from employers. They are usually defined-benefit schemes with workers receiving a share of their income based on a sliding scale with low-income earners receiving much larger percentages (up to 90 per cent) than high-income earners (as low as 25 per cent). Unlike the government plan (AHV/IV), funds are actually collected and assets accumulated.

Between 1987 and 1992 (the most recent year reported), the assets of occupational pension funds grew at a compound annual rate slightly in excess of 9 per cent, reaching Sfr254 billion (see Figure 6.5). Should this rate of growth continue until 2010 (the first year of retirement eligibility for individual males born in 1945), the pool of pension assets will slightly exceed Sfr1,200 billion. Should it continue at the 9 per cent rate until 2025, the pool will total approximately Sfr4.4 trillion.

The investments of occupational pension fund managers are clearly biased toward Swiss franc, domestic debt instruments (see Figure 6.6). In 1992, 51 per cent of total assets were accounted for by the combination of Swiss franc bonds (26 per cent), mortgages (9 per cent) and real estate (16 per cent). Equity comprised slightly under 10 per cent of the portfolio and foreign investments accounted for only a small minority (6 per cent) of all assets.

Allocation figures for Swiss pension funds are published infrequently, but the prevailing view is that they have significantly increased their equity investments above the 10 per cent level of 1992, but they are still considerably below the 30 per cent limit.[19] (Some pension funds have no equity investments). The superior return on Swiss equities has been an important stimulus for this change. Between 1985 and 1994, the annual return

[17] Stefan Hepp, The Occupational Pension Schemes in Switzerland - An Emerging Institutional Investment Force Dissertation Nr. 1149, Verlag Paul Haupt, (Bern/Stuttgart, 1990) Ch. 3.

[18] Hepp, Ch 3. Hepp's "worst case scenario" predicts a deficit of Sfr248 billion in 2025.

[19] See "Swiss Equities: Can the funds be tempted?" Euromoney Supplement: The superior returns of Swiss equities September 1995 pp. 4 & 13.

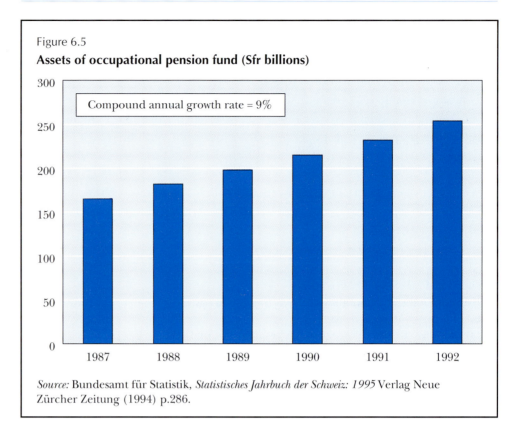

Figure 6.5

Assets of occupational pension fund (Sfr billions)

Compound annual growth rate = 9%

Source: Bundesamt für Statistik, *Statistisches Jahrbuch der Schweiz: 1995* Verlag Neue Zürcher Zeitung (1994) p.286.

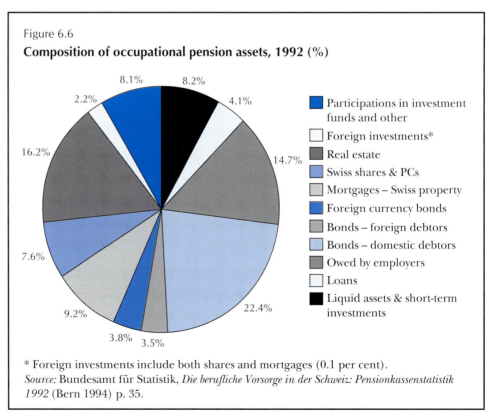

Figure 6.6

Composition of occupational pension assets, 1992 (%)

- Participations in investment funds and other
- Foreign investments*
- Real estate
- Swiss shares & PCs
- Mortgages – Swiss property
- Foreign currency bonds
- Bonds – foreign debtors
- Bonds – domestic debtors
- Owed by employers
- Loans
- Liquid assets & short-term investments

* Foreign investments include both shares and mortgages (0.1 per cent).
Source: Bundesamt für Statistik, *Die berufliche Vorsorge in der Schweiz: Pensionkassenstatistik 1992* (Bern 1994) p. 35.

Table 6.12

Total capital of Swiss state-run and private occupational pensions, 1992-1994 (Sfr millions)

Insurance programme	1992	1993	1994
Old age & survivors	22,456	23,266	23,827
Disability	240	-180	-805
Occupational pension	254,219	n/a	n/a
Health insurance	3,185	4,085[e]	n/a
Accident insurance	11,693	12,135[e]	n/a
Military service compensation scheme	3,243	3,662	n/a
Unemployment insurance	-207	-2,637	-4,878*
Total	**294,829**	–	–

[e] superscript indicates amounts estimated by authors based on a 4 per cent return on assets plus net contributions for 1993.
(n/a) indicates that no information was available for that year.
*Updated by phone in December 1995.

Source: Bundesamt für Sozialversicherung, *Sozialversicherung der Schweiz: Side 1 and 2* and Bundesamt für Statistik, *Statistisches Jahrbuch der Schweiz 1995* (Verlag Neue Zürcher Zeitung: 1994) pp. 277 & 283.

on Swiss equities (11.7 per cent) was higher than the return on foreign equities (5.6 per cent), cash (5.4 per cent), Swiss foreign bonds (5 per cent) and Swiss domestic bonds (4.8 per cent).[20]

There is a growing understanding in Switzerland that marginal differences in asset performance are important. Increasingly, studies have shown that Swiss equity portfolios have out-performed debt portfolios (see chapter 6). As a result, there is a discernible movement toward equity investments and international diversification. To a large extent, pension investments are limited by legal restrictions, but even these regulations are being relaxed. In 1993, Swiss investment rules governing pension funds were changed permitting funds to hold up to 50 per cent of their portfolio in equities (the previous ceiling was 30 per cent).[21]

Size of AHV and BV Assets

Table 6.12 summarizes the investment assets of the federal social security system and private, occupational pension plans from 1992 to 1994. The healthy net surpluses that existed over this period are deceiving and mask a looming problem in the future of the state-run, old age and survivors insurance scheme. The financing difficulties are well-known and will be the source of wide-ranging policy debates in the future.

---

[20] Euromoney Supplement: The superior returns of Swiss equities p 4 & 13.
[21] There is a 25 per cent ceiling on foreign shares and a 30 per cent ceiling on domestic shares as a percent of the total portfolio.

3. Mutual funds

Investment funds organized as mutual funds are an important part of the Swiss capital market and are subject to rigid legal regulations and supervision through the Federal Banking Commission. At the end of the first quarter 1995 there were 254 Swiss funds with combined assets of Sfr54.8 billion.[22] Unlike the US Mutual Fund, the Swiss Investment Fund has no corporate identity; it is based on a collective investment contract. The main growth period of Swiss investment funds was in the late 1960s and early 1970s, but the first fund was created in the 1930s, and at the time, it was the only continental European fund of its type. Foreign investment funds distributed in Switzerland are also governed by the Swiss law and supervised by the Swiss authorities.

An important peculiarity of the Swiss investment fund business is that it is part of the banking system. As a matter of law, a fund must be managed by a separate company whose sole business is managing the investment fund. Each fund must have a bank as a custodian (depot bank) that is responsible for the assets. Its major responsibilities are to safe-keep the investments of the funds and to execute all payments for it. The management of the fund has to be completely separated from that of the custodian. More important than these legal obligations is the moral obligation deriving from the public's identification of the fund with the name of the custodian. These custodians often advertise the funds under their own names, which virtually guarantees their professional management.

Foreign funds represented in Switzerland must have official permission by the Federal Banking Commission and a Swiss bank (or a Swiss branch of a foreign bank) as a representative (Vertreterbank). This representative bank's principal task is the supervision of the foreign fund's activities in Switzerland, and it is responsible for compliance in accordance with the new Federal Law on Investment Funds.

Certificates of foreign investment funds can be publicly offered in Switzerland. Such offerings also need the permission of the Federal Banking Commission, which establishes minimum requirements regarding organization, personal skills of the management and investment policy. Permission for public offerings can be obtained by any Swiss national or person legally established under Swiss law, who is responsible to the supervisory authorities and the investors. All Swiss mutual funds are open-end funds, which means that by law the investor has the right to sell back his/her certificates at a price equal to the book value minus sales costs. Closed-end funds are not permitted under federal law.

In 1994, Swiss real estate and foreign securities accounted for 80 per cent of the assets in all Swiss mutual funds (see Figure 6.7).

Real estate mutual funds

Real estate funds' investments in Switzerland are attractive to foreign investors who are not able to buy Swiss real estate directly because of the still-existing restrictions under Swiss law (Lex Friedrich). Unlike some Anglo-Saxon funds, Swiss real estate funds do not engage in mortgage finance but invest in revenue-earning properties. There are also certificates of certain real estate funds that cannot be bought by foreigners. Most real estate funds spread their risks by investing all over Switzerland. About Sfr8.8 billion, or close to 16 per cent of all trust fund assets, are invested in Swiss real estate.

---

[22] Swiss National Bank, *Monatsbericht* June 1995 p. 66.

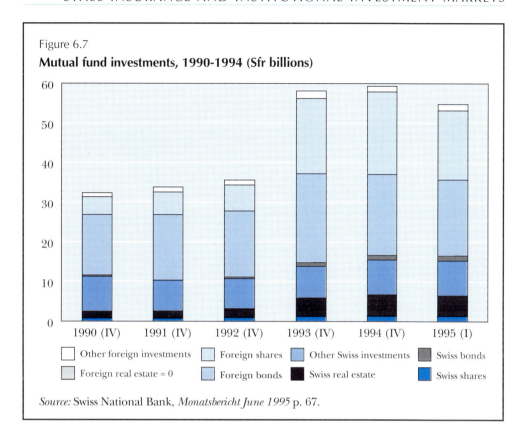

Figure 6.7

Mutual fund investments, 1990-1994 (Sfr billions)

Legend:
- Other foreign investments
- Foreign real estate = 0
- Foreign shares
- Foreign bonds
- Other Swiss investments
- Swiss real estate
- Swiss bonds
- Swiss shares

Source: Swiss National Bank, *Monatsbericht June 1995* p. 67.

Foreign security mutual funds

Another important area of investment opportunity is in foreign securities, which in 1994 represented about Sfr36.7 billion or 67 per cent of all funds' assets.[23] Dividends of funds deriving at least 80 per cent of their income from foreign sources are not subject to the 35 per cent Swiss withholding tax if paid to investors domiciled outside Switzerland. Foreign security mutual funds are also popular with Swiss investors because they have found it is easier to buy shares of Swiss funds investing abroad, than to create a diversified portfolio of foreign securities on their own. Only 11.9 per cent, about Sfr6.5 billion, of the assets of all Swiss investment funds are invested in Swiss securities.

Diversification of mutual funds

Most Swiss investment funds are mixed in the sense that they invest in shares and bonds, and often both in Switzerland and abroad (but the share of their investment in Switzerland is often kept below 20 per cent for tax reasons already explained). A few smaller funds specialize in either one country or one economic sector, where the risk and reward potential is considered to be higher.

Another difference between funds is the emphasis put on dividend yield versus capital appreciation (growth funds). Most Swiss investment funds are distributive funds, rather than accumulative funds that reinvest revenues. Funds perform valuable services for investors by lowering risk and increasing opportunities, usually through their research

---

[23] Swiss National Bank, *Monatsbericht* June 1995, p. 67.

departments which help to identify profit opportunities worldwide. For these services, the funds are paid commissions calculated as a percentage of asset turnover.

Certificates of virtually all existing funds can be purchased either on the stock exchanges, where the normal fee and tax structure applies, or on the over-the-counter market where the major funds and their banks maintain a market in the certificates managed by themselves.

Industry concentration

Switzerland's investment fund industry is dominated by the three Big Banks. As Figure 6.8 shows, Union Bank of Switzerland, Credit Suisse and Swiss Bank Corporation controlled 78 per cent of the domestic market in 1994. Neither foreign competitors nor insurance companies have gained significant shares of the Swiss markets, but these lines of competition are likely to increase in the future as banks and insurance companies (both domestic and foreign) continue to find overlapping business interests.[24] Moreover, increased competition in the asset management sector has caused Swiss private banks to increase their investment fund alternatives.

German players such as Bayerische Vereinsbank and Deka, France's Banque Paribas as well as American International Group and Merrill Lynch from the US are becoming more active competitors in the Swiss investment fund industry. Similarly, Swiss banks have set up operations in other nations (eg, England and Germany) largely to market their Luxembourg investment funds.

Figure 6.8

Concentration of Swiss investment fund industry, 1994

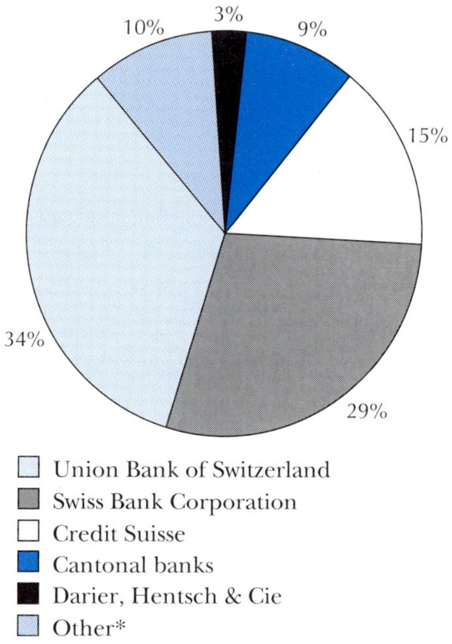

- ☐ Union Bank of Switzerland
- ☐ Swiss Bank Corporation
- ☐ Credit Suisse
- ☐ Cantonal banks
- ■ Darier, Hentsch & Cie
- ☐ Other*

* Among the leading "Other" investment funds are American International Group, Julius Baer, Merrill Lynch Bank, Vontobel Holding and Banque Scandinave en Suisse.

Source: Lipper Analytical Services International Corp., "Switzerland", *European Fund Industry Directory 1995* Fourth Edition, pp. 25.10 - 25.11.

New federal investment fund law

On 1 January 1995, Switzerland's revised Federal Law on Investment Funds came into force.[25] Article 1 of the new law states that its primary purpose is to protect investors, but

---

[24] American International Group holds a little over 1 per cent of total Swiss funds and is the largest foreign competitor in Switzerland. See, Lipper Analytical Services International Corp., "Switzerland", *European Fund Industry Directory 1995* Fourth Edition, pp. 25.10 - 25.11.

[25] The new legislation revised the 1966 Federal Law and the 1967 Ordinance on Investment Funds, as well as the 1971 Ordinance on Foreign Investment Funds.

important and potentially far-reaching additional benefits will also accrue to the Swiss financial industry.

Switzerland's taxes (eg, stamp duties), restrictive investment policies and its citizens' decision in 1992 not to join the EEA were major elements that encumbered the development of the domestic investment fund market. As a result of these disincentives, Swiss banks that wanted to maintain an international presence in this industry responded by setting up investment fund operations in Luxembourg. They were so aggressive that they grew in the 1990s to dominate the Luxembourg market for investment funds,[26] and a large portion (approximately 60 per cent) of the funds placed in Luxembourg were invested in money market instruments – investments that Swiss domestic funds were prohibited from making under the old Federal Law on Investment Funds.[27]

The new Investment Fund Law better harmonizes Switzerland's regulations with the current (and expected) European Union's Ucits Directive.[28] They also go a long way toward freeing Swiss fund managers to compete on the international markets by enabling (with limitations) the use of many of the new financial instruments (eg, derivatives, book entry instruments and money market instruments) that formerly were restricted. The Law is expected to diminish or eliminate many of the advantages that other countries (especially Luxembourg) have enjoyed.

Investor protection

The new Law mandates that the responsibility of a fund manager be limited to the investment fund and that the management of the investment fund be independent from the custodian bank. Investors are protected under the new law by enhanced transparency requirements that stipulate both semi-annual and annual reporting.[29] The law also defines more clearly the form these financial reports should take (eg, minimal reporting requirements are specified, such as a statement of financial position, off balance sheet transactions, profit and loss statement, change in net assets, number of units traded, valuation, names of valuation experts and a brief auditor's report on the aforementioned items), and it extends this reporting to both on- and off-balance sheet activities.

The new investment law mandates "adequate diversification" and limits investment in any single debtor or undertaking. The law identifies the Federal Banking Commission as the supervisory authority of the investment funds and defines the duties of fund managers, sales agents, representatives of foreign investment funds, custodians, auditors, valuers and supervisory authorities. Due to these legislative changes, competition will increase because foreign investment funds (ie, funds with management having their registered offices and principal places of business outside Switzerland) have been given

---

[26] Except for 1993 when German funds were the market leaders.

[27] Lipper Analytical Services International Corp., "Switzerland", *European Fund Industry Directory 1995* Fourth Edition, p. 25.5.

[28] Ucits stands for Undertakings for Collective Investments in Transferable Securities. The Directive governs open-ended funds that are sold across boundaries of nations belonging to the European Union.

[29] Investors who demonstrate a legitimate interest in obtaining more detailed information on specific investment fund transactions over the previous years have a right at any time to be provided with such information by the fund manager. The law also covers reporting responsibilities by the fund managers to the Swiss National Bank.

wider latitude to offer and sell units once they receive authorization from the Swiss Supervisory Authority.

Increased flexibility, competitiveness and cost savings

The new rules enable fund managers to use derivative instruments both for hedging and investment purposes. In passing this legislation, derivatives are recognized as useful financial instruments so long as they are controlled and investors are informed of the funds' risks. In addition to using novel and innovative financial instruments, the new law enables fund managers (within limits) to lend securities of the fund, effect borrowings and pledge fund assets.

In addition to the familiar securities funds[30] and real estate funds,[31] the law permits the creation of "other funds", that invest in securities having limited marketability, high price volatility, restricted diversification or problematic valuations. Investment in precious metals, commodities, options, futures, units of other investment funds and investments in other rights are examples of these "other funds". Permission is granted to offer the "other funds" so long as the risks are properly explained to the investor through the fund's name, a prospectus and accurate advertising.

Under the new law, banking groups will be able to form special in-house funds for the collective management of client assets.[32] By combining the fund management operations, economies of scale should reduce bank costs. Additional savings could result from the ability of fund managers (custodian banks) to have their rights and responsibilities assumed by other fund managers (custodian banks).

---

[30] Securities funds are European Union-compatible.

[31] A whole section of the new law relating to real estate funds covers areas such as permitted investments, diversification, special duties and special authorizations of fund management, participation of valuers, issuance, repurchase and trading.

[32] Public advertising of such funds is not permitted, there must be a written asset administration agreement, and these funds may not issue certificates.

SWISS NATIONAL BANK AND MONETARY POLICY

The Swiss National Bank (SNB) was founded in 1907. Its late appearance relative to other European central banks was due to moderate domestic credit demand and the lack of uniform currency laws. After 1848, the central government obtained the authority to administer the Swiss currency. The demand for funds increased rapidly, but federalist jealousies prevented the establishment of a central bank for another half century.

Over most of its lifetime, the SNB has acted passively rather than proactively, increasing the money supply when the economy was expanding and curtailing its growth as economic activity fell. Not until the 1960s did the Bank, under the pressure of events, start to take a more leading (rather than a guiding) role in the economy, and, only in 1978, when the Swiss National Bank Law was revised, did it gain the full range of central bank monetary tools. Prior to the revision, the SNB operated largely by gentlemen's agreements concluded with the banks and, in its early years, special legislation was needed to enact discretionary monetary policies.

Overview of the Swiss National Bank

The SNB is the financial arm of the Swiss federal government. With headquarters in both Zurich and Bern, it has exclusive rights to issue Swiss franc currency, tender federal debt issues and invest government funds held at the SNB. Among its other responsibilities, the central bank manages the national inter-bank clearing system and has the power to regulate bank reserves, foreign deposits in Switzerland, capital exports, foreign exchange transactions and domestic liquidity.[1] The SNB is a quasi-public, joint-stock institution. Its capital is two-thirds owned by the cantons, cantonal banks and other official institutions and one-third owned by private shareholders.[2] The federal government owns no part of the SNB.

The central bank is managed by a Governing Board (composed of a chairman, vice-chairman and one other member), whose members are appointed by the federal Parliament. The group meets regularly each week (every Thursday), though extraordinary meetings can be called easily and at any time.

Because it was created by the government, the SNB is ultimately accountable to the Swiss Parliament, but its dialogue is with the Federal Council. Formal reporting is to the

1. Functions, institutional structure and independence

---

[1] At present, the SNB exercises few of the powers at its disposal.
[2] Swiss National Bank, *87 Geschäftsbericht 1994* p. 70.

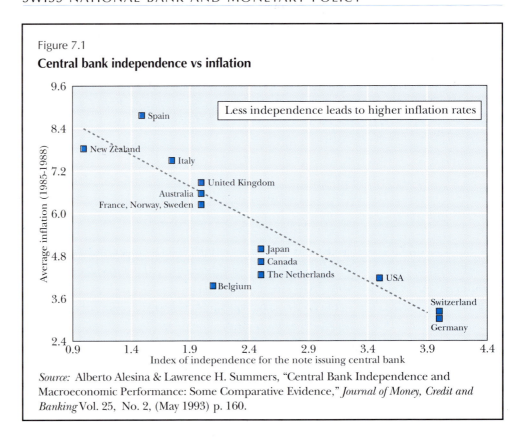

Figure 7.1

Central bank independence vs inflation

Source: Alberto Alesina & Lawrence H. Summers, "Central Bank Independence and Macroeconomic Performance: Some Comparative Evidence," *Journal of Money, Credit and Banking* Vol. 25, No. 2, (May 1993) p. 160.

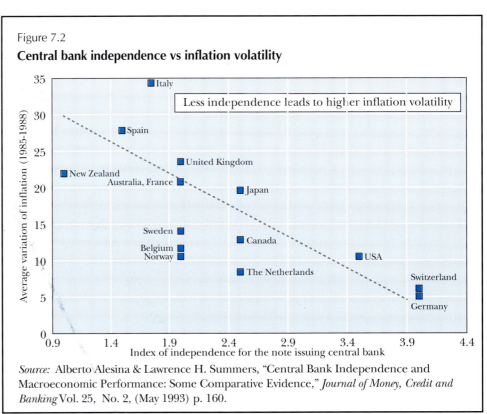

Figure 7.2

Central bank independence vs inflation volatility

Source: Alberto Alesina & Lawrence H. Summers, "Central Bank Independence and Macroeconomic Performance: Some Comparative Evidence," *Journal of Money, Credit and Banking* Vol. 25, No. 2, (May 1993) p. 160.

Swiss National Bank Council (Bankrat) consisting of 40 delegates from all segments of the Swiss economy. The members meet quarterly and are elected by the shareholders' assembly (15) and the Federal Council (25). This Bankrat delegates ten among its members to the Executive Committee (Bankausschuss) which meets once a month. Both bodies are more honourary in nature than operatively engaged and are used as a sounding board to check the *vox populi*. In the absence of a professional supervisory body, the main effective control is exercised by the press.[3]

Switzerland is considered to have one of the most independent central banks in the world. Political influence is not a constraint or a major factor in its day-to-day business. As Figures 7.1 and 7.2 show, there is a strong inverse correlation between central bank independence and both the rate of inflation and the volatility of inflation.

Switzerland separates the responsibility for supervising banks from the responsibility for controlling the money supply. The Federal Banking Commission[4] is charged with the former duty and the SNB with the latter. Article 2 of the Swiss National Bank Law empowers the central bank to 'regulate the country's money circulation, facilitate payment transactions and pursue credit and monetary policies in the overall interest of the country'. This charge has been interpreted by the SNB as a clear mandate to maintain the purchasing power of the Swiss franc without damaging the export sector.

From a domestic and international point of view, the long-term maintenance of Switzerland's purchasing power requires price stability, and the key to price stability is controlling the long-term growth of the money supply. The SNB's pursuit of an almost inflation-free economy has been easier to execute in Switzerland than in most nations because all political parties and an overwhelming majority of the Swiss unions and voters support a monetary policy that avoids inflation.

2. Mandate of the Swiss National Bank

The SNB operates with a philosophy of pragmatic monetarism. It believes there is a controllable and direct (long-term) relationship between money growth and inflation, and because this link occurs with extended and unpredictable lags, rules rather than human discretion should determine the growth in monetary targets. The only time this philosophy is substantially altered is when international capital flows force sharp movements in the value of the Swiss franc and dramatically change the price of Swiss exports. This concern is understandable in light of the fact that exports are approximately 40 per cent of Swiss GDP and imports comprise 30 per cent of the consumer price index.[5] When the SNB does target the exchange rate, it focuses more on the real rate than the nominal

3. Monetary philosophy and tools of the Swiss National Bank

---

[3] The SNB employed 564 persons on December 31, 1994 at a cost of Sfr76.5 million or Sfr135,638 per person.

[4] The Federal Banking Commission grants and withdraws banking licenses, as well as supervises banks, finance companies and investment trusts.

[5] A depreciation of the Swiss franc by a mere 1 per cent could result, theoretically, in a potential 0.3 per cent increase in inflation.

Table 7.1

Monetary tools of the Swiss National Bank

Tool	Description
Reserve requirements	The SNB sets minimum reserve requirements that are linked to bank liabilities. The length of the reserve accounting period is three months and the maintenance period is 1 month. The maximum reserve ratio is 2.5 per cent for maturities up to three months, and the highest ratio for other deposits is 0.5 per cent. Interest is not paid on bank reserves deposited with the SNB.
Lombard advances	Banks can borrow from the central bank on the collateral of approved securities. The interest charge on such loans is set by the SNB. Since 1989, the Lombard Rate has been a penal cost set at 2 per cent above the average interbank call-money rate from the two preceding days.[6]
Discount advances	Banks can borrow from the central bank at below market rates on the collateral of approved commercial loans or other securities. The interest charged on such loans is set by the SNB. Quotas are imposed, and most banks borrow to the limit of their quotas, rendering the discount window a poor source of new funds in times of financial difficulty.[7] The amount of funds borrowed using the discount window is not as important as changes in the discount rate, which signal changes (or maintenance) of SNB policy.
Foreign exchange intervention	The central bank purchases and sells foreign exchange (typically through swap transactions) to effect changes in the monetary base. Most swaps are dollars against Swiss francs with injections having maturities in the one to three month range.
Open market operations	In 1992, the SNB re-instituted its practice of transacting repurchase agreements to manage domestic short-term liquidity. Maturities ranged from overnight to one week.
Exchange controls	The SNB has the power to impose foreign exchange restrictions.
Suasion	Many of the SNB goals, particularly before 1978, are achieved through gentlemen's agreements sometimes called due diligence conventions. The effectiveness of these policies is enhanced by cooperation from the three Big Banks (Credit Suisse, Union Bank of Switzerland and Swiss Bank Corporation).

[6] See Organization of Economic Cooperation and Development, OECD, *Economic Surveys: Switzerland 1993-1994* p. 48.

[7] Bruce Kasman, "A Comparison of Monetary Policy Operating Procedures in Six Industrial Countries," *Federal Reserve Bank of New York Review* (Summer 1992) p. 17.

rate, and because of Switzerland's concentrated intra-European trade relations, the SNB targets the EU currencies (especially the Deutschmark) more than the US dollar.[8]

To accomplish its goals, the SNB pre-announces monetary targets that are consistent with Switzerland's long-run growth of real GDP and that will insure inflation remains within the desired 0 per cent to 1 per cent range. Since 1990, it has provided an intermediate-term (3- to 5-year) monetary target for the seasonally adjusted monetary base (M0, which is currency in circulation and bank sight deposits at the SNB).[9] This target is currently 1 per cent per annum, and the SNB has confirmed its intention to maintain this goal for the remainder of the decade.

Because of the lack of close correlation between the monetary base and economic activity, few other nations use bank reserves as their short-term operating objective, opting instead for short-term interest rates.[10] The SNB acts to smooth daily fluctuations in the short-term inter-bank interest rates, but does not, at present, set targets for them.

Many central banks control their monetary bases by purchasing and selling government securities. The SNB uses foreign exchange and foreign-denominated securities in place of government securities. In fact, foreign currency investments comprised over 70 per cent of the SNB's assets in 1994 (see Table 7.2). The foreign exchange market is relied upon by the SNB because of the relatively underdeveloped Swiss government securities market, which has been caused, in part, by the conservative management practices of the Swiss federal government.[11] Typically, federal budget deficits have been smaller than in other countries because of federalist spending patterns, causing the accumulated federal debt in 1994 to be about 21 per cent of Switzerland's GDP.[12]

Swiss monetary policy is considered to be a more flexible economic instrument (both in terms of timelines and impact) than Swiss fiscal policy, because SNB policies are not subject to popular referenda. At the same time, the SNB is conservative in its approach to monetary policy, following market forces more often than it leads them.

Generally, foreign exchange intervention is done by means of swap or reverse swap transactions (ie, the sale of Swiss francs for foreign currencies along with the simultaneous agreement to repurchase them in the future at an agreed upon price). Maturities range between 6 weeks and 8 months, and have become such a regular part of the SNB policy that existing trades expire virtually every week.

The SNB has resisted targeting the Swiss franc's international value, and for good reason. The effects such interventions would have on the domestic economy via changes in the monetary base could give rise to large swings in inflation and inflationary expecta-

---

[8] Georg Rich, "Exchange-Rate Management Under Floating Exchange Rates," *Journal of Banking and Finance* 14 (1990) p. 994. The SNB tries to avoid sharp fluctuations in the international value of the Swiss franc, but normally it sets no specific target ranges.

[9] Currency in circulation comprises approximately 90 per cent of the total Swiss monetary base. (See OECD, *Economic Surveys: 1993-1994 Switzerland* p. 42 & Swiss National Bank, *87 Geschäftsbericht 1994* pp. 74-75).

[10] Kasman, pp. 5-24.

[11] The Swiss stamp tax has also hindered the growth of the short-term capital market in Switzerland. To avoid these taxes, banks have channelled the bulk of these activities through the Euromarkets. See Chapter 9.

[12] Nevertheless, total debt at all three levels (federal, cantonal and municipal) amounted to 47.5 per cent of GDP in 1993. See Chapter 2. OECD, *Economic Surveys 1994-1995: Switzerland* p. 52.

Table 7.2

Swiss National Bank balance sheet: 31 December 1994

Assets	Amount (Sfr billions)	%
Cash	12.18	18.8
Gold	11.90	
Currency	0.28	
Foreign exchange investments	45.91	70.8
Reserve position at IMF	1.24	1.9
International payment funds	0.41	0.6
Currency credits	0.20	0.3
Domestic portfolio: money market paper	0.72	1.1
Lombard credits	0.01	0.0
Securities	3.03	4.7
Covered	0.49	
Other	2.54	
Participations	0.00	0.0
Correspondents domestic	0.57	0.9
Bills for collection	0.03	0.005
Postal check credits	0.0005	0.0
Coupons	0.0	0.0
Building	0.0	0.0
Furniture	0.0	0.0
Other assets	0.03	0.005
Accrued or deferred expenses	0.44	0.7
Not paid-in asset capital	0.03	0.005
Total	**64.8**	**100**

Liabilities	Amount (Sfr billions)	%
Currency in circulation	30.55	47
Domestic clearing account: banks & finance companies	3.84	6
Clearing account for foreign banks	0.05	
Federal administration	0.6	0.1
Depositors	0.10	1
Outstanding checks	0.003	0
Time liabilities	2.85	4
Other liabilities	0.63	1
Accrued or deferred expenses	0.10	
Provisions for currency risk	23.91	37
Other provisions	0.64	1
Revaluation of foreign exchange	0.81	1
Share capital	0.05	0.1
Reserve funds	0.06	0.1
Profit available for distribution **	0.61	1
Total	**64.8**	**100**

* Gold has been valued by the SNB since May 1971 at 1 kg pure gold = Sfr4,595.74
** Profit of the current year plus profit available for distribution from former years.

Source: Swiss National Bank, *87. Geschäftsbericht* (1994) pp. 74-75.

tions. Interventions, when the SNB has participated, have typically been in combination with the initiatives of other central banks.

4. The Swiss National Bank and Swiss short-term money markets

Since 1979, the SNB has purchased and sold federal debt with maturities one year or less in an effort to develop a domestic short-term money market. The federal government has helped in this effort by issuing short-term money market paper in the form of "book claims", also known as debt register claims. At first, maturities were limited to 3-months, but later 6-month and 1-month maturities were added. Buyers have been mainly domestic institutional investors whose minimum stake was Sfr100,000 (originally as much as Sfr500,000). In March 1982, the SNB announced that it intended to experiment by purchasing more domestic securities as a part of its open market operations. These purchases reached Sfr500 million in the first year and were intended to diversify the SNB's portfolio.

5. Monetary policy

The ability of a central bank to control its domestic money supply depends critically on the type of exchange rate system the nation has adopted. From 1946 to 1973, Switzerland was part of the Bretton Woods (1946-1971) and Smithsonian agreements (1971-1973), which committed the SNB to restrict its currency's movement within a narrow band around a parity rate.[13] By gearing its monetary policies to offset international market forces, the SNB relinquished virtually all control over the domestic money supply during this period. In large part, Switzerland's inflation rate and nominal interest rates for over two and a half decades until 1973, were influenced more by the economic events in foreign nations than the discretionary policies of the SNB. As a consequence, the Swiss franc was under-valued during this period.

In 1973, the Swiss franc was freed to float against all major currencies and, virtually overnight, the SNB gained control of its monetary base. For over two decades since this independence was regained, the SNB has vigorously sought to enact monetary policies aimed at keeping the domestic inflation rate low. The results have been dramatic. Switzerland's consumer inflation fell from 8.7 per cent and 9.8 per cent in 1973 and 1974, to 1.7 per cent, 1.3 per cent and 1.1 per cent in 1976, 1977 and 1978, respectively.

For the first five years after the collapse of the Bretton Woods system, the SNB policy targeted the M1 money stock growth rate. Occasionally the SNB intervened in the spot US dollar/Swiss franc market to reduce exaggerated fluctuations or to reverse unwanted exchange rate movements, and, for most of the 1970s, achieving domestic monetary targets was consistent with foreign exchange market developments.[14]

---

[13] The Bretton Woods system established the band at +/- 1 per cent and the Smithsonian Agreement widened it to +/-2.25 per cent.

[14] During this period, the SNB intervened in the spot market when it wanted to increase the monetary base and intervened in the forward exchange when it wanted to reduce it. Since 1980, the forward intervention technique has not been used. See Georg Rich, "Exchange-Rate management Under Floating Exchange Rates," *Journal of Banking and Finance* 14 (1990) p. 995.

In 1978, the Swiss franc strengthened considerably as a result of heavy international investment flows, putting the SNB on the horns of a dilemma. To reduce the value of the Swiss franc risked increasing the domestic money supply and fuelling inflation, but to refrain from intervening meant pricing many Swiss products out of the international markets. From April 1978 to March 1979, the SNB raised exchange rates from their penultimate position as an operating target to a top position in an effort to stave off the sharp appreciation of the Swiss franc.

Because of the elephantine size of the foreign exchange inflows, massive interventions were needed to have any significant influence. The resultant increase in the Swiss monetary base combined with the second oil price shock lifted Swiss inflation from 1.1 per cent in 1978, to 3.6 per cent in 1979.[15]

In reaction, the SNB swiftly returned to its policy of targeting monetary aggregates, using exchange rates as moderating influences, but without prescribing targets. Foreign exchange swaps were now used as the preferred vehicle for intervention. Controlling the money supply proved to be more difficult than expected, and, in 1980, the SNB switched from targeting the broader M1 aggregate to targeting the monetary base. From 1980 to 1982, inflation averaged 5.4 per cent, but dropped to a 3.1 per cent average rate from 1983 to 1985, and, by 1986, consumer price increases were brought under 1 per cent for the first time in over 20 years.

In 1987, the Swiss consumer price index began to climb above the central bank's target of 1 per cent and reached an unacceptably high rate of 5.8 per cent in 1991. The inflation levels experienced by Switzerland between 1989 and 1991 were not only high by Swiss historic standards, but they were in excess of neighbouring countries such as Germany and Austria.

There was controversy over the cause of Switzerland's inflation. Some analysts attributed the initial increase to non-monetary factors such as the advanced stage of Switzerland's economic expansion and the inflation anxieties from the Gulf Crisis during the second half of 1990. The majority opinion pointed most of the blame at monetary factors, in general, and the SNB's liberal increase in the money supply, in particular (see Figure 7.4).

The undesired increase in the money supply could be traced to a number of underlying causes. After the Plaza Accord of 1985, the dollar plummeted in value. Interventions by the SNB were undertaken to restrain the fall and resulted in unexpectedly high growth rates of the domestic monetary base. In 1987, a second shock hit the world economy when the stock market crashed causing share prices to nose-dive. Fearing a recession due to consumption and investment spending cuts, the SNB increased the money supply.

Other, more technical, factors also contributed to the monetary expansion. In 1988, the Swiss Interbank Clearing System (SIC) was introduced along with modifications in Swiss liquidity regulations governing banks. The SIC automated inter-bank clear-

---

[15] In 1978, the crisis year, SNB intervention amounted to Sfr22.5 billion after selling Sfr45.5 billion in the foreign exchange market during the previous 3 years.

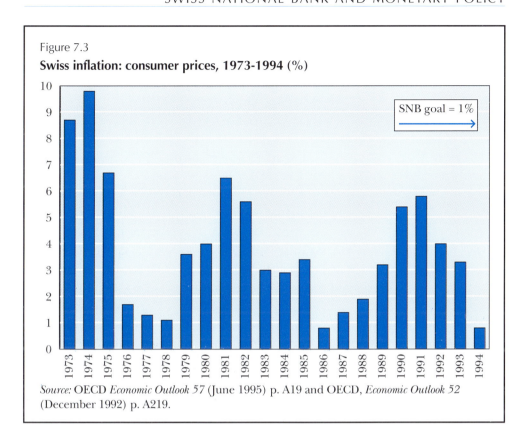

Figure 7.3

Swiss inflation: consumer prices, 1973-1994 (%)

Source: OECD *Economic Outlook 57* (June 1995) p. A19 and OECD, *Economic Outlook 52* (December 1992) p. A219.

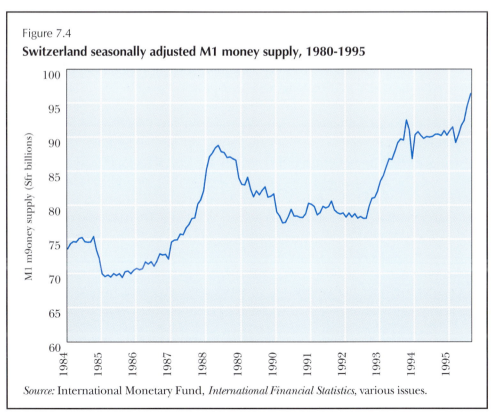

Figure 7.4

Switzerland seasonally adjusted M1 money supply, 1980-1995

Source: International Monetary Fund, *International Financial Statistics*, various issues.

Table 7.3

Summary of Swiss National Bank monetary targets since 1946

Date	Swiss National Bank monetary targets
1946-1973	Nominal exchange rates: Bretton Woods parity rate
January 1973-March 1978	Short-term money supply (M1) growth rate
April 1978-March 1979	Real exchange rates
January 1980-1988	Short-term monetary base growth (less than one year)
1988-Present	Medium-term monetary base growth (3-5 years)

ing and enabled banks to reduce their daily balances at the SNB.[16] These technical modifications broke the historic link between changes in Switzerland's monetary base and growth in its money supply, and money growth rates became less reliable indicators of monetary policy.

Criticisms of the SNB's laxness combined with problems gauging banks' demand for money caused the central bank to change, once again, its operating goals.[17] It abandoned short-term bank reserve targets, and, after a brief experiment using short-term interest rates and exchange rates, began to define its goals in terms of medium-term (3- to 5-year) changes in monetary base.[18]

In 1988 (about six months later than expected by many observers), the SNB began to curtail the growth rate of the monetary base (see Figure 7.5) in order to tighten the money supply and to quash inflationary expectations. These actions raised domestic interest rates (see Figure 7.6), led to an appreciation of the Swiss franc and precipitated a recession that began in the first part of 1991 and lasted nearly three years. The downturn was the longest in Switzerland's post-World War II experience. Inflation fell, albeit slowly, but unemployment rose to disturbing high levels. Interest-sensitive investment sectors, such as construction, machinery and equipment, were especially hard hit.

Swiss interest rates trended down during the 1990-1994 period (see Figure 7.6) in large part because of recession-induced decreases in the demand for funds. The decline was reinforced by a host of other events. Significant amounts of international capital

---

[16] As a result of the change, bank sight deposits have fallen to less than 9 per cent of the Swiss monetary base. In 1987, they were 25 per cent. At a more minute level of technical detail, there were measurement abnormalities, as well, in the M1 and M2 money supplies. For instance, salary accounts were not included in these measures when they should have been, and liabilities from bank security lending transactions were included when they should not have been. (See OECD, *Economic Surveys 1993-1994: Switzerland* p. 46).

[17] See OECD, *Economic Surveys: Switzerland* (Various issues starting in 1989).

[18] The SNB has researched which of the monetary aggregates provides the best policy prescriptions. It had little success finding a stable relationship between M2 or M3 and economic activity (ie, output, inflation, and interest rates). Investigations considering M1 Divisia and M2 Divisia were conducted to see if they outperformed alternative monetary aggregates that were used as leading indicators of inflation. Divisia monetary aggregates attach weights to individual money stock components reflecting the level of moneyness of the individual assets. See Piyu Yue and Robert Fluri, "Divisia Monetary Services Indexes for Switzerland: Are They Useful for Monetary Targeting?" *Federal Reserve Bank of St. Louis Review* Vol. 73, Issue 5, (September/October 1991) pp. 19-33.

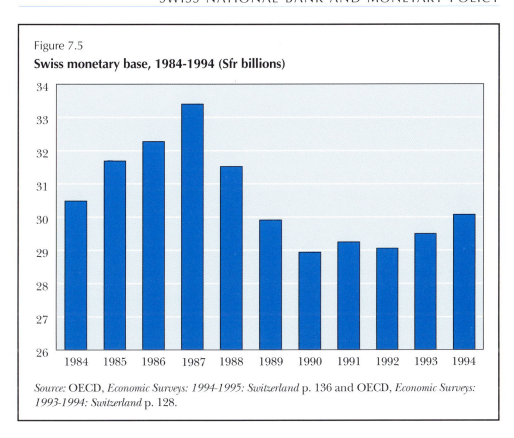

Figure 7.5

Swiss monetary base, 1984-1994 (Sfr billions)

Source: OECD, *Economic Surveys: 1994-1995: Switzerland* p. 136 and OECD, *Economic Surveys: 1993-1994: Switzerland* p. 128.

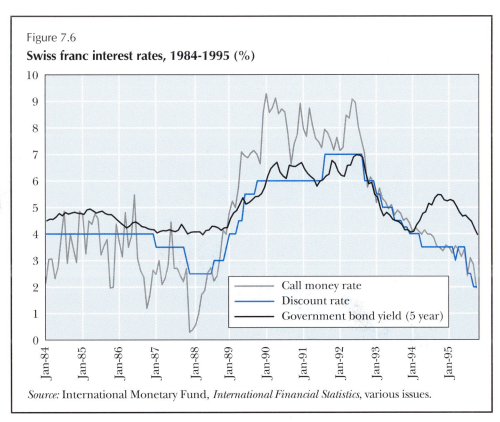

Figure 7.6

Swiss franc interest rates, 1984-1995 (%)

Source: International Monetary Fund, *International Financial Statistics,* various issues.

flowed to Switzerland in 1992 as a result of the turmoil surrounding the United Kingdom and Italy's exit from the European Exchange Rate Mechanism. In addition, the restrictive monetary policies of the SNB reduced inflationary expectations. Furthermore, Switzerland's strong current account balance and reductions in German interest rates all helped to stabilize Swiss interest rates at lower levels.

The 1991 recession confronted the SNB with a quandary. Unemployment rates increased much above desired levels, but the SNB was not convinced that inflationary fears had been fully suppressed. Officials worried that stimulation would reduce Swiss real interest rates even further below their German counterparts, resulting in a shift of financial capital that would lower the value of the Swiss franc and exacerbate domestic inflation.

Table 7.4

Swiss National Bank: targeted versus actual monetary base figures, 1990-1994 (Sfr billions)

Year	Targeted level	Actual level
1990	29.866	28.801
1991	30.164	29.204
1992	30.466	28.925
1993	30.771	29.724
1994	31.078	29.908

Source: OECD, *Economic Survey 1994-1995: Switzerland* p. 47.

When the Swiss recovery did begin during the second quarter of 1993, it was not strong enough to raise GDP for the whole year. Nevertheless, despite the slow progress of growth, it has persisted and is expected to last well into 1996.

Because of Switzerland's lacklustre economic growth, the strength of the Swiss franc and the high rate of domestic unemployment, businesses (especially the textile industry) and unions have put the SNB under considerable pressure to refuel the money supply. They have argued that the Swiss economy could handle more liquidity without a resurgence of inflation. They point to the fact that the yield curve has turned moderately positive, the monetary base has continued to grow below targeted levels and inflationary fears seem to have been subdued (see Table 7.4). Furthermore, real interest rates have been relatively high and unemployment has remained at levels above the Swiss norm.

There is every reason to believe that the SNB will continue to be reluctant to start another expansionary spiral.[19] It was fearful of repeating mistakes of the 1980s by raising domestic inflation and re-fuelling Switzerland's ever-more intransigent inflationary expectations.

Monetary policy in the 1990s

Because the international sector plays such a significant role in the Swiss economy, the SNB will continually face the tradeoff of either managing its monetary base or trying to manage its exchange rate. Evidence from the post-Bretton Woods period indicates that the Swiss Central Bank has had less success managing its exchange rate, but much better results controlling both the domestic monetary base and inflation. As the international

---

[19] A short-term spike in inflation during 1995 was anticipated by the implementation of the VAT tax. The SNB permitted the money supply to rise slightly faster in order to accommodate the new tax, but this increase played no significant role in the central bank's overall strategy for the 1990s.

capital markets become more liquid and the role of all central banks (including the SNB) becomes increasingly trivialized, the ability of the SNB to influence the foreign exchange rate (without risking inflation) will be further diminished.

The SNB's philosophy of pragmatic monetarism frames its role as an inflation fighter rather than a creator of jobs. It is abundantly clear that Swiss inflation during the 1970s and 1980s was stimulated by excessive monetary expansion, and after each bout with inflation, its reduction was caused by a contraction in the growth of the monetary base. In the mid-1990s, the SNB, therefore, resisted the temptation to relax its restrictive monetary policy in order to lower the Swiss franc's value – fully aware that with a time lag of 2-3 years, it would have to pay the price in the form of a higher inflation rate.

To the extent that restrictive monetary policy curtails real economic growth, it brings to the surface an inherent conflict between income generation and value conservation. Low money growth reduces demand for resources and prevents their prices from rising as fast as they otherwise would. In contrast, low inflation keeps nominal interest rates down and protects bondholders from valuation losses. It also protects foreign investors, many of whom have bought Swiss francs to escape the ravages of inflation and devaluation. The SNB believes that money is not the cause of long-term increases in real economic growth, but a lack of it surely restricts growth. The proper mixture is a delicate balance. Further liberalization of world-wide capital flows will make achieving it a more demanding – if not impossible – task for a small country.

Appendix 7-A

Table 7-A.1

Swiss discount rate and Lombard rate, 1936-1995

Year of change	Day & month of change	Discount rate (%)	Lombard rate (%)
1936	9 September	2.00	3.00
	26 November	1.50	2.50
1957	15 May	2.50	3.50
1959	26 February	2.00	3.00
1964	3 July	2.50	3.50
1966	6 July	3.50	4.00
1967	10 July	3.00	3.75
1969	15 September	3.75	4.75
1973	22 January	4.50	5.25
1974	21 January	5.50	6.00
1975	3 March	5.00	6.00
	20 May	4.50	5.50
	25 August	4.00	5.00
	29 September	3.50	4.50
	29 October	3.00	4.00
1976	13 January	2.50	3.50
	8 June	2.00	3.00
1977	15 July	1.50	2.50
1978	27 February	1.00	2.00

Table 7-A.1 *continued*

Swiss discount rate and Lombard rate, 1936-1995 *continued*

Year of change	Day & month of change	Discount rate (%)	Lombard rate (%)
1979	5 November	2.00	3.00
1980	28 February	3.00	4.00
1981	3 February	3.50	4.50
	20 February	4.00	5.50
	11 May	5.00	6.50
	2 September	6.00	7.50
	4 December	6.00	7.00
1982	19 March	5.50	7.00
	27 August	5.00	6.50
	3 December	4.50	6.00
1983	18 March	4.00	5.50
1987	23 January	3.50	5.00
	6 November	3.00	4.50
	4 December	2.50	4.00
1988	1 July	2.50	4.50
	26 August	3.00	5.00
	19 December	3.50	5.50
1989	20 January	4.00	6.00
	14 April	4.50	7.00
	26 May	4.50	Floating
	30 June	5.50	
	6 October	6.00	
1991	16 August	7.00	
1992	15 September	6.50	
	25 September	6.00	
1993	8 January	5.50	
	19 March	5.00	
	2 July	4.50	
	22 October	4.25	
	17 December	4.00	
1994	15 April	3.50	
1995	31 March	3.00	
	14 July	2.50	
	22 September	2.00	
	15 December	1.50	

Source: Swiss National Bank, *87 Geschäftsbericht 1994* p. 94 & updated by authors.

8

THE SWISS FRANC

Overview of the
Swiss franc market

In 1995, the Swiss franc was the sixth most actively traded currency in the world (behind the US dollar, Deutschmark, Japanese yen, Sterling and Hong Kong dollar).[1] It was a counter-currency in 7 per cent of all foreign exchange transactions, and annual turnover per day amounted to US$86.5 billion.[2]

The deepest Swiss franc markets are against Deutschmarks and US dollars. Under normal conditions, the enormous volume of trade produces thin bid/ask spreads. For the interbank markets, representative spreads in 1995 were 5 basis points for dollar/Sfr, 3 basis points for Deutschmark/Sfr, and 5-10 basis points for ¥/Sfr.[3] There are also considerable Swiss franc volumes in the derivative markets (ie, forwards, futures, options on futures, interest rate swaps and cross-currency swaps). In the forward market (Swiss franc against both the US dollar and the Deutschmark), highly active trading takes place in maturities up to one-year. On the Philadelphia Exchange, the Swiss franc is the third largest cash option contract, comprising about 15 per cent of the market. In the swap market, the Bank for International Settlements reports outstanding Swiss franc interest rate swaps at the end of 1993 were equal to US$182.2 billion, the sixth largest notional principal amount (behind the US dollar, Yen, Deutschmark, French franc and Sterling). Outstanding Swiss franc currency swaps were equal to US$146.5 billion, third behind the US dollar and the Yen.[4]

Among the Swiss banks, only Union Bank of Switzerland, Swiss Bank Corporation and Credit Suisse compete at the highest ranks in the foreign exchange markets. Table 8.1 shows that Union Bank of Switzerland and Swiss Bank Corporation have two of the top ten international slots when ranked on the basis of global market shares.

A 1995 *Euromoney Magazine* poll[5] on the foreign exchange market ranked international banks by their performance in the: interbank markets, regional markets, currency

---

[1] The facts presented in this paragraph are based on: Bank for International Settlements, Central Bank Survey of Foreign Exchange Market in April 1995: Preliminary Global Findings (Basel, October 24, 1995).

[2] Turnover increased from US$65.5 billion per day in 1992 when the Swiss franc was a counter currency in 9 per cent of all foreign exchange transactions. Bank for International Settlements, Central Bank Survey of Foreign Exchange Market in April 1995: Preliminary Global Findings (Basel, October 24, 1995) & Bank for International Settlements, *Central Bank Survey of Foreign Exchange Market in April 1992* (Basel, 1993) p. 9.

[3] "Euromoney Supplement: Euromoney Guide to Currencies — Swiss Franc", *Euromoney* (March 1994) pp. 54-55.

[4] Bank for International Settlements, *International Banking and Financial Market Development* Appendix Tables 16A and 16B, (May 1995) pp. 56-57.

[5] "Foreign Exchange: Treasurers put their views on banks", *Euromoney Magazine* (May 1995) pp. 65-84.

regions, currency pairs, out-of-hours services, short-term forward contracts, major currency deals, EMS cross transactions, options, research and advice and expertise in risk management. In general, the details indicate a strong presence for Union Bank of Switzerland and Swiss Bank Corporation in the North American, European and Asian interbank markets. All of Switzerland's Big Banks showed strength in the Swiss franc-related currency trading areas, but only Union Bank of Switzerland ranked among the top ten in any of the regional markets (Asia and the EMS currency area). Finally, Swiss Bank Corporation was ranked either the best, or among the best in the world for options, research and advice and risk management expertise.

Table 8.1

Top 20 foreign exchange dealers, 1994 and 1995 (ranked by market share)

Rank 1995	Bank	Rank 1994
1	Citibank	1
2	Chase Manhattan	2
3	HSBC Markets/Midland	3
4	Chemical	5
5	Union Bank of Switzerland	10
6	Bank of America	6
7	NatWest	7
8	JP Morgan	8
9	Swiss Bank Corporation	13
10	Standard Chartered	–
11	Barclays	12
12	First Chicago	14
13	BNP	–
14	SE Banken	–
15	Indosuez	–
16	Credit Suisse	16
17	Bankers Trust	4
18	ABN Amro	15
19	Royal Bank of Canada	8
20	Svenska Handelsbanken	–

Source: "Treasurers put their views on banks," *Euromoney Magazine* (May 1995) p. 66.

1. The Swiss franc and the Swiss National Bank[6]

The Swiss franc's reputation for stability and external strength is due largely to the Swiss National Bank's independence, its adherence to monetary rules rather than discretion and its success at curbing inflation. Since 1980, the Swiss National Bank has set its monetary targets in terms of the monetary base. Nevertheless, it pays close attention to the real international value of the Swiss franc and occasionally acts to smooth erratic fluctuations in the foreign exchange market.[7] Moreover, because of the nation's sizable volume of trade with Germany, the Swiss National Bank focuses more on the Swiss franc's real value against the Deutschmark than the US dollar. Figure 8.1 reveals how the real exchange rate has varied among Switzerland's major trading partners over the 1982-1995 period. The relative stability of the Swiss franc-Deutschmark relationship is apparent.

Rarely does the Swiss National Bank intervene directly in the spot market to affect the value of the Swiss franc. In part, its decision to avoid direct intervention is due to the absence of any officially recognized exchange rate target. Equally important is the perceived futility of doing so.[8] Switzerland's monetary base is small relative to the foreign exchange market. To have a significant impact, the magnitude of the intervention

---

[6] For a more detailed treatment of the Swiss National Bank, see Chapter 7.

[7] Georg Rich, "Exchange-Rate management Under Floating Exchange Rates," *Journal of Banking and Finance* 14 (1990) p. 994.

[8] M. Obstfeld, *The Effectiveness of Foreign Exchange Intervention: Recent Experience* National Bureau of Economic Research Working Paper, No. 2796 (1988).

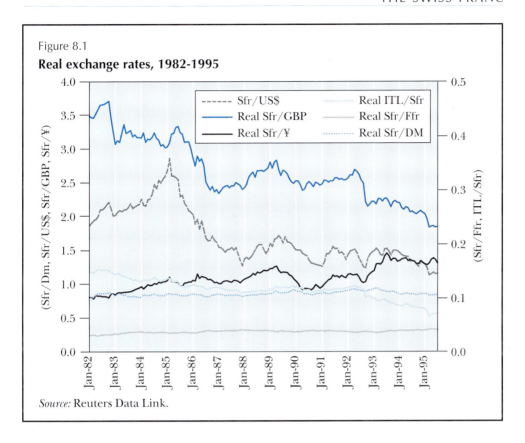

Figure 8.1

Real exchange rates, 1982-1995

Source: Reuters Data Link.

could cause the domestic monetary base to fluctuate wildly. When adjustments are made, they are typically undertaken in reaction to market changes rather than in anticipation of them.

Figure 8.2 shows the Swiss franc's effective exchange rate from 1982 to 1994. This measure weights nominal exchange rates using a system that considers both the import and export competitiveness of each nation.[9] Over the eleven years observed, Switzerland's effective exchange rate fell slightly in some years (eg, 1984, 1988, 1989, 1991 and 1992),[10] but on average showed strong appreciation.

2. Effective exchange rate

Switzerland's birth as a major international finance centre dates to 1926, when the Swiss franc became the nation's exclusive currency.[11] Since then, the Swiss franc has greatly appreciated in value against all other major European currencies (see Figure

3. Factors accounting for the Swiss franc's strength since 1982

[9] *OECD Economic Outlook,* Vol. 57, (June 1995) p. A41.
[10] Most of these declines were associated with Switzerland's relatively high inflation rate in the late 1980s and early 1990s.
[11] Between 1865 and 1926, Switzerland was a member of the Latin Currency Union.

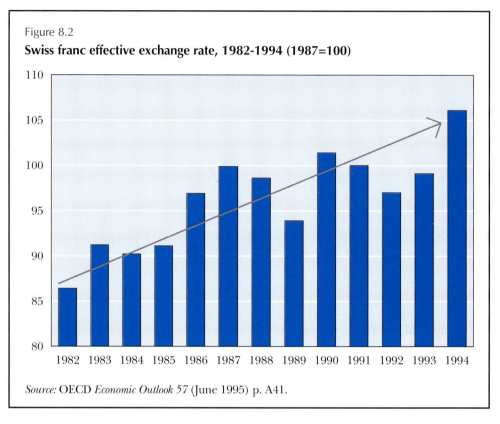

Figure 8.2

Swiss franc effective exchange rate, 1982-1994 (1987=100)

Source: OECD *Economic Outlook 57* (June 1995) p. A41.

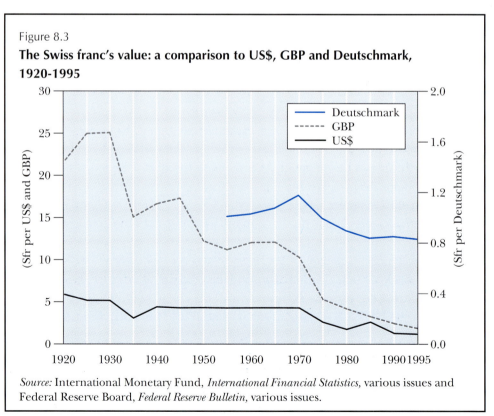

Figure 8.3

The Swiss franc's value: a comparison to US$, GBP and Deutschmark, 1920-1995

Source: International Monetary Fund, *International Financial Statistics,* various issues and Federal Reserve Board, *Federal Reserve Bulletin,* various issues.

8.3). Its continued strength has earned the Swiss franc 'safe haven' status in the international community.

The Swiss franc's status as a safe haven currency has been a mixed blessing for the Swiss economy. On the positive side, billions of Swiss francs worth of international investment funds have been attracted to Switzerland each year because of the confidence global investors have in the stability of both the nation and its currency. These flows have helped to create jobs in areas such as banking and investment management, and they have provided the wherewithal for Swiss financial institutions to develop competencies in asset management. On the negative side, strong international capital flows have, on occasion, overwhelmed the relatively small Swiss franc financial sector causing volatile shifts in the value of the Swiss franc. For this reason, policy makers are fearful of having Swiss francs serve as an international reserve currency. Their apprehensions revolve around the consequences of ever-magnified Swiss franc capital flows that are not connected to the health of the Swiss economy.[12]

The business media is filled with articles trying to explain the causes of the Swiss franc's twists and turns. Factors such as capital inflows due to the nation's safe haven status, its current account surpluses, inflation rate differentials, differences in money supply growth rates (M1 and M2), interest rate differentials (long- and short-term) and gold prices have all been the focus of attention.

Figure 8.4 shows the three major parts of Switzerland's balance of payments – the current account, capital account and official reserves account – from 1985 to 1994.[13] In each of the 10 years, Switzerland's current account was positive reflecting the nation's ability to sell more goods and services abroad than it purchased and to earn more investment income than it paid. For most observers, the image of a Swiss current account surplus is consistent with their general image of the nation and a strong Swiss franc.

Current account surpluses, capital inflows and the appreciation of the Swiss franc

The deficits in Switzerland's official reserves account, except for 1988, are also consistent with expectations. The Swiss National Bank expands the domestic money supply by purchasing currencies (mainly US dollars) in the foreign exchange market. These purchases increase the supply of Swiss francs on the foreign exchange market and lower its international value. Figure 8.5 shows the increase in the Swiss National Bank's international reserves from 1984 to 1993.

Switzerland's capital account is less transparent, but a glance at Figure 8.4 reveals why international capital flows have not been the cause of the Swiss franc's long-term appreciation. Each year, Switzerland is the temporary destination of billions of Swiss francs worth of foreign capital flows, but Switzerland is not the ultimate destination for these funds. Swiss intermediaries re-export and invest these funds in other nations.

---

[12] Fritz Leutwiler, *Swiss Monetary and Exchange Rate Policy in an Inflationary World* American Enterprise Institute Studies in Economic Policy, (Reprint and extension of a speech delivered at the Swiss National Bank on April 17, 1978) (1978) pp. 5 & 12.

[13] Prior to 1983, the Swiss National Bank did not publish quarterly estimates of Swiss international capital transactions. Consequently, analyses of the Swiss balance of payments are limited by this lack of information.

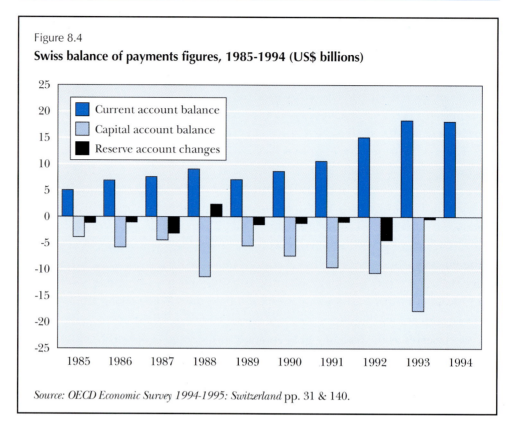

Figure 8.4

Swiss balance of payments figures, 1985-1994 (US$ billions)

Source: OECD Economic Survey 1994-1995: Switzerland pp. 31 & 140.

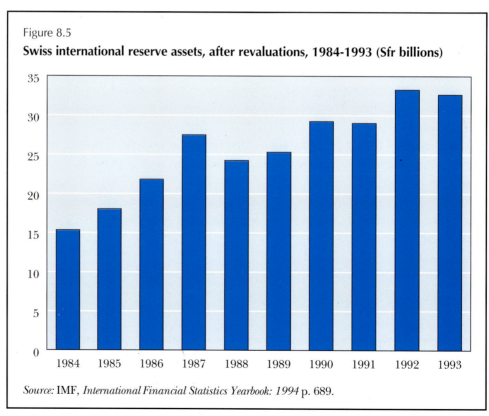

Figure 8.5

Swiss international reserve assets, after revaluations, 1984-1993 (Sfr billions)

Source: IMF, *International Financial Statistics Yearbook: 1994* p. 689.

If Switzerland were only a financial intermediary, these inflows would match the outflows and the net capital account would be zero. Figure 8.4 reveals that for each of the 10 years between 1984 and 1993, the Swiss invested more abroad than was invested in Switzerland. The additional source of funds for these foreign investment uses came from the net saving of Swiss residents, and these net outflows served to reduce (not raise) the Swiss franc's value. Therefore, if outflows are higher than inflows, international investments in Switzerland could not be the source of the Swiss franc's overvaluation.

At the end of 1994, the Swiss National Bank valued its gold holdings at Sfr11.9 billion, representing a 39 per cent gold coverage of Swiss notes in circulation and 13 per cent coverage of the M1 money supply (notes in circulation plus demand deposits other than those of the central government). These ratios understate the true level of gold backing for the Swiss franc. Since May 1971, the Swiss National Bank has priced its gold reserves at Sfr4,595.74 per kilogram of fine gold,[14] implying its physical reserves equal 2,590,205 kilograms of gold. Recalculating the value of these reserves with the market price of Sfr475 per troy ounce produces gold reserves valued at Sfr39.6 billion.[15] Using the revalued gold reserves as the base, the gold coverage of notes in circulation and M1 rises to 130 per cent and 44 per cent, respectively. Moreover, if Switzerland's international currency reserves of Sfr44.3 billion[16] are added to the gold reserves, the coverage ratios rise further to 275 per cent and 92 per cent, respectively. In part, the security the world feels about the value of the Swiss franc is derived from the assurance that there is ample gold and foreign currency backing to the currency.[17]

The Swiss franc and gold

The timetable decided by the EU members at the Maastricht summit of 1991 calls for a common currency by 1999. Though the probability of this occurring on schedule changes frequently, the potential impact on Switzerland is worth considering because of these nations' vital importance to the Swiss economy.

The success of a common currency arrangement will depend heavily on Europe's future political structures, its institutions and their tasks. Will the union be a centrally-focused federal state like the US, or a loose confederation of largely independent states, each with its own priorities and taxes to finance them? The history of Europe with its diversity of cultures would not suggest a centralized super-state, but rather a mutual organization that takes care of those responsibilities national member states are unable to perform successfully.

4. How will European Monetary Union affect the Swiss franc?

---

[14] Swiss National Bank, *87. Geschäftsbericht 1994* p. 88.

[15] Calculation: Sfr11,903,906,919 worth of gold owned by the Swiss National Bank valued at Sfr4,595.74/kg = 2,590,205 kg of gold. (2,590,205 kg worth of gold)x(US$380/troy oz) x (Sfr1.25/US$) x (1 troy oz/31.103 grams) x (1000 grams/kg) = Sfr39,554,649,574. Swiss National Bank, p. 88.

[16] Swiss National Bank, *Schweizerische Nationalbank: 87. Geschäftsbericht 1994* p. 62.

[17] Using the Granger Causality test, our statistical analysis indicates that a low degree of confidence (35 per cent) can be placed in gold prices as an explanatory variable in the Swiss franc-Deutschmark market within a six month time frame. In the Swiss franc-US dollar market, the level of confidence (92 per cent) is much higher.

Adopting a common currency means that participating nations would have to abandon monetary policy as an independent tool of economic adjustment. Because interest rates would also be closely linked, such an economic environment will function only if the capacity of each country to borrow is curtailed. They would have limited freedom to tax financial transactions because such business could easily be done elsewhere.

If members of the European Union can agree in 1996 on a constitution with a clear political structure, tasks and institutions, an independent central bank, a prohibition of central bank-financed deficits and limitations on member states' indebtedness, the introduction of a common European currency is possible by the end of the century. Its success after introduction will depend on strict enforcement of the Maastricht Treaty rules and the toughness of the supra-national monetary body in charge of maintaining price stability.

The effect of a European monetary union on the Swiss franc is problematic. A common currency will force global re-evaluation of the currency weightings in both private and institutional investment portfolios, and it will act to create greater convergence in the economic performance of the member nations. If Switzerland decides not to join, the Swiss franc will be among a handful of major currencies available for portfolio diversification. To the extent that investors might choose to make the Swiss franc a larger part of their portfolios, its value should rise.

At the same time, the Swiss franc's vulnerability to massive movements out of the European currency and into the Swiss franc will also be elevated. The Swiss franc has been one of the strongest currencies in the world over an extended period of time, or, to put it differently, it is the currency that has lost the least purchasing power in this century. In a Europe where capital transfers are free, any mistrust of the European central bank's independence will result in huge capital flows into the Swiss franc, thereby pushing up its value and severely reducing Switzerland's export vitality.

These expectation-led movements in financial capital threaten to cause greater volatility of the Swiss franc's external value. Under such circumstances, the Swiss National Bank would have three choices. It could sit idly by and watch the economic disruption occur; it could intervene causing a rapid increase in the monetary base and introducing another type of damage in the form of inflation,[18] or it could repeat the unsuccessful actions of 1979, artificially stopping the inflow and imposing punitive negative real interest rates. Under the worst scenario – where all the countries of Europe except Switzerland join a common currency and the field was left to free market forces – the price of the Swiss franc would behave like a pond connected to the sea with the ebb and flood cycle pushing and pulling on the Swiss economy. The central question, whether there will be one common currency for all of Europe is thankfully not the subject of this book.

---

[18] The same result would occur if it fixed the Swiss franc to the EU's currency .

9

SWISS DEBT MARKETS

Switzerland's high domestic saving rate, substantial placing power, low inflation, open capital markets, lack of exchange controls, low cost legal system and reputation as a safe haven are just a few of the ingredients that have enabled it to become a leading international financial centre.

Swiss franc debt instruments are attractive to foreign investors because they offer the safety of a hard currency and the possibility of earning capital gains (non-taxable in Switzerland)[1] on its appreciation. Moreover, because Switzerland is not a part of the European Union, Swiss franc assets provide a means of diversifying international portfolios, especially in light of the prominent position the Swiss franc has in the international capital markets. These instruments are attractive to borrowers because of their relatively low cost and an abundance of long-term funding. In 1995, over 2,500 different bonds were listed on the Swiss exchanges.

In spite of obvious strengths, the Swiss franc's position in the international debt markets is not evenly balanced among the various maturities (short-, medium- and long-term) and the major markets (domestic, foreign and Euro). In general, the Swiss debt markets have depth and breadth in the medium- to long-term maturities (see Table 9.1). Except for the Euromarkets which are outside the reach of the Swiss tax authorities and the short-term portion of Swiss franc foreign bonds, short-term Swiss franc debt instruments are not competitive internationally.

Overview of the Swiss debt market

The federal stamp duty is one of the most obvious reasons for the weak development of the Swiss money market. Until 1993, this flat tax was imposed on all security issues and transfers (both long-term and short-term) in Switzerland.[2] For long-term Swiss franc instruments, the tax burden has only a minor impact because it can be amortized over many years of the instrument's life. By contrast, short-term instruments bear the full burden of the tax, pricing the Swiss franc instruments out of the broader international markets. Furthermore, the stamp duty has encouraged investors to hold their instruments to maturity rather than bear the charge again. As a result, potential liquidity in the secondary markets has evaporated.

1. Reasons for Switzerland's underdeveloped money market

---

[1] Except in the Canton Graubünden.
[2] The stamp tax was revised in 1993 to exempt foreign issues and bank trading. Domestic issues are still subject to the stamp tax.

Table 9.1

An overview of the Swiss franc money and capital markets

	Short-term	*Medium- & long-term*
Domestic market[a]		
Public issues	Restricted by the Swiss stamp duties & withholding taxes	Very active market
Private issues	Restricted by the Swiss stamp duties & withholding taxes	Very active market
Foreign market[b]		
Public issues	Restricted by the Swiss stamp duties (until 1993)	Very active market
Private issues	Restricted by the Swiss stamp duties (until 1993)	Very active market
Government market[c]		
Public issues (Exchange-traded)	Restricted by the Swiss stamp duties & withholding taxes	Limited market: low federal debt level
Private issues (OTC)	Restricted by the Swiss stamp duties & withholding taxes	Limited market: low federal debt level
Euromarket [d]		
Swiss franc deposits/ liabilities (Mainly inter-bank & fiduciary accounts)	Very active market	Shallow market
Private issues	Shallow market	Swiss National Bank has not sanctioned Euro-Swiss franc notes[e]
Public issues	Shallow market	Swiss National Bank has not sanctioned public Euro-Swiss franc bonds[e]

[a] *Domestic market:* Swiss residents borrowing Swiss francs within Switzerland
[b] *Foreign market:* Foreign residents borrowing Swiss francs within Switzerland
[c] *Government market:* Swiss federal, cantonal & municipal governments borrowing Swiss francs in Switzerland)
[d] *Euromarket:* Swiss franc debt incurred outside Switzerland
[e] Except in the context of medium-term note programmes

The diminutive size and lopsided composition of the Swiss federal debt level is a second reason for Switzerland's anaemic money market development. Because of Switzerland's federalist government structure, its federal government debt has been much lower than in nations with more centralist government systems. As a result, sufficient quantities of federal government bonds do not exist to make markets in all but a few issues. Moreover, a large majority (66 per cent in 1994) of the federal government debt has a medium- or long-term maturity.[3]

---

[3] Swiss National Bank, *Monatsbericht June 1995*, p. 82.

The Swiss National Bank is not a regular buyer or seller of federal debt instruments because it uses the foreign exchange market to influence the domestic monetary base. Since 1979, the Swiss National Bank has tried to take a more active role in the domestic debt market, but the government debt market remains small.

Adding to the list of reasons for Switzerland's relatively undeveloped money market is the structure of the domestic banking system. Though an active inter-bank market exists, it is relatively small when compared to other nations because three major banks dominate the Swiss banking system, and many of their financing needs are solved by inter-branch lending rather than tapping the external markets. Furthermore, the Raiffeisen banks have their own interbank credit system, and the regional banks have recently organized a similar interbank market.

In a similar sense, Swiss corporate demand for short-term credit (and, therefore, the supply of tradeable, short-term credit instruments) is small due to the tendency of Swiss companies to finance their needs internally. When short-term funds are desired, they are secured ordinarily through bank loans rather than the issuance of tradeable commercial paper.

Currency risk is another major factor that has restricted the growth in foreign demand for short-term Swiss franc debt. There can be significant risks associated with unhedged positions in foreign currencies. Over longer time periods, changes in the value of the Swiss franc have tended to closely parallel international interest rate differentials, reducing both the foreign exchange risk facing borrowers/lenders and the need to cover exposed positions. In the short-run, significant deviations can and do occur. Even though these risks can be hedged, the added cost reduces demand for Swiss franc money market financing.

2. Quality of Swiss franc borrowers

A wide range of national and international borrowers – corporations, governments, central banks and supranational organizations – tap the Swiss capital markets each year. Though Switzerland has a reputation for financing borrowers with impeccable international credit standing, there is also a thriving market in privately-placed, equity-linked notes of low-capitalized, high-growth foreign companies (mostly from Asia).

Name recognition and rarity are also important factors in the Swiss franc debt markets. Foreign companies, and countries, rated Single- and Double-A have been able to achieve very competitive borrowing terms due to the Swiss market's familiarity with their names. Corporations, like Philip Morris, and sovereigns, such as New Zealand and Sweden, have been very successful at taking advantage of opportunities in Switzerland. In a similar sense, those issuers who come to the market often and over-saturate it, tend to pay higher rates than less frequent borrowers. Even the anticipation of more frequent appearances or irresponsible fiscal management can make Swiss franc financing more expensive.

The regional distribution of international borrowers who tap the Swiss capital markets is relatively narrow. As Table 9.2 and Figure 9.1 show, approximately 85 per cent of total issuance originates in the developed nations of the US, Canada, Japan, the European Union and EFTA.

Table 9.2

Geographic distribution of Swiss franc debt issuers (Sfr millions)

Nation/region	Amount of debt issues	
	1993	*1994*
European Union	14,884.2	12,065.3
EFTA	7,510.1	3,374.0
Other European nations	43.9	227.4
Middle & Eastern Europe	300.0	150.0
USA & Canada	1,990.0	3,457.0
Caribbean	2,654.2	2,523.9
Latin America	150.0	–
Middle East	–	–
Africa	–	–
Japan	14,560.5	7,970.0
Australia & New Zealand	370.0	175.0
Asia & Oceania	728.7	1,093.5
Developing organizations	2,250.0	600.0
Total	**45,441.6**	**31,636.1**

Source: Swiss National Bank, *Monatsbericht: June 1995* p. 61.

Figure 9.1

Foreign Swiss franc bonds by debtor country, 1994

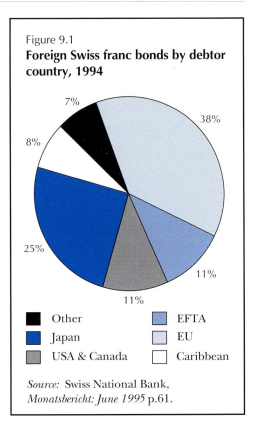

Source: Swiss National Bank, *Monatsbericht: June 1995* p.61.

In the domestic market, there are no official credit rating services for Swiss companies, and in the past, due to Swiss accounting standards, domestic company performance was often not transparent. Many of the Swiss multinational companies have now adopted International Accounting Standards (IAS) and other companies have made significant strides toward the new Swiss FER or the European E-4 and E-7 standardized reporting. To this end, the 1992 Swiss Company Law improves transparency by permitting hidden reserves, but requiring companies to notify auditors when hidden reserves are created or dissolved. Companies that are listed on the stock exchange also have to report if hidden reserves are dissolved.

3. The size of the Swiss franc domestic and foreign debt market

At the end of 1994, the total volume of outstanding foreign and domestic Swiss franc debt was Sfr 420.9 billion. Foreign issues and placements accounted for 61 per cent of total Swiss franc borrowing, while non-federal government, domestic issues and Swiss federal government issues accounted for 32 per cent and 7 per cent, respectively. Of this volume, notes (non-exchange-traded private placements) constituted 25 per cent and bonds (exchange-traded public placements) made up the remaining 75 per cent (see Figure 9.2).

The overwhelming majority (91 per cent) of outstanding Swiss franc issues in 1994 were fixed-rate instruments. Convertible instruments accounted for 7 per cent of the

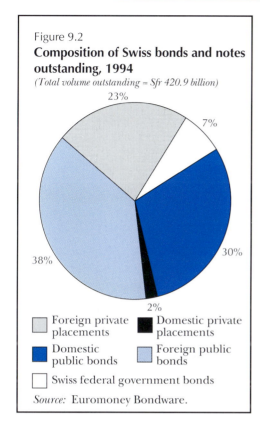

Figure 9.2
Composition of Swiss bonds and notes outstanding, 1994
(Total volume outstanding = Sfr 420.9 billion)

- Foreign private placements
- Domestic private placements
- Domestic public bonds
- Foreign public bonds
- Swiss federal government bonds

Source: Euromoney Bondware.

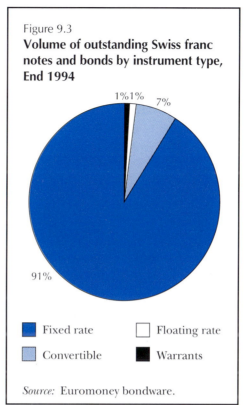

Figure 9.3
Volume of outstanding Swiss franc notes and bonds by instrument type, End 1994

- Fixed rate
- Floating rate
- Convertible
- Warrants

Source: Euromoney bondware.

market and both floating rate securities and warrant issues took a 1 per cent share of the market each (see Figure 9.3).

In 1994, almost Sfr61 billion worth of Swiss franc bonds and notes were floated on the Swiss franc market. Of them, 68 per cent were foreign issues (32 per cent were domestic issues), and approximately 74 per cent were raised with public bonds (the remaining 26 per cent with private placements).

4. Major Swiss franc debt markets

Swiss franc public issues

By far the most developed and internationally active Swiss financial market is in the medium- to long-term maturities (see Figure 9.4). Domestically, this market is well used by banks, the three levels of government, utilities, the construction industry and individual investors. A cocktail of convenient and flexible bond arrangements are available and placement or issues costs are among the lowest in the world.

Because of the high level of saving, there is a continuous flow of medium- and long-term loanable funds providing both breadth and depth to the financing markets.[4] Domestic borrowers favour straight fixed-rate issues with maturities between 7- and 10-

[4] Even though the bond market is the main source of capital in Switzerland, at the medium-term level (ie, 1-5 years) many corporate financing needs are satisfied with term loans, and leasing, which in 1994 accounted for approximately 6 per cent of Swiss capital goods financing needs. Longer term installment loans are also used to finance capital expenditures. See, The Economic Intelligence Unit, *Country Reference: Financing Foreign Operations: Switzerland: 1994* p. 17.

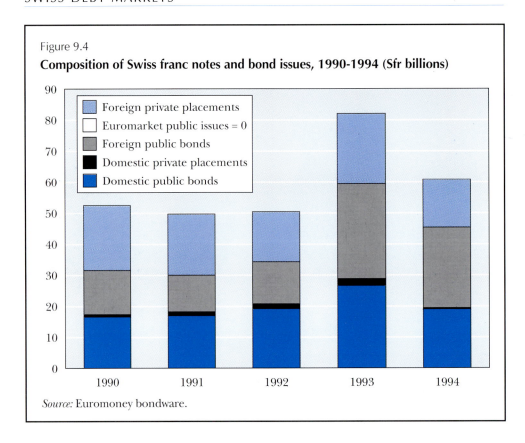

Figure 9.4

Composition of Swiss franc notes and bond issues, 1990-1994 (Sfr billions)

Legend:
- Foreign private placements
- Euromarket public issues = 0
- Foreign public bonds
- Domestic private placements
- Domestic public bonds

Source: Euromoney bondware.

years, but in years of healthy stock markets, convertible bonds and bonds with warrants have grown increasingly popular. A large portion of the debt issued in the foreign Swiss franc market is combined with interest-rate and cross-currency swaps permitting borrowers to switch to the currency and interest terms of their choice. Because of this swap/debt combination, demand for new Swiss franc issues is dependent not only on Swiss franc interest rate, but the all-in cost of Swiss francs and currency swap rates, as well.

Swiss franc private placements

Private placements or notes are unadvertised, high denomination bonds issued (usually through a syndicate) to a limited number of investors,[5] with very competitive issuance costs.[6] They are interesting alternatives for investors willing to place funds in multiples of units of Sfr50,000 for medium- to long-term maturities. The yield on these instruments is usually higher than the yield on bonds because their marketability is lower. Swiss franc bearer notes are not listed on any stock exchange, but the issuing banks are usually willing to acquire customer notes at prevailing yield levels.

Usually, coupons are paid on an annual basis, and investors wishing to purchase such notes buy them during the underwriting period.

---

[5] In Switzerland, a note is not defined by the type of security or its maturity but rather by the method of its issuance.

[6] Fees in 1994 were between 0.125 per cent and 0.25 per cent lower than public bonds with comparable maturities. (see The Economic Intelligence Unit, *Country Reference: Financing Foreign Operations: Switzerland: 1994* p. 3.)

In 1994, over 87 per cent of the total Swiss franc foreign debt was accounted for by 10 countries (Japan, US, Germany, France, Austria, the Netherlands, Luxembourg, Cayman Islands, United Kingdom and Sweden).[7]

Foreign private placements are an invention of the late 1960s and early 1970s. Unlike public bonds, Swiss law does not specifically deal with such notes, but they fall under the general legal framework of securities in OR Art. 965-989. The absence of bureaucratic restrictions has made them very popular and has allowed costs to be kept very low. Most of the once decisive limitations established by the Swiss National Bank under its currency and monetary responsibilities in connection with capital exports were lifted in May 1986. As of January 1995, the Swiss National Bank must be notified of all bond and note issues. No approval procedures remain in force.

The foreign bond and note market in Switzerland has thrived (see Tables 9.3 and 9.4). Because they have relatively few reporting requirements, companies do not need

Table 9.3

Geographic composition of foreign Swiss franc bond and note issuers (Sfr billions)

	1990	*1991*	*1992*	*1993*	*1994*
Supranational	4.43	3.25	4.50	4.26	1.60
USA & Canada	6.43	4.16	2.67	6.04	8.21
Europe	27.55	28.90	34.13	56.05	39.84
Asia	13.72	13.30	8.95	14.85	10.93
Latin America	0	0	0.02	0.15	0
Others	0.29	0.04	0.08	0.58	0.15
Total	**52.42**	**49.65**	**50.35**	**81.93**	**60.73**

Source: Euromoney Bondware

Table 9.4

Composition of foreign Swiss franc bonds and notes by instrument: 1989-1994

	1989	*1990*	*1991*	*1992*	*1993*	*1994*
Straights	8,925.3	20,706.1	17,096.0	18,191.5	25,859.3	17,183.1
Floating rate bonds	50.0	30.0	143.0	381.0	2,033.0	3,226.3
Convertible issues	17,706.0	8,827.0	4,206.5	2,081.0	4,008.2	4,273.5
Warrants	3,874.0	2,219.9	6,425.0	5,411.0	11,331.2	6,182.0
Other	670.0	300.0	1,067.0	937.5	2,210.0	771.3
Total	**31,225.3**	**32,083**	**28,937.5**	**27,002**	**45,441.7**	**31,636.2**

Source: Swiss National Bank, *Monatsbericht: June 1995* p. 61.

Foreign private placements

---

[7] Swiss National Bank, *Monatsbericht June 1995* p. 61.

141

formal credit ratings and issuers are exempt from paying the 35 per cent Swiss withholding tax. Moreover, since 1993, foreign bonds have been exempt from paying the Swiss stamp duty on new issues. As a result, they are particularly attractive to foreign investors – especially from countries with no, or inadequate, double taxation agreements.

As notes are usually not printed (for cost reasons), they must remain in the issuing banks on the account of the investor. In contrast to the United States, there is no Swiss limitation on the number of purchasers (35 in the US) of privately placed notes, no prospectus is required, and purchasers are given only the most important information about the debtor. Generally, the execution of either bond, and particularly note, issues on the Swiss capital market is straight forward and uncomplicated.

Government bond market

The Swiss government bond market is relatively small in comparison to most other developed nations. For years, the federal government ran budget surpluses, thereby avoiding the need to borrow. In the early 1990s (see Figure 9.5), the deficit rose sharply.[8] At the end of 1994, the federal debt stood at Sfr78 billion up from Sfr55 billion in 1992. The low yield on government bonds indicates a lack of sufficient government debt in relation to the legally prescribed obligation of certain institutional investors to buy such government papers.

Public bonds are traded on the Swiss stock exchange and the notes are traded on the OTC market. Only three outstanding issues of federal notes exist, and they will

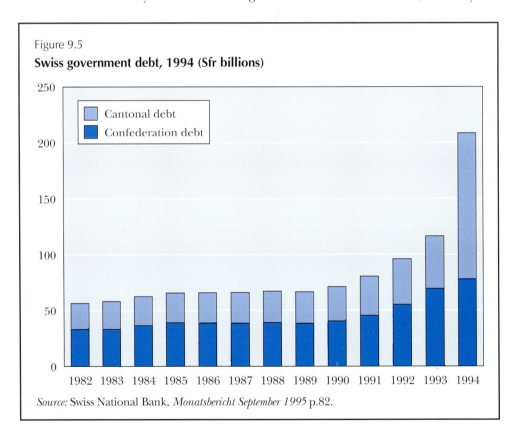

Figure 9.5

Swiss government debt, 1994 (Sfr billions)

Source: Swiss National Bank, *Monatsbericht September 1995* p.82.

---

[8] A large proportion of these deficits was recession-induced, rather than structural in nature.

mature by 1997. These fixed-income securities are issued by the Swiss National Bank, the federal government's fiscal agent, with bond maturities between five and twenty years.[9] Virtually all of the most recent government bonds have reopening clauses, and new issues are avoided when the terms of existing debt are close to current market conditions. In 1980, the federal government began issuing 10-year bonds using a Dutch auction system. Ten-year bonds are issued bimonthly on the fourth Tuesday of the respective month with payment on the following Thursday.

Federal government bonds are traded on a clean-price basis with bid/offer spreads between 0.1 per cent and 0.5 per cent. Many federal bonds have call features, but this feature is becoming less frequent in new issues. Because of the 35 per cent Swiss withholding tax imposed on the interest earnings of these bonds (like private sector Swiss bonds), they are generally not attractive to foreign investors. Nevertheless, foreigners can participate in this market by purchasing government bond futures contracts on SOFFEX. This derivative market has high liquidity, low transaction costs and is subject to neither withholding taxes nor income taxes.

Swiss federal, cantonal and municipal governments issue promissory notes (*Kassascheine, Reskriptionen, Schatzscheine*) to cover short- to medium-term deficits. They are normally placed with banks, that use them for liquidity purposes. These instruments are mentioned here for the sake of completeness, but they are of little interest to the non-bank investor. This is also true for the relatively new money market instrument, *Buchforderung*, which represents a non-documented claim against the Treasury that was introduced to avoid the taxes on securities.

Swiss banks participate actively in the multifaceted Eurocurrency markets (see Table 9.5). *The Euromarkets*

Table 9.5

Swiss bank participation in the Euromarkets

	Swiss franc Euromarket	*Non-Swiss franc Euromarket*
Short-term	Swiss banks are very active. The domestic stamp duty has forced Swiss banks into this Swiss franc market.	Swiss banks are very active (especially investing fiduciary deposits).
Medium/long-term	The Swiss National Bank has not sanctioned the issuance of Swiss franc bonds outside Switzerland (except in the context of medium-term note programmes).	Swiss banks are very active and Swiss residents are active buyers of these Eurobonds. There is a growing demand for non-Swiss franc Eurobonds developing within Switzerland.

[9] The most liquid issues are in the eight- to ten-year period.

143

Swiss participation in the short-term Euro-Swiss franc market

Because the Swiss stamp duty has severely retarded the development of all the domestic, short-term markets, Swiss banks are large participants in the Euro-Swiss franc markets. Participation gives them not only access to a large pool of short-term, Swiss franc funds, but links them to the broad international money markets.

Swiss participation in the short-term Euromarkets for non-Swiss franc currencies

Swiss banks are large participants in the non-Swiss franc Eurocurrency money markets – largely through their investments of fiduciary deposits. Fiduciary deposits are funds placed in Swiss banks and invested in the name of the bank for the account and risk of the depositor. Since 1980, they have grown at a compound annual rate of 6 per cent to over Sfr300 billion (see Figure 9.6), but have fallen in value since 1992.

Foreign currencies account for most of the Swiss fiduciary accounts (see Figure 9.7). Approximately 90 per cent of these funds are invested in the Euro-interbank market (mostly in the UK, Belgium, Luxembourg, the Netherlands and France). About two-thirds of the funds are from European depositors. In 1994, foreign banks and the three Big Banks accounted for almost three-quarters of all Swiss fiduciary deposits. Typically, banks match their fiduciary liabilities with assets of identical maturity and currency denomination.[10]

Fiduciary accounts are popular from depositors' points of view because, if placed abroad, they are not subject to Swiss withholding taxes. Moreover, since the funds are invested in the name of the bank, they offer depositors a larger degree of anonymity. The main risks associated with Euro deposits are transfer and counterparty risk (ie, the risk that the redemption money cannot be transferred out of the borrowers' country of domicile and the risk of a bank failure).

From the bank's point of view, fiduciary deposits are popular because of the fees they earn (about 0.5 per cent per annum for investments of over Sfr500,000). Since they are invested in the name of the bank, but at the client's risk, they are recorded off balance sheet. As a result, the liabilities do not enlarge banks' reserve requirements.[11]

Swiss participation in the medium/long-term Euro-Swiss franc market

For medium- and long-term maturities, Swiss participation in the Euromarkets is asymmetric. Since 1963, the Swiss National Bank has not sanctioned the issue of Swiss franc-denominated Eurobonds.[12] Moreover, the Swiss National Bank is empowered to deter Swiss participation in these prohibited Swiss franc issues. As a result, all Swiss franc issues are transacted within Swiss borders.

---

[10] See the asset and liability composition by currency in: Swiss National Bank, *Das Schweizerische Bankwesen im Jahre 1994* p. A157.

[11] Mario A. Corti, "Switzerland: Banking, Money and Bond Markets," *Banking Structures in Major Countries* ed. George G. Kaufman, (Kluwer Academic Publishers, 1992) p. 27

[12] The Swiss National Bank has no power or jurisdiction to prohibit foreign banks from issuing Swiss franc bonds. Nevertheless, an agreement among the European central banks effectively accomplishes this end. Under the agreement, Euro-issue restrictions by any participating central bank (eg, Switzerland) are supported by the other central banks (eg, Bank of England) for the financial intermediaries under their jurisdiction. Moreover, in the absence of multilateral agreements among central banks, these sanctions could be enforced if the Swiss National Bank delayed or prohibited the transfer of Swiss franc funds, as the US did during the Iran Crisis in 1980.

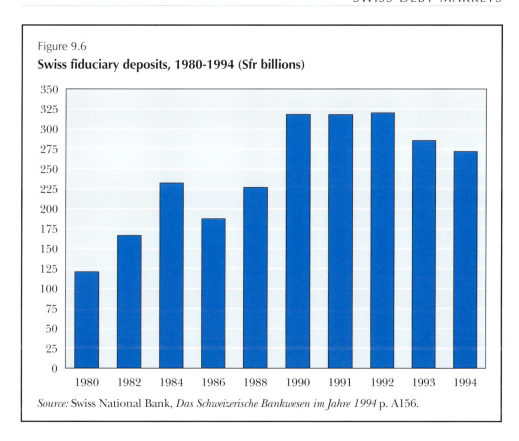

Figure 9.6

Swiss fiduciary deposits, 1980-1994 (Sfr billions)

Source: Swiss National Bank, *Das Schweizerische Bankwesen im Jahre 1994* p. A156.

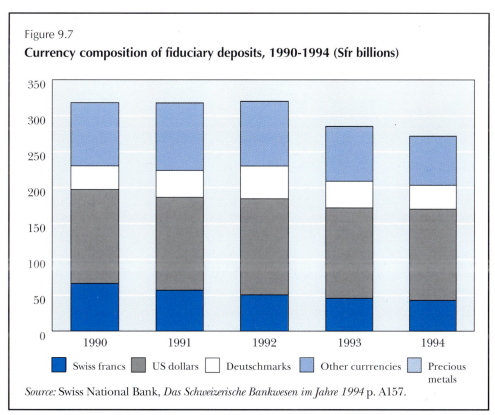

Figure 9.7

Currency composition of fiduciary deposits, 1990-1994 (Sfr billions)

Swiss francs   US dollars   Deutschmarks   Other currrencies   Precious metals

Source: Swiss National Bank, *Das Schweizerische Bankwesen im Jahre 1994* p. A157.

145

Swiss participation in the medium/long-term Euromarket for non-Swiss franc currencies

The Swiss National Bank policy for Swiss franc Eurobond issues does not prevent Swiss banks from participating in the non-Swiss franc Eurobond market. Indeed, non-Swiss franc denominated Eurobond issues are among the most popular medium/long-term fixed income securities offered in Switzerland. An important reason for their popularity among foreign investors is, as is the case with Swiss franc foreign bonds and notes, the absence of withholding tax on the interest income.

A large proportion of traditional, plain vanilla Eurobonds is ultimately placed with banks and portfolio managers in Switzerland. Swiss banks, through their special foreign subsidiaries, are very active in both the primary and secondary markets. The ultimate placement of new issues is, however, done directly through the Swiss banking community in Switzerland. It is, therefore, not surprising that the three major Swiss banks are represented in the majority of all Eurobond issues as either lead- or co-managers. The secondary market in Eurobonds is somewhat peculiar because bonds themselves are listed on the London and/or Luxembourg stock exchanges, but the actual trading is done almost exclusively over the phone by banks, brokers and other institutions.

Swiss participation in the medium/long-term market for non-Swiss franc currencies in Switzerland

An active Euromarket is developing in Switzerland for convertible, foreign issues denominated in non-Swiss franc currencies. The stimuli behind this Alpine market are the 1993 repeal of the Swiss stamp duty (ie, issue tax) on foreign issues and the desire of borrowers to avoid home country regulatory burdens (eg, Eurodollar bonds were popular because they enabled borrowers to issue dollar debt outside SEC rules). Between 1993 and September 1995, eighteen Alpine issues were brought to the market. All but one were denominated in US dollars and the other one in yen. Issuers were from nations such as Japan, Korea, Germany, Thailand, Hong Kong and the Cayman Islands.[13]

5. Issuing procedures

Regulation, the Swiss National Bank and Swiss syndicates

The Swiss authorities do not regulate the timing of bond issues. Since 1980, the Swiss federal government's bonds have been issued under a tender system organized by the Swiss National Bank. Other issuers use one bank or a syndicate of banks.

Until 1991, these issues were managed, generally, by four syndicates. Those syndicates were the Big Banks syndicate, the HandelsBank syndicate, the Nordfinanz syndicate, and the Gutzwiller, Kurz, Bungener syndicate. Non-resident banks were prevented from participating in, or leading new issues (See Appendix 9-A.1). In the 1980s, Switzerland's Big Banks controlled approximately 80 per cent of the new issue business. In 1989, the Swiss Cartel Commission recommended the abolition of the oligopolistic cartel system in an effort to increase Switzerland's competitiveness. At first the new structure caused a drop in the Big Banks' lock on the market, but in 1995, their share of the market was back to approximately 80 per cent of all new issues.

---

[13] All issues as of September 1995 were drawn from the Euromoney Bondware database.

146

Only in April 1993, did the Swiss National Bank liberalize its syndication rules for public bond issues,[14] enabling non-resident banks to participate in, but not lead-manage, syndicates for foreign issuers of Swiss franc bonds. Residency requirements (in either Switzerland or Liechtenstein) still apply to all domestic issues.

The Swiss franc bond market is largely a retail market, in which bonds are placed with end-users within a couple of days after launch. As a result, bond issues are typically not traded in big volumes over long periods of time. Because they soon become seasoned with relatively thin secondary market trading, the secondary market prices of selected issues can only serve for a limited period of time as the basis for pricing new issues. In addition, because of the paucity of Confederation bond issues, Switzerland lacks a sufficient benchmark security (eg, treasury bonds) to use as a basis for pricing new Swiss franc issues.[15] Consequently, the "fixed price re-offer" system that depends on benchmark issues has not developed in Switzerland.

No fixed price re-offer system for distributing bonds

There is no longer a formal re-allowance system in Switzerland for distributing Swiss franc bonds. A substantial portion of the underwriting commission is usually included in the issue price and co-distributors earn their profits from the difference between the purchase price of the bonds allocated to them and the price at which they place the bonds with investors. In the late 1980s, Swiss lead managers abandoned the formal "real-lowance" system because, too often, co-distributors sold their allocations directly into the secondary ("grey") markets causing prices to weaken. In these cases, lead managers, who are responsible for the "success" of their issues, felt forced to buy back the securities to prevent their prices from falling exorbitantly.

No formal reallowance system for distributing bonds

During the 1990s, few Swiss franc bond issues have had early redemption clauses (ie, embedded options).[16] As the Swiss capital market has grown more sophisticated and the ability to price call options has become more accurate, lead managers have recommended against their use. Bonds with early redemption clauses seldom offer savings, and they are clearly not the preference of institutional investors.[17] As a result, early redemption clauses in bonds are now an insignificant part of the new issue business in Swiss francs.

Early redemptions

Swiss capital market rules permit any borrower to repurchase his/her own debt in the open market. Instances where a company has formally approached debt holders in an

Bond buybacks

---

[14] Syndication rules do not exist for notes.

[15] In the 1990s, this situation has changed somewhat as Swiss Confederation deficits have increased (see Chapter 2).

[16] Such clauses were more frequently used prior to 1990s and 1980s. As a result, in 1995, when Swiss franc interest rates fell, many of these bonds were called and new ones re-issued at lower interest rates.

[17] Calculating such a bond's duration is problematic causing difficulties for structured portfolio management.

attempt to buy back outstanding issues are very rare, and when they occur, they are usually connected to corporate restructuring.

Trading Swiss franc bonds

Trading in Swiss franc bonds begins immediately after the terms of the new issue have been fixed and before the actual securities have been printed. Trading in this grey market is done over the Reuters system on a reallowance basis in denominations of Sfr250,000 and more. Active Vorbörse trading occurs shortly after the end of the subscription period. Both the grey market and Vorbörse trading are popular because the transactions are off-balance sheet, forward trades that do not require immediate cash payments and are not subject to the Swiss stamp duty (ie, issue tax) on new issues if such trading occurs before the payment date.

6. Clearing and settlement

Security settlement can be transacted by either SEGA (Schweizerische Effekten und Giro AG), Intersettle or custodian banks. SEGA was started by Swiss banks to streamline and consolidate the domestic settlement process for its members.[18] It warehouses securities and banks have custodial accounts in SEGA where book-entry changes can be made to account for changes in security ownership.[19] In this way the time-consuming physical transfer of securities is avoided. Transfers of funds are made through the Swiss Interbank Clearing (SIC) system of the Swiss National Bank. Intersettle is the Swiss custodian for international transactions.

Since October 1993, settlement for securities in SEGA have been transacted via the SECOM system that electronically links SEGA, the Swiss National Bank's SIC and Intersettle.[20] SECOM is a new and improved version of the old settlement system, providing not only more efficient clearing but additional services (eg, value date monitoring and cash-planning).

Custodial banks are used in Switzerland for securities that do not qualify for SEGA warehousing (certain registered shares are not eligible) or, at the request of the customer, shares are held in the bank. The names of registered share owners are not revealed to SEGA. Most of these new issues are held in book-entry form at SEGA and physical certificates are printed only at the request of the customer's bank.[21]

Intersettle was created to streamline and consolidate the settlement process with securities worldwide. In contrast to SEGA, which has only bank members, Intersettle is open to other market participants such as brokers, finance companies and insurance companies. Rather than each bank having independent international settlement networks, banks now have an account at Intersettle, and Intersettle uses its network to settle

---

[18] Members must be subject to the Swiss Banking Law.
[19] Institutions may deposit all their securities with SEGA or only enough to clear daily trades. See International Society of Securities Administrators, *ISSA 1994 Handbook*, Fifth edition (1994) p. CH-50.
[20] SECOM was phased in over a three year period.
[21] Starting in 1997, all registered securities on SEGA must be SEGA eligible "one-way" certificates. These certificates come with no coupon sheets attached and are held in dematerialized form until a customer specifically requests them. See International Society of Securities Administrators, *ISSA 1994 Handbook*, Fifth edition (1994) p. CH-55.

the transactions. This system allows the Swiss banks to reap economies of scale in transactions and reduce the transaction costs to customers.

Settlement for domestic bonds (government and private securities), foreign securities and notes takes place over a three workday period. All Swiss securities can be cleared through Cedel or Euroclear. Forward transactions are settled on the last trading day of the month with security delivery through SEGA and payment via SIC.

The stock exchange listing regulations are published under the title Kotierungsreglement, which contains all procedures and conditions for listing a public bond issue. The new draft of Kotierungsreglement was in the last stages of approval in late 1995 and was expected to become effective in early 1996. A full discussion of these listing requirements and their administration is included in Appendix 1 of this book, but the major provisions for debt market participants are:

7. Listing requirements for debt securities

- To qualify for listing, the Swiss Admissions Board requires that debt securities have a minimum nominal value equal to Sfr20 million;

- Publicly disclosed information for listing purposes must cover a period of three complete financial years. Exceptions can be made by the Admissions Board;

- A full prospectus must be published in at least one nationally-circulated newspaper and written in any one of the three national languages (German, French or Italian) or English. The prospectus must contain all relevant information to allow a judgment on the securities, as well as the financial situation, organization and legal status of the issuer;[22]

- To ensure an adequate distribution, issuers must provide proof to the Swiss Admissions Board that a sufficient quantity has been issued to permit a properly functioning market;

- Securities with transfer restrictions may be listed on the Swiss Stock Exchange so long as the restrictions do not affect the proper functioning of the market. Furthermore, the Swiss Admissions Board permits the issuance of permanent global certificates so long as issuers comply with the Swiss requirements stated in the Admissions Board directives;

- Special reporting requirements exist for convertible debt securities because they have characteristics of debt, equity and derivative instruments;

- The issuing company and guarantor, if any, must issue a printed annual report, available for investors.

---

[22] Disclosure requirements for public bonds on the Swiss debt markets are somewhat less detailed than in the US, but more demanding than in other European countries. The disclosures contain all material relevant for informed investor decisions. Listing companies must comply with the internationally accepted standards such as IAS, Swiss FER, EU-4 or EU-7. Most large Swiss corporations observe International Accounting Standards which are somewhat more conservative than US GAAP rules (eg, amortization of goodwill and intangibles is 20/40 years). Local companies are more likely to observe the Swiss FER or European EU-4 or EU-7 rules.

8. Secondary markets

The secondary market for Swiss franc bonds and notes is not as deep as the US and UK markets, in part, because a majority of the issues are held to maturity rather than becoming liable to pay the Swiss stamp duty (ie, transfer tax). Furthermore, there are no official market makers in the Swiss capital markets to ensure sufficient liquidity in various issues. With the introduction of EBS (Elektronische Börse Schweiz – expected to be working fully in 1996), secondary market liquidity should increase substantially.[23]

9. Other debt instruments

Floating rate notes and bonds

Periods of high and fluctuating interest rates during the 1970s and 1980s prompted the use of floating rate notes (FRNs). These issues are less subject to capital losses (gains) if interest rates rise (fall) and are thus preferred by many investors – particularly banks and other institutions – as long as the interest rate outlook remains uncertain. Swiss private investors have generally not been large buyers of FRNs, although there are periods when they become more popular (eg, in periods of rising interest rates). Investors are protected because the erosive effects of inflation on real rates of return are offset by inflation-induced changes in their nominal rates of return.

The rates on floating-rate bonds are usually fixed every 6 months as a certain spread over Libor (London Interbank Offered Rate), depending on the credit risk of the borrower.[24] At the time of the issue, only the premium over the reference rate – which reflects the credit standing of the borrower – is agreed to and published. Subsequently, the interest rate is changed at the agreed regular intervals according to market conditions.

Such issues often set a minimum interest rate, or provide a fixed interest rate for an initial period, for example for three years, after which the rate starts to float. Different parts of an issue may also have different conditions. In times of increasing interest rates, a floating rate protects the investor from capital losses, but it often also prevents capital gains, should interest rates fall, unless there is a minimum interest rate. Commission rates in 1994 were 1.75 per cent to 2 per cent for a 5-year, Sfr100 million public bond issue. The commission rate for comparable private placements ran from 1.5 per cent to 1.625 per cent.

Convertible bonds and notes

Convertible bonds – bonds with provisions allowing the holder to convert them into shares of the borrowing company at a certain pre-agreed conversion price – have become a permanent and popular part of the Swiss financial markets. The market originated in the early 1970s and surged in the 1980s with the flow of business from Japan – mainly in equity-linked notes, often with guarantees from Japanese banks – which explains the large number of Japanese banks in Switzerland.[25] In the 1990s, the convertible note market has been dominated by relatively low-rated, fast-growing Asian corporate borrowers.

---

[23] EBS began trading foreign shares on December 8, 1995. It is expected that Swiss shares, Swiss options and all bonds will be traded beginning the latter part of 1996.

[24] The Swiss interbank rate and the mortgage rate have also been used as reference rates.

[25] In the 1990s, Japanese demand has been falling as Japanese companies mature and have less need for these sources of financing. This decline in demand has been substantially offset by a rise in demand from other Asian nations (eg, Thailand and Korea).

Convertible securities carry a lower interest rate than fixed-rate bonds of equal maturity and rating, but if the share prices rise, they offer the possibility of capital gains that are not taxed by most Swiss cantons. If the company's share does not perform well on the stock exchange, losses are limited to the interest differential.[26] The conversion premium of notes is typically between 5 per cent and 15 per cent and the term five years. Japanese convertible notes have typically had very low premiums.

In difficult market conditions, a put-option is negotiated which allows the holder to request repayment of the note after, for instance, four years, with a premium that would give the investor nearly the yield of a straight note. Many investors tended to convert at a low gain, but the absence of a capital gains tax in Switzerland makes the investment attractive even at a modest level.

The secondary market in most convertible bonds is thin and volatile. In general, these securities are held to maturity (again, tax-induced) or more likely, held until the conversion price is reached, at which time they are converted to equity.

A speciality of the Swiss market are mortgage bonds (Pfandbriefe), which are issued by two institutions for periods of approximately 12- to 15-years for the purpose of refinancing their members' mortgages (see Figure 9.8). The Pfandbriefzentrale der Schweizer-

Mortgage bonds

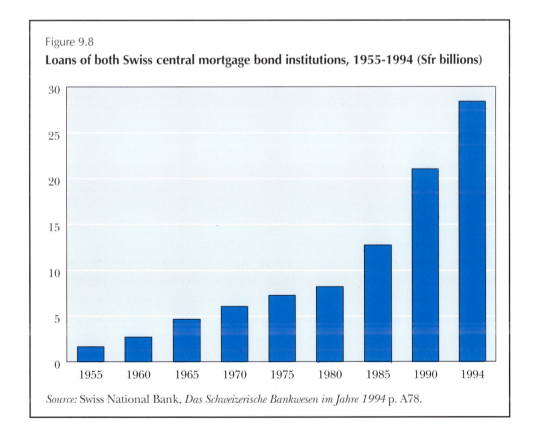

Figure 9.8

Loans of both Swiss central mortgage bond institutions, 1955-1994 (Sfr billions)

Source: Swiss National Bank, *Das Schweizerische Bankwesen im Jahre 1994* p. A78.

---

[26] Plus capital losses if market interest rates increase.

ischen Kantonalbanken was created by the cantonal banks and the Pfandbriefbank Schweizerischer Hypothekarinstitute was created by the regional mortgage institutes.[27] Mortgage bonds are bought mainly by financial institutions that hold mortgages as security. Their long-term nature combined with the Swiss withholding tax make them unattractive instruments for foreign investors.

Dual-currency bonds

In general, the popularity of dual-currency issues depends on prices in the foreign exchange markets because the currency denomination of interest payments on dual-currency bonds is different from denomination of the principal. Dual-currency bonds have lost their importance due to the creation of new financial instruments (derivatives).

Hybrid bonds

The Swiss capital market has been highly innovative in the range of debt instruments offered. There have been many highly successful zero-coupon bond issues, bonds with put options, drop-lock bonds, fixed-rate bonds with variable or extendible maturity, bull spreads, knock-outs and convertibles with double dividend equivalent pay-outs.

Commercial paper

Other developed nations have commercial paper markets, but there is no such market in Switzerland. Commercial paper issuance has been restricted because most of the short-term financial needs of companies are satisfied by bank borrowing which can be arranged without security tax implications.

10. Major assets of Swiss financial intermediaries

Mortgage loans

Mortgage loans – amounting to about Sfr468 billion in 1993 – are the most important single category of long-term loans in Switzerland. Switzerland has the highest per capita mortgage indebtedness in the world (see Figure 9.9). In Switzerland, the typical loan with mortgage security has an indefinite duration but can be terminated with six months' notice by either party. In practice, they last forever. Interest rates are adjusted periodically to reflect market conditions and corrected by political considerations. The banks began to introduce amortization on a major scale only in the late 1970s.

Swiss mortgage loans have traditionally been the domain of the cantonal and regional banks as well as the savings and loans associations. Nevertheless, the Big Banks have actively pursued this area since the 1980s, and, in 1995, Union Bank of Switzerland was ranked as the largest Swiss mortgage lender.

Multicurrency loans

Multicurrency loans on a floating-rate basis are common in Switzerland. They give a borrower the option of switching from one currency to another at specified interest periods. Banks granting loans wish to know exactly what their exposure is. Therefore, the amount of the credit facility is usually stipulated in the home currency. Depending on the credit

---

[27] Chapter 3 has a fuller discussion of these institutions.

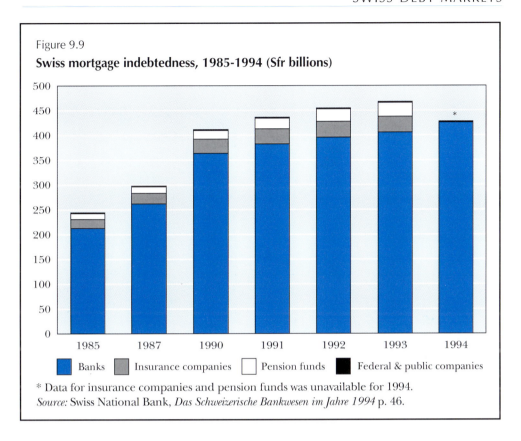

Figure 9.9

Swiss mortgage indebtedness, 1985-1994 (Sfr billions)

Legend: ■ Banks ▨ Insurance companies □ Pension funds ■ Federal & public companies

* Data for insurance companies and pension funds was unavailable for 1994.
Source: Swiss National Bank, *Das Schweizerische Bankwesen im Jahre 1994* p. 46.

standing of the borrower, Swiss banks might require a bank guarantee as collateral. Typically, such guarantees would also be in local currency (Swiss francs). If the guarantee is issued in foreign currency, the guaranteed amount has to be larger than the Swiss franc equivalent at the time of contracting the loan.

For a 10-year loan (bullet), the guaranteed amount has to be sufficiently high to cover the potential currency risk for the whole period, which might require a 200 per cent guarantee for inflation-prone countries. A borrower may be unwilling to give his own bank a 200 per cent collateral, thereby blocking his credit capacity over a 10-year period. As a consequence, the most important multicurrency borrowers are the very large corporations which do not need to offer bank guarantees.[28]

Cash bonds (Kassenobligationen) are a Swiss speciality. They are issued in the form of medium-term notes or CDs by banks for periods of between two and eight years and carry individual issue and maturity dates. Cash bonds are issued on tap, only in Swiss francs, with minimum denominations of Sfr1,000, and are tailored to investors' needs. In practice, they resemble savings accounts, because they are sold on the banks' premises

11. Major liabilities of Swiss financial intermediaries[29]

Banks' cash bonds

---

[28] Where securities, such as foreign currency bonds or shares, are used as collateral, a provision must be made for both the stock exchange price risk plus the foreign exchange risk.
[29] See Figure 9.10.

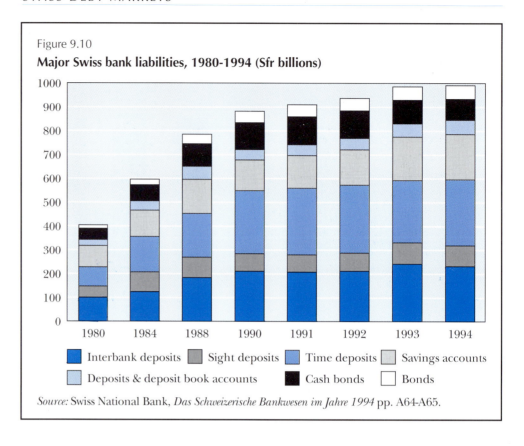

Figure 9.10

Major Swiss bank liabilities, 1980-1994 (Sfr billions)

Legend: Interbank deposits, Sight deposits, Time deposits, Savings accounts, Deposits & deposit book accounts, Cash bonds, Bonds

Source: Swiss National Bank, *Das Schweizerische Bankwesen im Jahre 1994* pp. A64-A65.

and not traded on the stock exchange. Nevertheless, liquidity is provided by banks' willingness to buy back their own cash bonds.

Cash bonds carry higher interest rates than savings deposits. The higher interest rate compensates for their lower liquidity and the 0.15 per cent federal issue tax on securities which has to be paid when they are bought. Although they accounted for Sfr88.5 billion in 1994, or about 7.5 per cent of all Swiss banks' balance sheets (ie, liabilities and net worth), only negligible amounts are bought by foreigners, mainly because of the taxation (see Figure 9.10).[30]

Insurance companies and pension funds are large holders of cash bonds, and banks use them mainly as an instrument to fund Swiss export finance and mortgages. The interest rate on cash bonds is, therefore, important for the Swiss export industry. The rates at which banks finance most Swiss exports are directly linked to the rate they pay on cash bonds.

Current accounts

Portfolio investors normally open current accounts as an operational base for their investments. Swiss banks will keep the accounts in any major convertible currency. As an alternative, portfolio investors may use a deposit account, since withdrawal restrictions do not usually apply to the purchase of securities.

---

[30] Switzerland's federal government, some cantons and companies issue three to six month instruments (money market book entries) similar to commercial paper, but the volume is very low. These issues are exempt from the Swiss turnover tax

Savings accounts in different forms (called Spareinlagen, Depositenhefte or Sparheft) are very popular forms of investment for the Swiss. Because of the 35 per cent withholding tax on interest earnings and the typically low interest rate, only a small fraction of all savings accounts are held by foreigners. The withholding tax is waived only for interest amounts below Sfr50. Banks usually do not charge any fees for opening or keeping the account. There are limitations on withdrawals (eg, Sfr25,000 in any one month), but these rules are liberally interpreted. Securities can usually be bought through these accounts, without any restrictions.

Savings accounts

Savings accounts are popular with non-sophisticated investors who prefer risk-free investments, and for whom the limited liquidity and low interest rate are not decisive factors. Private individuals hold 90 per cent of all Swiss savings deposits. For the more sophisticated investors with available amounts of, say, over Sfr50,000, there are other opportunities, which are almost as safe and earn usually a higher interest rate, such as time deposits, cash bonds and fiduciary placements.

For larger sums (ie, Sfr100,000 or the equivalent in foreign currency) there are time deposits. Normally, they are non-transferable and, therefore, illiquid until maturity. At the same time, if this period is one month, they are technically more liquid than savings deposits, for which several months' notice may be required for withdrawal of major amounts.

Time deposits

Time deposits are available in all major currencies. Swiss banks place the counter-value of time deposits in foreign currencies either in the Euromarket, or in the country of the currency's origin. About 50 per cent of all Swiss time deposits are denominated in foreign currencies. For foreign investors who wish to place their funds in the Euromarkets, the 35 per cent Swiss holding tax applicable does not apply if they use fiduciary deposits, which have become more popular than standard time deposits.

Call money is mentioned here only because investors may put money on call between two longer-term investments. Apart from the very short-term, Euro-call money has the same conditions as fiduciary accounts: there is a small commission and the usual, minimum amount is Sfr500,000 or its equivalent. No withholding tax applies and investments in any major currency are available.

Call money

For investors interested in currency speculation, call money may be a more useful instrument than a current account, because it will usually earn interest on funds while waiting for favourable currency movements.

At the end of the first quarter 1995, Switzerland's 254 investment funds had combined assets totalling Sfr54.8 billion,[32] and certificates for most of them could be purchased

Investment (mutual) fund certificates[31]

---

[31] A fuller discussion of Switzerland's mutual funds industry is included in Chapter 6 (Swiss Insurance and Institutional Investment Markets).

[32] Swiss National Bank, *Monatsbericht June 1995* p. 66.

either on the stock exchanges or over-the-counter with the major funds and their banks. All Swiss investment funds are open-end funds,[33] and for tax reasons, foreign security funds have captured the clear majority (67 per cent) of Swiss mutual fund business.[34] Real estate funds were a popular way for many foreigners to invest in Swiss real estate without violating Swiss law (Lex Friedrich).

The Big Banks are the major players in the Swiss mutual fund industry and have taken a leading position in Luxembourg. Swiss private banks are also active in this market. Over the 1990s, increased domestic and international competition in the asset management sector has caused Swiss private banks to increasingly offer investment fund alternatives.

Due to its stamp duties, confining investment policies and the 1992 referendum decision not to join the EEA, the development of Switzerland's domestic investment fund market has been greatly impeded. There is hope that recent revisions in the stamp duty law and new Federal Investment Funds Law will increase Switzerland's international competitiveness and either curtail or reverse the flow of mutual fund investments to foreign financial centres (especially Luxembourg).[35]

The new Federal Investment Funds Law better protects investors, increases competition in the Swiss market and at same time, gives Swiss investment funds a greater capacity to compete in the international marketplace. In addition to securities funds and real estate funds, the law permits the creation of "other funds" that are able to invest in assets having limited marketability, high price volatility and restricted diversification (eg, precious metals, commodities, options, futures, units of other investment funds and investments in other rights). It also permits banking groups to establish special in-house funds for the collective management of client assets, and thereby enables them to take advantage of potential economies of scale in fund administration.

12. Taxes, commissions and brokerage fees

The relative absence of bureaucratic regulations has kept average new issue costs quite low if calculated on a yearly basis, particularly for initial debt offerings which tend to be more expensive elsewhere. Lawyers' fees and auditors' costs, in particular, are substantially lower in Switzerland than in other international financial markets, especially in the US or UK. Because of the simplicity of the Swiss laws, one large corporation expects to have three to ten times higher legal fees in the US than in Switzerland.

Brokerage fees

Since 1 January 1991, fixed brokerage commissions have been abolished. This change resulted in fees for large transactions falling considerably and those for small investors have not changed appreciably. Large transactions generally pay approximately a 0.1 per cent flat fee.

---

[33] Closed-end funds are prohibited by federal law.

[34] Switzerland does not impose a 35 per cent withholding tax on dividends paid to investors domiciled outside Switzerland if the Swiss funds derive at least 80 per cent of their income from foreign sources.

[35] Switzerland's revised Federal Law on Investment Funds came into force on January 1, 1995.

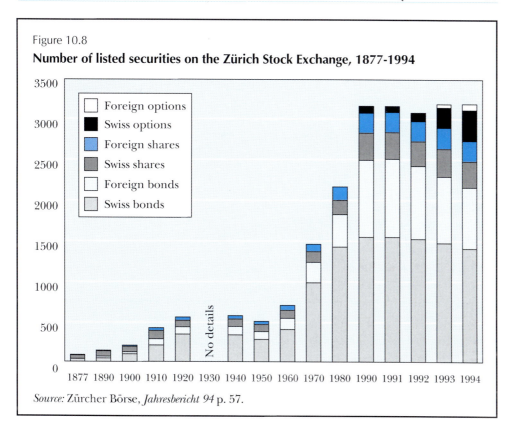

Figure 10.8

Number of listed securities on the Zürich Stock Exchange, 1877-1994

Source: Zürcher Börse, *Jahresbericht 94* p. 57.

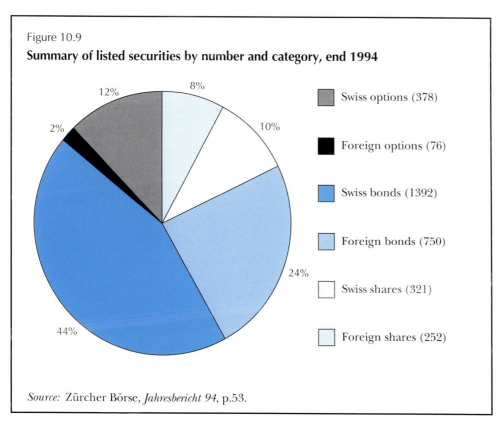

Figure 10.9

Summary of listed securities by number and category, end 1994

Swiss options (378)

Foreign options (76)

Swiss bonds (1392)

Foreign bonds (750)

Swiss shares (321)

Foreign shares (252)

Source: Zürcher Börse, *Jahresbericht 94*, p.53.

Table 10.8

Listed foreign stocks: categorized by country

Country	Status: 31/12/94		Change in 1994	
	Stocks	Issuers	Stocks	Issuers
USA/Canada	115	115	-3	-3
Germany	40	35	-1	-1
The Netherlands	21	21	0	0
Japan	16	16	0	0
Great Britain	14	13	0	0
South Africa	10	8	0	0
Other countries	36	34	-5	-3
Total listed foreign shares	**252**	**242**	**-9**	**-7**

Source: Zürcher Börse, *Jahresbericht 94* p. 51.

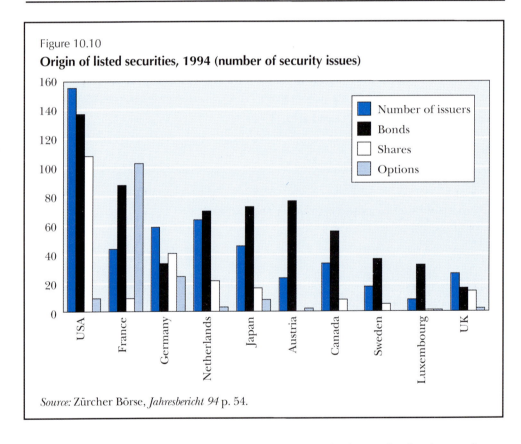

Figure 10.10

Origin of listed securities, 1994 (number of security issues)

Source: Zürcher Börse, *Jahresbericht 94* p. 54.

Swiss security issues (see Figure 10.9). The US is, by far, the largest foreign issuer of securities on the Swiss capital market, followed by Germany, the Netherlands and Japan (see Table 10.8 and Figure 10.10).

Restrictions on foreign stock purchases

In some cases, foreigners are quantitatively restricted from voting when they buy registered shares of certain Swiss companies. These restrictions were originally introduced in the by-laws of corporations during World War II. Later, the system was continued, allowing registered shares to protect companies or their management against unfriendly takeovers.[12] Since 1988, there has been a significant trend in Switzerland toward liberalization (especially among large companies) and share structure simplification that has opened the Swiss capital market to foreigners. Foreigners can purchase unlimited quantities of bearer shares of Swiss companies. Typically, the overall performance of bearer and registered shares of the same company has been the same.

Foreigners have indirect access to investing in registered Swiss equity by purchasing the certificates of Swiss investment funds, which in turn buy registered shares. Furthermore, by purchasing participation certificates or non-voting equity securities, they can share in dividend and subscription rights, but are not entitled to vote at the shareholders' meetings. Options on registered shares are not subject to registration.

7. Venture capital

As a general rule, newly-listed companies on the Swiss stock exchange are well-established enterprises that may, for instance, need additional capital for growth. Because of legal or stock exchange requirements (such as the publication of a 5-year track record),[13] venture capital offers are made infrequently in Switzerland. This practice is in sharp contrast to the United States, where venture companies going public raise billions of dollars each year on the stock markets.

8. Costs and taxes associated with direct investments in Swiss common stocks

Transaction costs and withholding taxes are major factors influencing global portfolio decisions. Transaction costs can be divided into two major categories: custodial charges and execution costs.

Custodial fees[14]

World-wide competition and computerization have greatly reduced custodial fees. They vary depending on factors such as the size and market value of positions, but, in general, they have been reduced to approximately 0.1 per cent.[15] Custodial turnover and settlement charges (levied on a per transaction basis) have also been sharply reduced.[16]

Execution costs

Fixed commissions in Switzerland were abolished in 1991. Since their abolition, the level of efficiency and the potential for greater gains through the new electronic stock exchange have increased Switzerland's competitive international position.

---

[12] During the petrodollar excesses of the 1970s, some companies, like UBS, introduced protective measures against takeovers.

[13] The preliminary draft of the new admission regulations requires a 3 year track record.

[14] Swiss domestic custody and global custody are discussed in more detail in Chapter 8.

[15] Swiss Bank Corporation, *SBC Research: Equity Investment Across Borders: Cutting the Costs* (1993) p. 3.

[16] Most or all of these fees can be offset by the earnings from stock loan agreements.

Table 10.9

Typical portfolio execution costs per round trip, 1992 (%)

Cost	US	Canada	Switzerland	Germany	France	UK	Japan	Australia
Commission	0.09	–	–	–	0.40	–	0.05	0.60
Bid/ask spread	0.56	0.85	1.00	1.00	0.80	0.80	1.50	0.80
Exchange tax	–	–	–	–	–	0.50	0.30	0.60
Total	0.65	0.85	1.00	1.00	1.20	1.30	1.75	2.00
Portfolio size (US$ millions)	25	10	10	10	10	10	15	10

Source: Swiss Bank Corporation, *SBC Research: Equity Investment Across Borders: Cutting the Costs* (1993) p. 5.

Execution costs vary by stock, country and portfolio type (ie, diversified or undiversified). Table 10.9 compares these costs among the major industrialized nations for offshore investors with portfolios ranging in size from US$10-US$25 million. Among the surveyed countries, Switzerland tied with Germany for the third lowest charges, 1 per cent.

Withholding taxes

In addition to custodial charges and execution costs, withholding taxes are important factors influencing international investment flows. Each country has its own tax laws regarding the payment of taxes on corporate profits and dividends, and most of these laws differentiate between the treatment of domestic and foreign residents. Complicating the picture further are negotiated bilateral double taxation treaties that vary their treatment by the type of investment instrument. Among the developed nations, the range of net withholding taxes is from 0 per cent to 15 per cent (see Table 9.6). In 1992, foreign investors in Switzerland paid a net withholding tax of 0.33 per cent, the third lowest of the studied nations (see Table 10.10).

9. Listing requirements for equities

The listing rules for equities are published in the Admissions Regulations (*Kotierungsreglement*) of the Swiss Stock Exchange. These equity requirements are very similar to the listing conditions for debt instruments discussed in Chapter 9.[17] The most important equity provisions are:

- Issuers of equity (or their guarantors) must have consolidated own funds equal to at least Sfr25 million and disclosure must cover a period of three complete financial years. If the issuer already has listed shares in some other category, the minimum threshold is Sfr10 million of

---

[17] A fuller discussion of the listing requirements for equity, debt and derivatives can be found in Appendix 1 at the end of this book.

Table 10.10

Typical dividend yields and dividend withholding taxes (%)

Country	Index	Expected dividend yield 1992	Withholding treaty tax rate	Net withholding tax cost per year
United Kingdom	FTSE	3.95	15 [a]	0.59
Australia	All-Ordinaries	3.80	0-15 [c]	0.57
Canada	Toronto 35	3.48	0-15	0.52
France	CAC	3.00	15	0.45
United States	S&P 500	2.85	0-15	0.43
Switzerland	SMI	2.20	15	0.33
Germany	DAX	2.70	0-15 [b]	0.27
Japan	Nikkei	0.93	15 [a]	0.14

[a] There is no withholding for tax-exempt funds under the US-Canada Bilateral Treaty.
[b] There is no withholding tax for charitable organizations. A 10 per cent rate applies to other tax-free investors in the US and a 15 per cent rate applies to many other cross-border investors.
[c] Taxable accounts may face withholding taxes on dividends not paid out of after-tax profits.

Source: Swiss Bank Corporation, *SBC Research: Equity Investment Across Borders: Cutting the Costs* (1993) p. 4.

additional issues. Exceptions to these rules can be made by the Swiss Admissions Board.

- To fulfil the distribution requirements for public share issues, at least 25 per cent of the total amount must be in the hands of the public, or proof must be supplied to the Swiss Admissions Board that a lower percent will not affect the market's operation.

- A full prospectus must be published in at least one nationally-circulated newspaper and written in any one of the three national languages (German, French or Italian) or English. This prospectus must contain all relevant information allowing a judgment on the securities, as well as the financial situation, organization and legal status of the issuer;

- Equities with transfer restrictions may be listed if it can be shown that the restrictions will not affect the proper functioning of the market.

10. Development of the stock price indices

The Swiss stock market has several important indices that vary from one another according to the number of shares included, frequency of tabulation and stock weightings. Two of the most widely-followed indices are the Swiss Performance Index (SPI), which is dividend-adjusted and measures the price movements of all securities listed on the main Swiss exchanges and the Swiss Market Index (SMI), a non dividend-adjusted index that tracks the prices of the 20 to 24 of the most liquid, blue-chip, Swiss stocks.

Table 10.11

Swiss stock indices

Swiss Performance Index

The SPI, the Swiss Performance Index, was introduced on June 1, 1987 and indexed at 1,000. It is based on the prices of all securities listed on the main Swiss exchanges (Zürich, Geneva and Basel, until they are replaced by EBS) and on the parallel markets in Zürich, Geneva and Basel. The SPI is a dividend-adjusted index with shares weighted by market capitalization. For calculation purposes, the relevant number of shares included in the index is based on the number issued rather than the number in circulation. SPI is divided into two group sector indices (services and industry), and subdivided further into 5 sub-indices for services (banks, insurance, transportation, retail trade and other industries) and 7 sub-indices for industry (machine, energy, chemical/pharmaceutical, food, electrical, construction and other industries). The index is also partitioned into four security categories (bearer shares, registered shares, bearer/participation certificates/non-voting equity securities and participation certificates/non-voting equity securities). Since 1993, sub-indices for small, middle and large companies have also been calculated.

SPIX

SPIX is identical to the SPI without dividend adjustments.

SMI

SMI, the Swiss Market Index, is a non dividend-adjusted index calculated continuously (real time – updated with each new price) based on the 20 to 24 most liquid Swiss shares. Shares are weighted by market capitalization, and for calculation purposes, the relevant number of shares is based on the number in circulation rather than the number issued. It was developed in tandem with the founding of SOFFEX and is the basis for the SOFFEX stock index option and futures. The index began on June 30, 1988 indexed at 1500.

SMIC

SMIC is identical to the SMI with dividend adjustments. It has been calculated since January 4, 1993. Its base was fixed at 1500 as of June 30, 1988.

SSCI

SSCI is the Swiss Small Company Index. In October 1994, it included approximately 60 per cent of the companies listed on the Swiss stock exchanges and accounted for 4 per cent of the exchanges' market capitalization.

SMCI

SMCI is the Swiss Medium Company Index. In October 1994, it included approximately 33 per cent of the companies listed on the Swiss stock exchanges and accounted for 20 per cent of the exchanges' market capitalization.

SLCI

SLCI is the Swiss Large Company Index. In October 1994, it included approximately 7 per cent of the companies listed on the Swiss stock exchanges and accounted for 76 per cent of the exchanges' market capitalization.

SNCI

SNCI is the Swiss Small and Medium-Sized Company Index.

SBAI

SBAI, the Swiss Bid/Ask Index, is a double index – one based on the bid prices and the other on the ask prices of securities included in the SMI. Because it reflects bid/ask

Table 10.11 *continued*

Swiss stock indices *continued*

prices rather than the last prices paid (like the SMI), the SBAI gives a better reflection of hedging costs and current market conditions, especially in periods of high volatility. Its share structure is identical to the SMI.

SBV Index
(Swiss Bank Corporation)
The SBV Index (ie, Schweizerischer Bankverein Index or Swiss Bank Corporation Index) – one of the most popular – is a market-weighted index based on 396 listed shares. The index started in December 1958.

SKA Index
(Credit Suisse)
The SKA Index (ie, Schweizerische Kreditanstadt Index or Credit Suisse Index) began in 1959 with an index number of 100, and is both calculated and published daily by Credit Suisse based on 25 listed shares.[18]

Datastream-Vontobel Index
(Vontobel Bank)
The Datastream-Vontobel general index (base: December 31, 1972 = 100) includes most of the Swiss stocks traded on the Zürich Stock Exchange and the parallel market. Equities in this index are weighted by market capitalization.

OZX
(OZ Zürich)
OZX was constructed so that it reflected the market performance of the Zürich Stock Exchange and could be replicated by investors holding a small basket of different Swiss stocks. Only the largest companies in each industry group were chosen for the index and within this selection, each company's share was weighted by its capitalization level.

* Note: These indices are reported daily in the Neue Zürcher Zeitung.

Source: Schweizer Börse, *SWISSINDEX: The Index Family of Swiss Stock Exchanges* December 1994, OZ Zürich Optionen und Futures Aktiengesellschaft, *OZX: The New Swiss Stock Index* (undated), and descriptions updated by authors.

Figure 10.11 shows these indices (ie, SMI, SPI, SBV/SBC and SKA/CS) vary in almost identical patterns. Figures 10.12, 10.13 and 10.14 display the movement of the Swiss Performance Index relative to other major international indices on a normal and exchange-weighted basis for the 1986-1994 and 1989-1994 periods. Figures 10.12 and 10.13 are included to highlight the sensitivity of Switzerland's ranking to the base year chosen (ie, a number one ranking when 1989 was used and a third ranking when 1986 was used).

---

[18] Zürcher Börse, *Zürcherbörse Jahresbericht 94* (1994) p. 92.

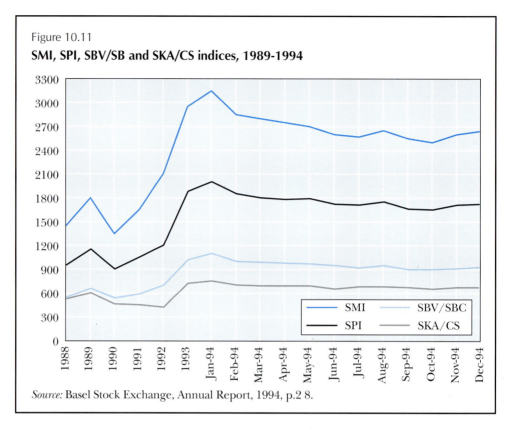

Figure 10.11

SMI, SPI, SBV/SB and SKA/CS indices, 1989-1994

Source: Basel Stock Exchange, Annual Report, 1994, p.2 8.

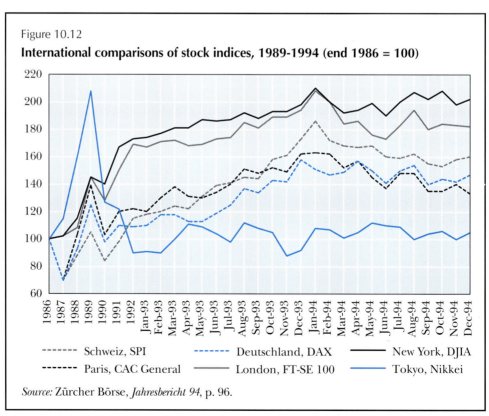

Figure 10.12

International comparisons of stock indices, 1989-1994 (end 1986 = 100)

Source: Zürcher Börse, *Jahresbericht 94*, p. 96.

Figure 10.13

International comparisons of stock indices, 1986-1994 (end 1989 = 100)

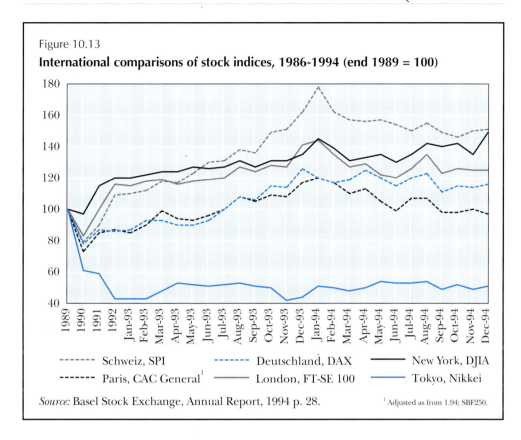

Source: Basel Stock Exchange, Annual Report, 1994 p. 28.

[1] Adjusted as from 1.94; SBF250.

Figure 10.14

International comparisons of foreign exchange, 1986-1994 (end 1986 = 100) adjusted stock indices

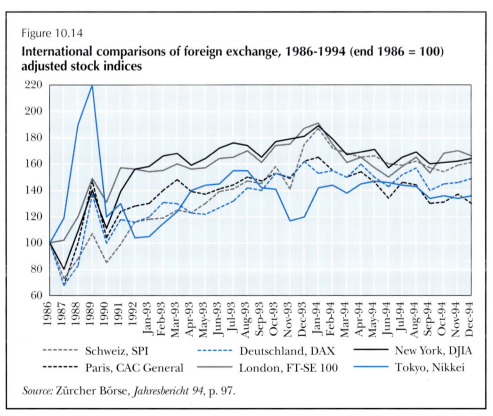

Source: Zürcher Börse, *Jahresbericht 94*, p. 97.

SWISS DERIVATIVE MARKETS

Just as necessity is the mother of invention, volatility is the mother of all derivatives. For years, banks have offered derivatives in the form of forward currency contracts and forward interest rate agreements, but the flowering of current-day derivative alternatives (both over-the-counter and exchange-traded) is mainly a by-product of the post Bretton Woods period.[1] As exchange rates and nominal interest rates began to fluctuate wildly and swiftly due to changes in macroeconomic polices and inflationary expectations, businesses demanded effective, low-cost means of transferring these risks (see Figure 11.1).

Derivatives are perfect examples of how markets and products are created without government intervention to solve problems associated with time, risk and information. Their innovation lies in the capacity to uncouple risks (eg, interest and currency)

Overview of the Swiss derivative markets

Figure 11.1

Swiss franc interest rate variability, 1960-1995 (monthly percentage change)

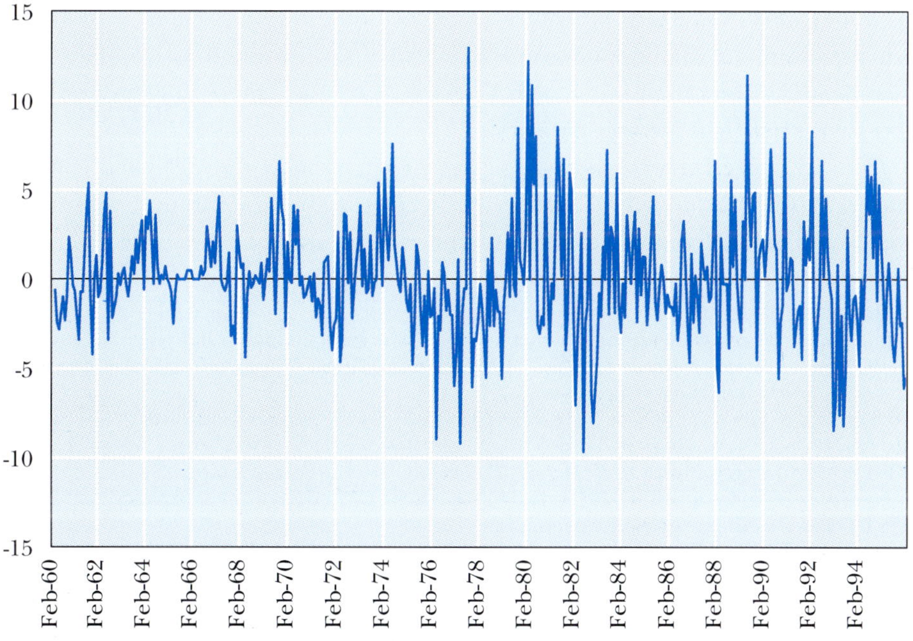

Source: Reuters Data Link.

---

[1] International trends toward deregulation and securitization also helped to fuel their growth.

enabling users to transfer the ones they are unwilling to bear, keep those they can handle and, if desired, take on additional risks in search of higher returns.[2] Generally, these instruments provide a liquid and convenient means of trading, hedging and arbitraging markets. They give users the flexibility to diversify, leverage and protect their portfolios not only at a point in time, but dynamically over time as their risk preferences and financial positions change.

Cost-conscious corporate treasurers, private investors, portfolio advisers, bankers, and pension fund managers have used derivative instruments to alter cash flows on existing assets and liabilities. They have also been employed to lower or lock-in future interest payments and enhance returns. Speculators and arbitrageurs use them as low-cost, high-leverage means of increasing exposure to risk and profiting from small imperfections in the pricing of these instruments. If usage is any measure of value, they have provided, in a very short time period, a substantial benefit to the international financial community.[3]

In the 1990s, the use of derivatives has become controversial due to some spectacular losses associated with users' failure to control and understand position risk. The collapse of Barings in 1995 and the Orange County California losses were two relatively recent examples. Table 11.1 highlights some others.[4]

In the early 1990s, various major reports were published focussing on derivatives, in general, and OTC derivatives, in particular.[5] Further studies were initiated in 1995 by the Futures Industry Association, International Swap Dealers Association, Bank for International Settlements and other groups[6] to examine the derivative markets in terms of their safeguards, control mechanisms, codes of conduct and macroprudential risks.[7]

One of the most visible signs of the new financial age has been the rise of derivative exchanges. By interposing the exchange (and its total capitalization) as the counterparty to all trades, credit risk has been virtually eliminated on these transactions. Equally, if not more important, are the liquidity and the orderly market conditions. Positions can be traded at a lower cost than in the cash markets. As a result, these standardized instruments have gained considerable popularity.

There has been an explosion of derivative contracts over the 1980s and 1990s (see Table 11.2). On 31 March 1995 (after adjustment for double counting), the notional value of outstanding foreign exchange, interest rate, equity and commodity contracts on

---

[2] Originally, users were able to transfer all but credit risk. Recently, derivatives have been developed that enable the transfer of credit risk, as well. (See Aline van Duyn, "Credit risk for sale. Any buyers?" *Euromoney Magazine* April 1995: pp. 41-43.)

[3] See Kenneth A. Froot, David S. Scharfstein and Jeremy C. Stein, "A Framework for Risk Management," *Harvard Business Review* (Nov.-Dec. 1994) pp. 91-102. Also see, David Weinberger, "Using Derivatives: What Senior Managers Must Know" *Harvard Business Review* (Jan.-Feb. 1995) pp. 33-41.

[4] A *Euromoney Magazine* survey in 1994 indicated there were US$6 billion in losses related to derivatives, US$4.5 billion within the previous 12 months.

[5] Bank for International Settlements, *Recent Developments in International Interbank Relations* (Basel: 1992); Bank of England, *Derivatives: Report of an Internal Working Group* (London: 1993); G-30, *Derivatives: Practices and Principles* (Washington: 1993); Commodity Future Exchange Commission, *OTC Derivative Markets and Their Regulation* (Washington: 1994); and Bank for International Settlements, *Risk Management Guidelines for Derivatives* (Basel: 1994).

[6] For example the Derivatives Policy Group (formed by 6 US investment firms) proposed a framework for OTC oversight by security firms.

[7] See for instance, Bank for International Settlements, *Issues of Measurement Related to Market Size and Macroprudential Risks in Derivatives Markets* February 1995.

Table 11.1

Famous losses associated with derivatives, 1983-1995 (US$ millions)

Rank	Losses	Company	Derivative
1	1,700	Orange County	Interest derivatives *
2	1,580	Showa Shell Sekiyu	Foreign exchange forwards
3	1,450	Kashima Oil	Currency derivatives
4	1,340	MG Corporation (Metallgesellschaft)	Energy derivatives
5	1,240	Barings Singapore	Futures & options on Nikkei 225
6	600	Askin Securities	MBS model
7	500	Many UK local authorities	Interest rate swaps & swaptions
8	380	Klöckner	Commodities hedging
9	335	Merrill Lynch	Principal-only MBS volatility
10	275	Allied Lyons	Currency Options
11	260	Volkswagen	Foreign exchange futures
12	200	Codelco, Chile	Copper & precious metals futures & forwards
13	157	Procter and Gamble	Leveraged swaps
14	150	Glaxo	Structured bonds & MBS
15	130	Nippon Steel	Foreign exchange derivatives
16	100	Cargill (Minnetonka Fund)	Mortgage derivatives
17	99.6	Florida State treasury & Florida League of Cities	Mortgage derivatives
18	90	AIG	Derivatives revaluation
19	70	ABN Amro	Marked-to-market valuation
20	67.9	Pacific Horizon Funds (BoA)	Structured notes
21	51.3	Harris Trust & Savings Banks (Bank of Montreal)	Mortgage derivatives
22	50	JP Morgan	Mortgage strips
23	50	First Boston	Bond option volatility
24	50	Medani	Structured notes
25	34.6	Dell Computer	Leveraged swaps & options
26	33	Chemical	Options model error
27	25	Louisiana State Retirement Fund	IOs/POs
28	25	Laszlo Tauber	Foreign exchange derivatives
29	22	Arco (Pension Fund)	Structured notes
30	20	Paramount Communications	Interest rate swaps
31	19.7	Gibson Greetings	Leveraged swaps
32	12.1	Mead Corp.	Leveraged DM/US$ spread

* Most of Orange County's losses were the result of leveraged positions. It borrowed heavily and purchased inverse floaters.

Abbreviations

MBS = Mortgage-backed securities; IO and PO = Interest-only and principal-only/ mortgage strips

Note: All losses are in pre-tax equivalency (assumes 35 per cent tax rate for US companies)

Source: David Shirreff, "Fill that gap!" *Euromoney Magazine* (August 1994) p. 29 and updated by the authors.

Table 11.2

Markets for selected financial derivative instruments worldwide (US$ billions)

Instruments	Notional principal outstanding					
	1990	*1991*	*1992*	*1993*	*1994*	*1995*
Exchange traded instruments	2,290.2	3,518.8	4,632.5	7,760.8	8,837.8	16,439.0
Interest rate futures	1,454.5	2,156.7	2,913.0	4,942.6	5,757.4	12,436.0
Interest rate options	599.5	1,072.6	1,385.4	2,362.4	2,622.8	3,238.0
Currency options	16.9	17.9	24.9	32.2	33.0	81.0
Currency futures	56.5	62.8	70.9	75.4	54.5	39.0
Stock market index futures	69.1	76.0	79.7	109.9	127.7	195.0
Stock market index options	93.7	132.8	158.6	238.3	242.4	450.0
Over-the-counter instruments[a]	3,450.3	4,449.4	5,345.7	8,474.6	na	20,257.0
Interest rate swaps	2,311.5	3,065.1	3,850.0	6,177.3	na	18,283.0
Currency swaps	577.5	807.2	860.4	899.6	na	1,974.0
Other swap-related derivatives [b]	561.3	577.2	634.5	1,397.6	na	na

[a] Note: The data in this table only partially capture the OTC market activity. Forward contracts, option-related instruments on currencies, fixed income, equity securities, as well as cross-product swaps and structured securities are not included.
[b] Caps, collars, floors and swaptions.

Source: Bank for International Settlements, *Bank for International Settlements 65th Annual Report, 1st April 1994-31st March 1995* (Basel: 12 June 1995) p. 184, and Bank for International Settlements, *Central Bank Survey of Derivatives Market Activity: Release of Preliminary Global Totals* (Basel: 18 December 1995) p. 6 (Tables 2A & 2B).

the over-the-counter derivative markets was US$40.7 trillion.[8] Of these outstanding OTC contracts, single-currency interest rate instruments accounted for 65 per cent, foreign exchange contracts for 32 per cent and equity and commodity contracts for 1 per cent each. For the month of April 1995, daily turnover of foreign exchange and interest rate derivatives on the OTC derivative markets was US$839 billion.[9]

In the exchange-traded derivative markets, the notional value of outstanding contracts (not adjusted for double counting) at the end of March 1995 was US$16.6 trillion, and the daily turnover for interest rates and futures contracts over April 1995 was US$1.1 trillion. Futures and options on interest rates accounted for 95 per cent of the total volume;[10] contracts involving equity and stock indices accounted for 4 per cent, and less than 2 per cent of the total outstanding contracts were composed of commodity and foreign exchange contracts (less than 1 per cent each).[11]

---

[8] Gross market value (ie, replacement cost) of these contracts was US$1.7 trillion. Of this outstanding gross market value, 59 per cent were foreign exchange contracts, 37 per cent interest rate contracts, 3 per cent equity contracts and 2 per cent commodity contracts.
[9] All figures used in this paragraph were taken from: Bank for International Settlements, *Central Bank Survey of Derivatives Market Activity: Release of Preliminary Global Totals* (Basel: 18 December 1995) pp. 1-2.
[10] Nearly all of the turnover on the exchange-traded market involved interest rate contracts.
[11] Bank for International Settlements, pp. 2 & 4.

Of the outstanding foreign exchange derivative contracts, 83 per cent involved the US dollar on one side of the transaction, and only 5 per cent of these contracts involved a currency other than the US dollar, Deutschmark or Japanese yen. Of the outstanding single currency interest rate derivative contracts, the dollar accounted for 35 per cent, and 31 per cent was accounted for by currencies other than the US dollar, Deutschmark or Japanese yen.[12] The Swiss franc's portion of the notional amount of global turnover on the OTC markets for foreign exchange and interest rate derivatives was about 4.6 per cent and 1 per cent, respectively. The Swiss franc accounted for 0 per cent and 0.4 per cent, respectively, of the global turnover in exchange-traded foreign exchange and interest rate contracts.[13]

In the early years of exchange-traded derivatives, the US held nearly total control of the world-wide market. In the 1990s, the US is still the world's largest marketplace, but, over the intervening years, other nations have established derivative exchanges eroding the US' share to nearly 50 per cent of global volume. The Swiss Options and Financial Futures Exchange (SOFFEX) was established in 1988, and, since its introduction, volume has grown rapidly. Nevertheless, because it is still relatively young, it lacks the breadth and depth (in terms of liquidity) of the larger international exchanges, especially those of the US and Japan.

The Swiss franc derivative markets are used by different institutions and individuals for functionally different purposes. Banks, other financial intermediaries and large corporations are the most frequent users, followed by institutional investors and, distantly, by private investors. Banks, other financial intermediaries and private individuals use derivatives primarily for trading purposes.[14] Both corporations and institutional investors use them mainly for hedging exposures (ie, transaction, translation and economic exposures), as well as fund-raising and yield enhancement. Banks and other financial intermediaries are the only major users of these markets for arbitrage transactions (see Table 11.3).

One group of institutional investors that, at present, is clearly under-represented in the Swiss (and international) derivative markets is the pension fund sector. From 1985, Swiss law has required most employed people in Switzerland to contribute to a private pension insurance programme. Yet, of the more than 5,500 Swiss pension funds that existed in the early 1990s, only 17 per cent used SOFFEX.[15] Between 1990 and 2001, these institutions are expected to double in size to almost 110 per cent of Switzerland's GDP.[16] As a result, future demand could be significant once (and if) pension fund man-

1. The Swiss derivative markets: major users

---

[12] Bank for International Settlements, p. 3.

[13] Bank for International Settlements, p. 10 (Table 6).

[14] Trading is profiting from buying and selling without the intention of hedging on- or off-balance sheet positions.

[15] Heinz Zimmermann, *Preisbildung und Risikoanalyse von Aktienoptionen* Schweizerisches Institut für Aussenwirtschaft-, Struktur- und Regionalforschung an der Hochschule St. Gallen (Grüsch Switzerland, Verlag Rüegger, 1988).

[16] Stefan Hepp, *The Swiss Pension Funds – An Emerging New Investment Force* Bankwirtschaftliche Forschungen Band 126 (Bern/Stuttgart: Verlag Paul Haupt, 1990).

Table 11.3

Major uses and users of derivative Swiss franc instruments

	Trading	Hedging	Arbitrage	Total
Banks/financial intermediaries (own account)	Regularly (70-80%)	Regularly (20-25%)	Occasionally (0-5%)	100%
Large corporations	Occasionally (5-20%)	Regularly (80-95%)	Not used (0%)	100%
Institutional investors *	Regularly (20-30%)	Regularly (70-80%)	Not used (0%)	100%
Private investors	Regularly (80%)	Occasionally (20%)	Not used (0%)	100%

* Institutional investors = pension funds, insurance companies, (semi-) government agencies, local/state authorities, investment funds and supranationals.

Source: Marcel Erni, *Derivative Swiss Franc Interest Rate Instruments: Pricing, Market Structure, Market Potential* (Bern: Verlag Paul Haupt, 1992) pp. 107-109.

agers are convinced that risk administration can be facilitated by the prudent use of derivative instruments.

2. Swiss over-the-counter derivatives versus exchange-traded derivatives

Competition between traditional over-the-counter derivatives and exchange-traded derivatives has added a new dimension to the Swiss financial markets. If customized, tailor-made service is a priority and participants are not as concerned with paying rock-bottom prices, the over-the-counter markets will prevail. The standardized exchange-traded derivatives compete generally on the basis of broad liquidity, price transparency, negligible counterparty risk and low costs. However, increasing user sophistication and the proliferation of new derivative instruments have caused a convergence between the OTC and exchange-traded markets.

Over-the-counter derivatives

OTC derivatives are generally tailored to the individual needs of a customer. Marketing them requires a firm understanding of clients' financial positions which makes them expensive in terms of technical service and selling costs. In the Swiss markets, the major types of OTC derivatives are forwards, swaps, forward rate agreements, interest rate guarantees and options. OTC derivatives have evolved to solve a variety of specific institutional, private, corporate, governmental and supranational needs.

In part because of their large minimum size and variety, only banks and other financial intermediaries are regular users of all the OTC instruments. Large corporations, due to their hedging and financing needs are active players, as well, and both institutional and private investors are only occasional users of any derivative instrument (see Table 11.4).

188

Table 11.4

Users of derivative Swiss franc interest rate instruments

	Exchange traded	*OTC derivatives*			
	Futures	*FRAs*	*Swaps*	*Interest rate guarantees*	*Futures/ options*
Banks/financial institutions					
(own account)	Regular	Regular	Regular	Regular	Regular
Large corporations	Occasional	Regular	Regular	Regular	Regular
Institutional investors	Regular	Occasional	Occasional	Not used	Regular
Private investors	Not used	Not used	Not used	Not used	Regular

Source: Marcel Erni, *Derivative Swiss Franc Interest Rate Instruments: Pricing, Market Structure, Market Potential,* (Bern: Verlag Paul Haupt: 1992) p. 107.

Table 11.5

Demand structure of wholesale Swiss franc & interest rate-related instruments (%) *

	Forward rate agreements	*Interest rate swaps*	*Interest rate guarantees*
Banks/financial institutions	90-95	68	50
Large corporations	3-7	21	40
Institutional investors	2-3	0	5
Government/supranational	0	11	0
Private investors	0	0	5
Total	100	100	100

* Wholesale market = Professional market.

Source: Marcel Erni, *Derivative Swiss Franc Interest Rate Instruments: Pricing, Market Structure, Market Potential,* (Bern: Verlag Paul Haupt, 1992) pp. 111.

In the OTC market for interest-related derivatives, banks and other financial intermediaries tend to be the major users of forward rate agreements, interest rate swaps and interest rate guarantees. Institutional investors are the major source of demand for interest rate options to hedge portfolios, and large corporations focus their demands on both interest rate options and interest rate guarantees. Private investors, who account for a relatively small part of the OTC markets, are concentrated in the interest rate options market (see Table 11.5).

OTC derivatives are offered by a wide variety of domestic and foreign financial institutions. Table 11.6 lists the primary domestic and foreign suppliers of these derivative instruments (as of September 1995). In Switzerland's retail market,[17] Swiss banks domi-

---

[17] The retail market includes small- and medium-sized corporations, institutional investors, small and other medium-sized banks and financial intermediaries, as well as other non-market makers.

Table 11.6

Major Swiss franc OTC derivatives and their major suppliers, 1995

Forward rate agreement	*Interest rate swaps*	*Currency swaps*	*Interest rate guarantees*	*OTC options*
In Switzerland				
1. CS Holding	1. CS Holding	1. CS Holding	1. CS Holding	1. CS Holding
2. Union Bank of Switzerland	2. Union Bank of Switzerland	2. Union Bank of Switzerland	2. Union Bank of Switzerland	2. Union Bank of Switzerland
3. Swiss Bank Corporation	3. Swiss Bank Corporation	3. Swiss Bank Corporation	3. Swiss Bank Corporation	3. Swiss Bank Corporation
4. Bank Leu	4. Paribas Suisse	4. Paribas Suisse	4. Paribas Suisse	
5. Bank Julius Baer				
6. Paribas Suisse				
Outside Switzerland				
1. ABN Amro Bank	1. Bank of America	1. Bank of America	1. Bank of America	1. Bank of America
2. Barclays Bank	2. Barclays Bank	2. Barclays Bank	2. Barclays Bank	2. Barclays Bank
3. BNP	3. BNP	3. BNP	3. Chase Manhattan Bank	3. BNP
4. Chase Manhattan Bank	4. Chase Manhattan Bank	4. Chase Manhattan Bank	4. Citicorp	4. Chase Manhattan Bank
5. Citicorp	5. Citicorp	5. Citicorp	5. Commerzbank	5. Citicorp
6. Commerzbank	6. Commerzbank	6. Commerzbank	6. Deutsche Bank	6. Commerzbank
7. Deutsche Bank	7. Deutsche Bank	7. Deutsche Bank	7. Dresdner Bank	7. Deutsche Bank
8. Dresdner Bank	8. Dresdner Bank	8. Dresdner Bank	8. JP Morgan	8. Dresdner Bank
9. JP Morgan	9. JP Morgan	9. JP Morgan	9. Lloyds Bank	9. JP Morgan
10. Lloyds Bank	10. Lloyds Bank	10. Lloyds Bank	10. Merrill Lynch	10. Lloyds Bank
11. National Westminster Bank	11. Merrill Lynch	11. Merrill Lynch	11. Morgan Stanley	11. Merrill Lynch
12. Paribas	12. Morgan Stanley	12. Morgan Stanley	12. National Westminster Bank	12. Morgan Stanley
13. Société Générale	13. National Westminster Bank	13. National Westminster Bank	13. Paribas	13. National Westminster Bank
	14. Paribas	14. Paribas	14. Salomon	14. Paribas
	15. Salomon	15. Salomon	15. Société Générale	15. Salomon
	16. Société Générale	16. Société Générale		16. Société Générale

Source: Authors' tabulation.

Table 11.7

OTC derivative suppliers: the Big Banks versus all other Swiss banks,1992 (%)

	FRAs	*Swaps*	*IRGs*
Switzerland's three Big Banks	40	45	35
All other banks	60	55	65

Source: Marcel Erni, *Derivative Swiss Franc Interest Rate Instruments: Pricing, Market Structure, Market Potential,* (Bern: Verlag Paul Haupt, 1992) p. 124.

Table 11.8

Specialized brokers of derivative Swiss franc interest rate & currency instruments

Interest rate derivatives

1. Astley & Pearce
2. Babcock Fulton Prebon
3. Bierbaum & Co. GmbH
4. Cedef
5. CMS Capital Market Services Ltd.
6. Euro Brokers Ltd.
7. Exco, Godsel, Astley & Pearce (Capital Markets) Ltd.
8. Finaco
9. Finarbit AG
10. GeldHandel GmbH
11. Gottex SA
12. Guy Butler
13. Harlows Ltd.
14. Interacor
15. Intercapital Brokers Ltd.
16. Karl Kliem
17. Mayflower CMTS
18. RP Martin
19. Sihaco Finanz AG
20. Tradition SA
21. Tullet & Tokyo
22. Velcor SA

Currency derivatives

1. Astley & Pearce
2. Cantor Fitzgerald, London
3. Exco, London
4. GFI, London
5. Kliem FFT
6. Tullet Tokyo/London
7. Tradition

Source: Marcel Erni, *Derivative Swiss Franc Interest Rate Instruments: Pricing, Market Structure, Market Potential,* (Bern: Verlag Paul Haupt, 1992) p. 118. Updated and expanded by authors.

nate, with little foreign competition. By contrast, in the more competitive wholesale markets, foreign domiciled banks have considerable shares of the market (see Table 11.7).

Switzerland's Big Banks are leaders in the Swiss franc derivative markets. CS Holding acquired a specialist team from Bankers Trust derivative group in 1990, to create Credit Suisse Financial Products (CSFP). Swiss Bank Corporation boosted its position in this market through a 1992 alliance with Chicago-based O'Connors & Associates. Union Bank of Switzerland chose to develop its own talent in-house. In large part, Swiss banks have become major players in the derivatives market because of their solid credit ratings and widespread concerns about counterparty risk.[18] Moreover, these banks enjoy a broad customer base and some can use their balance sheets to hedge a large volume of transactions.

Because of the specialized nature of OTC derivatives and the high search costs associated with selling them, brokers play an important role in this market. Table 11.8 lists the major brokers in the Swiss franc interest rate and currency derivative markets.

The Swiss Financial Futures and Options Exchange (SOFFEX) has the distinction of being the world's first totally electronic, nation-wide exchange for trading, clearing and settling American-style option contracts, and it has developed into one of the key building blocks for Switzerland's integrated financial system. In January 1995, SOFFEX became a wholly-owned subsidiary of the Swiss Stock Exchange Association (SSE), allowing for a com-

Exchange-traded derivatives

---

[18] The need for superior credit ratings in the wholesale market has erected a formidable barrier to entry that has helped the well-capitalized Swiss banks.

Table 11.9

Derivatives traded on SOFFEX, end November 1995

Equity-related options

1. Short-term options on shares
- Alusuisse-Lonza Holding (Registered)
- Holderbank (Bearer)
- BBC-Brown Boveri (Bearer)
- Swiss Bank Corporation (Bearer)
- Ciba (Registered)
- Swiss Re (Registered)
- CS Holding (Registered)
- SMH (Registered)
- Nestlé (Registered)
- Union Bank of Switzerland (Bearer)
- Roche Holding (Non-Voting Equity Security)
- Zürich Insurance (Registered)
- Sandoz (Registered)
- Winterthur Insurance (Registered)

2. Long-term options on shares
- Ciba-Geigy (Registered)
- Roche Holding (Non-Voting Equity Security)
- CS Holding (Registered)
- Swiss Bank Corporation (Bearer)
- Nestlé (Registered)
- Union Bank of Switzerland (Bearer)

3. Low exercise price options on shares (LEPOs) – Same shares as under heading #1

Stock index-related options & futures

1. Short-term SMI options
2. Long-term SMI options
3. SMI futures

Interest rate-related options & futures

1. Options on confederation bond futures
2. Futures on confederation bonds

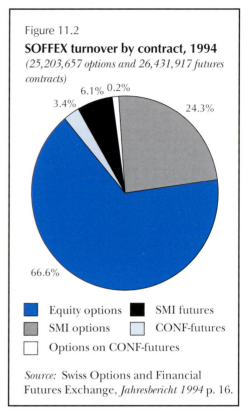

Figure 11.2

SOFFEX turnover by contract, 1994
(25,203,657 options and 26,431,917 futures contracts)

- Equity options
- SMI options
- Options on CONF-futures
- SMI futures
- CONF-futures

Source: Swiss Options and Financial Futures Exchange, *Jahresbericht 1994* p. 16.

mon organizational structure with the Swiss Electronic Stock Exchange (EBS – Elektronische Börse Schweiz). In 1995, it had 52 Swiss and non-Swiss members, of which 33 were clearing members.

In 1995, eight categories of options and futures were traded on SOFFEX (see Table 11.9). Active markets existed for options on the fourteen leading Swiss company shares, short-term and long-term options on the SMI, futures on the SMI, as well as options and futures on Swiss government bonds (CONF-futures and options on CONF-futures). Figure 11.2 shows the relative composition of transactions on the exchange in 1994.

Trading volumes have increased to levels that made SOFFEX the third largest derivatives exchange in Europe in 1994, behind the Deutsche Termin Börse (DTB) and the London International Financial Futures Exchange (LIFFE) (see Figure 11.3). In contract volume, SOFFEX options ranked first among all European exchanges, third in stock index contracts and sixth in futures transactions.

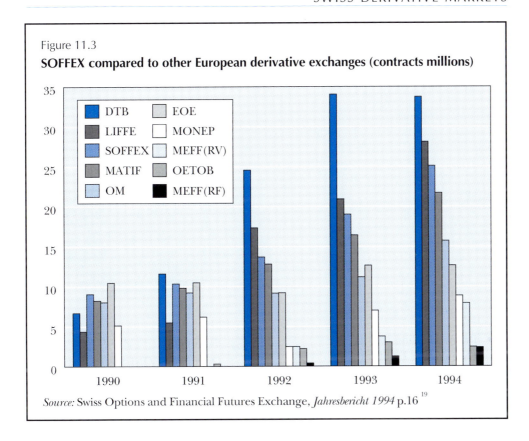

Figure 11.3

SOFFEX compared to other European derivative exchanges (contracts millions)

Source: Swiss Options and Financial Futures Exchange, *Jahresbericht 1994* p.16 [19]

In 1994, total volume on SOFFEX reached 27.9 million contracts.[20] This derivative activity was helped by a new fee schedule introduced in 1993 that not only reduced fees by 66 per cent, but also simplified them. Further cuts in fees were also made in 1995 in anticipation of synergies from the integration of SOFFEX into the Swiss Stock Exchange.

Trading volume and capitalization levels on SOFFEX vary substantially among the various contracts. In 1994, stock option contracts were clearly the leading products among all the future and option alternatives (see Table 11.10).

Options on shares are latecomers to the Swiss capital markets. Today, three broad types are traded on the Swiss markets: covered warrants (*Stillhalter Optionen*), OTC options and exchange-traded options (SOFFEX). The Swiss covered options market leader is OZ Zürich, a specialized option boutique and subsidiary of BZ Bank in Zürich (See Chapter 4). The OTC market is the domain of about 20 banks, visible among which are

3. Equity-related derivatives in the Swiss market

Options

---

[19] DTB = Deutsche Termin Börse in Frankfurt; EOE = European Options Exchange in Amsterdam; LIFFE = London Financial Futures Exchange; MATIF = Marché à Terme International de France; MEFF(RF) = (Madrid) MEFF Holding Corporation Renta Fija (Equity Derivatives); MEFF(RV) = (Madrid) MEFF Holding Corporation Renta Variable (Fixed-Income Derivatives); MONEP = Marché des Options Négotiable de Paris; OETOB = Österreichische Termin und Optionsbörse; OM = Stockholm Options Exchange); SOFFEX = Swiss Options and Financial Futures Exchange.

[20] Swiss Options and Financial Futures Exchange, *Jahresbericht 1994* p. 16.

Table 11.10

Turnover information on SOFFEX derivative products, 1994

	Average daily turnover	*Record daily turnover*	*Record date*
Options contracts			
Equity	74,336	145,839	16 December 1994
SMI	26,009	69,862	1 February 1994
CONF	214	2,190	2 March 1994
Total	101,159	181,758	11 February 1994
Futures contracts			
SMI	6,750	16,116	17 November 1994
CONF	3,754	16,772	2 March 1994
Total	10,504	31,536	2 March 1994

Source: Swiss Options and Financial Futures Exchange *Jahresbericht: 1994* p. 16.

Table 11.11

Swiss equity derivatives, 27 July 1995 (Sfr millions)

	Capitalization of open contracts	*Capitalization of option premium*	*Delta[b] adjusted open contracts*	*Stock exchange capitalization*	*% of market capitalization*
Covered warrants[a]	73,837	9,858	41,417	–	10.8
OTC options	40,000	1,400	20,000	–	5.2
SOFFEX options	11,556	231	5,778	–	1.5
Total Swiss market	**125,393**	**11,489**	**67,195**	**383,100**	**17.5**

[a] 100 per cent collateralized and delta-hedged warrants
[b] The "delta" of an option is its price sensitivity to a change in the price of the underlying asset.

Source: Estimates, 27 July 1995

Switzerland's Big Banks, as well as subsidiaries of large US banks. Finally, SOFFEX deals in standardized contracts of shares for fourteen leading Swiss companies and the SMI stock index.

In mid-1995, the total value of all open Swiss option contracts equalled over Sfr125 billion. On a delta-adjusted basis its size was about Sfr67 billion, amounting to 17.5 per cent of the market capitalization of all listed Swiss shares (See Table 11.11).

Covered equity warrants

Among Swiss investors, covered warrants on single shares are the largest and most popular segment of the Swiss equity derivatives market. In mid-1995, the market capitalization of open contracts on them was estimated at almost Sfr74 billion, approximately 60 per cent of the total Swiss share option market, over 19 per cent of the total Swiss stock market value and almost 11 per cent of the total Swiss stock market value on a delta-adjusted basis. These instruments are distinctive because of their longer duration, typically maturing between one and five years. They complement SOFFEX options where typical durations range between 3 and 9 months.

Covered warrants can be either 100 per cent collateralized or synthetic covered options. Options that have 100 per cent collateralization, allow buyers to focus almost exclusively on market risk, since counterparty risk is no longer an issue. Written call options are backed by shares deposited with banks, and written put options are often backed by government securities. By contrast, issuers of synthetically covered options cover only the option delta[21] causing the buyer to face both the market and counterparty risk.

A Primer on writing covered warrants

Fully covered equity warrants (ie, warrants with 100 per cent collateral) provide investors with a means of purchasing financial instruments without the risk of counterparty default or non-performance. For the writers of such warrants, there is the opportunity to tailor the risk/return profile of their portfolios. An example will help to clarify the incentives in this market.

Writing call options

Suppose a share of XYZ Company costs Sfr1,000, a one-year call option with a Sfr1,100 strike price has a Sfr50 premium and that government securities earn 5 per cent a year. The sale of a covered call option obligates the seller to deposit the share in a bank, assuring the buyer that delivery can be made in the future. In exchange, the seller receives the Sfr50 premium and invests it at the risk-free annual rate of 5 per cent, earning Sfr2.5 a year. If the share price remains at or below the strike price, the call option expires unexercised. As a result, the writer keeps the share and enhances his/her total return (ie, dividends plus price appreciation up to the strike price) by 5.25 per cent, the option premium of Sfr50 and interest earnings of Sfr2.5. Since the option is not exercised, delivery is not an issue and the buyer loses the premium paid.

By contrast, suppose the share price rises 20 per cent to Sfr1,200. The call warrant would be exercised requiring the writer to sell for Sfr1,100 a share that was bought for Sfr1,000. For the seller, the total return would equal 15.25 per cent. Of this return, 10 per cent was derived from the difference between the purchase- and the strike prices, 5 per cent came from the Sfr50 premium and 0.25 per cent was the premium-invested earnings of Sfr2.5. The seller sacrificed only the opportunity to earn above 15.25 per cent. Because the shares were deposited in a bank when

---

[21] The delta of an option is its price sensitivity to a change in the price of the underlying asset.

the deal was originally transacted, the buyer is assured that delivery can/will be made. For the option buyer, the 20 per cent appreciation in price netted a return of 100 per cent (ie, Sfr50/50 = 100 per cent). He/She earned Sfr100 from the difference between the purchase price and the market price.[22]

Writing put options

The logic behind writing covered put warrants is symmetrical to writing covered calls. Sellers of puts are typically the owners of interest earning securities looking for ways to enhance their return. Suppose an investor owns Sfr1,000 of government securities earning 5 per cent a year and that a one-year stock put option with a Sfr900 strike price has a Sfr40 premium. Upon selling a stock put option, the writer deposits 100 per cent collateral (Sfr900) in the form of government securities (or other acceptable collateral) in a bank.

In exchange, the seller receives the Sfr40 premium and invests it at the risk-free annual rate of 5 per cent (ie, Sfr2 per year). If the share price remains at or above the strike price, the put option expires unexercised. The writer keeps the government securities and earns a before tax return of 9.2 per cent (ie, 5 per cent from the government securities, 4 per cent from the premium (ie, Sfr40/Sfr1,000 = 5 per cent) and 0.20 per cent from the interest return on the invested premium (ie, Sfr2/Sfr1,000)). Since the option is unexercised, the issue of whether the seller can afford to pay for the shares never arises.

By contrast, suppose the share price falls to Sfr830. The put option would be exercised, requiring the writer to purchase for Sfr900 what the market values at Sfr830 (ie, a Sfr70 loss). Offsetting (part or all of) these losses is the Sfr40 premium and the interest earnings on the principal and invested premium (ie, Sfr50 and Sfr2, respectively). As a result, the net return to the seller is 2.20 per cent. The seller would have earned more by remaining in government securities and could have actually had a negative return if the price of the shares fell below Sfr808. But regardless of how far the market falls and how much the seller loses, the buyer would have no fear of contract non-performance because of the 100 per cent collateral that was deposited at contract initiation.

The ideal world for covered option writers

The ideal world for covered option writers is one where the market expects stock prices to be volatile, but the turbulence never materializes. The expectation of volatility will increase option prices enhancing stock and security returns, but without substantial movement, the options would expire unexercised. Institutions that sell covered options and provide investment advice must take precautions to ensure that their vested interest in projecting disruptive markets does not interfere with their obligation to give objective advice.

---

[22] Minus any interest payments if the funds to buy the stock\warrants were borrowed.

OTC stock options

The second largest segment of the Swiss stock options market is the OTC market where many of the contracts are tailored to the individual needs of clients. They are usually synthetically constructed with only the delta covered by physical underlying shares. Because they are not fully collateralized, the number of shares that must be held to stay delta hedged varies with the stock price. As a result, sellers' positions must be tracked and adjusted continually.

Effective delta hedging requires that prices move incrementally and that liquid markets be available for all trades (both large and small). In such an environment, the risks of human error are quite large. Equally, if not more important, because they are not fully collateralized, the risk of non-delivery or contract non-performance is significantly greater than with covered options (due to both default and systemic risk).[23] In the OTC market, there are no limits on the number of options that can be written on the same underlying share and there is no way to accurately measure default risk with so many independent bilateral contracts.[24]

An example may help to clarify the point. If the delta were 0.50, call option sellers could cover their positions by purchasing half of the underlying shares of the options they sell. A sharp rise in the price of the underlying shares would force many of them into the spot market to cover their positions as their call options gained intrinsic value. These forced purchases could (and usually do) cause spot market share prices to rise even further.

Similar problems occur with a sharp drop in prices. Sellers of option puts would have only 50 per cent collateral in securities backing their positions. A substantial drop in price would put many options in-the-money, forcing writers to sell securities to hedge their open positions. Such distress sales can and do cause further reductions in prices of the underlying security.

Exchange-traded equity options and futures

SOFFEX trades equity contracts for 14 major Swiss companies and the SMI index (see Table 11.9). Of the actively traded securities on this market, the largest volumes during 1994 were in the shares of Union Bank of Switzerland, Swiss Bank Corporation, CS Holding, Nestlé, Ciba and Roche Holding (see Figure 11.4).

One of the trends in the international financial markets is to offer long-term put and call contracts. Standardized long-term options were first offered by Amsterdam's EOE exchange in 1986. They spread quickly to the US in 1987, and on May 2, 1994, SOFFEX introduced the Long-Term SMI option. Because of its success, SOFFEX introduced in 1995 long-term options on individual shares.[25] These new contracts should increase the competition between the exchange-traded options and the covered warrants market.

---

[23] Of the risks (market, settlement, legal, credit and systemic) considered by the six reports cited in footnote 5, systemic risk (the possibility that an unpredictable event will cause a chain reaction of interrelated financial problems) and credit risk (the chance that a counterparty will fail to deliver on the derivative instrument) were considered to be the most important.

[24] Appendix 11-A.1 shows the information reported to the Swiss National Bank on derivative activities.

[25] Many of these options are held until expiration date, which accounts for the large open interest.

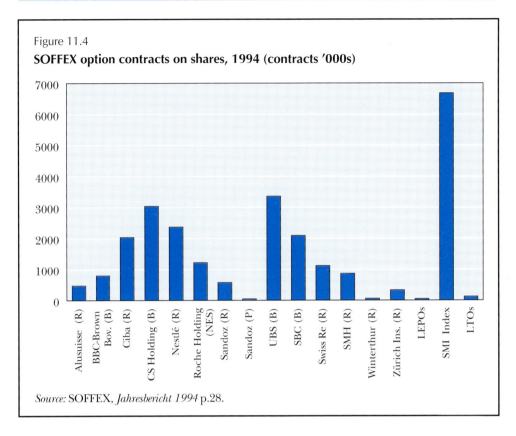

Figure 11.4

SOFFEX option contracts on shares, 1994 (contracts '000s)

Source: SOFFEX, *Jahresbericht 1994* p.28.

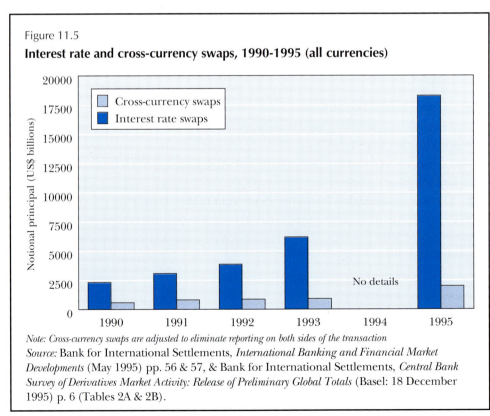

Figure 11.5

Interest rate and cross-currency swaps, 1990-1995 (all currencies)

Note: Cross-currency swaps are adjusted to eliminate reporting on both sides of the transaction
Source: Bank for International Settlements, *International Banking and Financial Market Developments* (May 1995) pp. 56 & 57, & Bank for International Settlements, *Central Bank Survey of Derivatives Market Activity: Release of Preliminary Global Totals* (Basel: 18 December 1995) p. 6 (Tables 2A & 2B).

The SMI Future contracts accounted for only a little over 6 per cent of the contract volume on SOFFEX in 1994 (an increase from 4.5 per cent in 1993) with volume of approximately 1.7 million contracts (ie, 6,750 per day). Relative to other European exchanges, SOFFEX futures volume is relatively thin.

4. Interest rate-related derivatives

Swaps

Since their initiation in the early 1980s, interest rate and cross currency swaps have become significant parts of the international financial markets (see Figure 11.5).[26] These instruments have given market participants a means of changing interest rate exposures over a longer time horizon than could be accomplished in the futures or options markets. Through these off-balance sheet instruments, financing terms and interest receipts can be converted from fixed to floating, floating to fixed or floating on one basis to floating on some other basis.

Interest rate swaps

Swaps, and in particular, interest rate swaps, have gained popularity because they provide a cheaper, more flexible and convenient means of changing exposures than could be accomplished in the cash markets. Because these markets are so competitive and broad (especially in comparison to the Swiss franc bond market), swap rates have become bellwether indicators of the Swiss financial markets.[27] In 1993, the Swiss franc interest rate swap market was the sixth largest interest rate swap market in the world (see Figure 11.6).

Unlike options and futures, interest rate swaps have longer maturities, enabling users to hedge bonds and long-term loans, as well as change the stream of interest earnings on long-term assets. Figure 11.7 shows that 60 per cent of these instruments in 1993 had maturities of over 2 years.

Swiss franc interest rate swap use is almost evenly split between banks and other end-users. Unlike the cross-currency market, where users are primarily non-bank participants using swaps to change the financing terms of foreign bond issues, interest rate swaps have a wider customer base among institutions using them for financial engineering purposes (see Figure 11.8).

The uses for interest rate swaps vary, but their major employment is for portfolio management (48 per cent) – especially among banks (see Figure 11.9 for a breakdown in 1988). In contrast to hedging liabilities (26 per cent of the users), participants have made limited application of swaps for hedging assets (6 per cent of users). This lopsidedness could be due to the illiquidity of the domestic, Swiss franc bond market. Capital market transactions (20 per cent) made up the remaining portion of the demand.

Cross currency swaps

Swiss franc-related cross currency swaps were ranked third behind only the US dollar and

---

[26] The first ever major cross currency swap occurred in August 1981 between the World Bank and IBM using US dollars and Swiss francs.

[27] Adrian Ryser and Thomas Wilson, "Swiss Franc Currency Swaps," in R.J. Schwartz and C.W. Smith (eds.): *The Handbook of Currency and Interest Rate Risk Management* (New York: New York Institute of Finance, 1990) Chapter 14, p. 14-13.

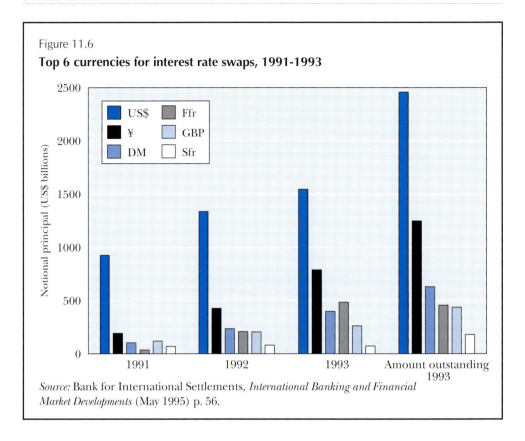

Figure 11.6

Top 6 currencies for interest rate swaps, 1991-1993

Source: Bank for International Settlements, *International Banking and Financial Market Developments* (May 1995) p. 56.

the yen from 1991 to 1993 (see Figure 11.10). In contrast to interest rate swaps, where users are more evenly split between banks and non-bank users, cross currency swaps are dominated by non-bank users, because a large proportion of Swiss franc currency swap business is designed to alter the financing and currency terms of Swiss franc foreign bond issues (see Figure 11.11).

In common with interest rate swaps, cross currency swaps have longer maturities than most derivative instruments. Moreover, because of their close connection to the foreign bond market, they have, on average, longer maturities than interest rate swaps. Nearly three-quarters of them mature in more than 2 years compared to interest rate swaps where only 60 per cent have maturities of over 2 year (see Figure 11.12).

Other interest rate-related derivatives

Unlike exchange-traded derivatives, there

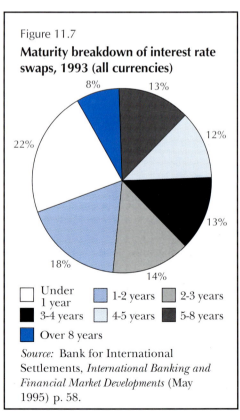

Figure 11.7

Maturity breakdown of interest rate swaps, 1993 (all currencies)

Source: Bank for International Settlements, *International Banking and Financial Market Developments* (May 1995) p. 58.

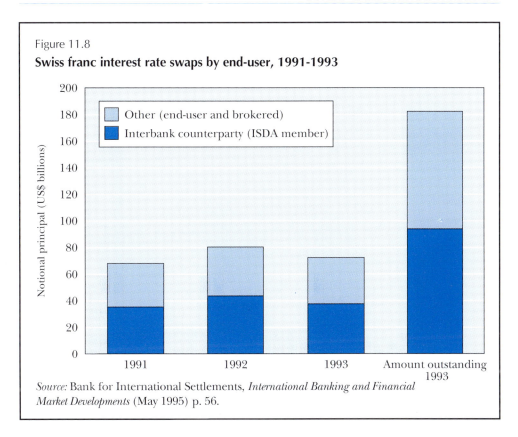

Figure 11.8

Swiss franc interest rate swaps by end-user, 1991-1993

Source: Bank for International Settlements, *International Banking and Financial Market Developments* (May 1995) p. 56.

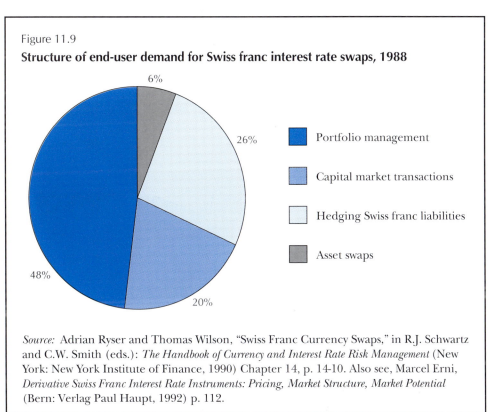

Figure 11.9

Structure of end-user demand for Swiss franc interest rate swaps, 1988

Source: Adrian Ryser and Thomas Wilson, "Swiss Franc Currency Swaps," in R.J. Schwartz and C.W. Smith (eds.): *The Handbook of Currency and Interest Rate Risk Management* (New York: New York Institute of Finance, 1990) Chapter 14, p. 14-10. Also see, Marcel Erni, *Derivative Swiss Franc Interest Rate Instruments: Pricing, Market Structure, Market Potential* (Bern: Verlag Paul Haupt, 1992) p. 112.

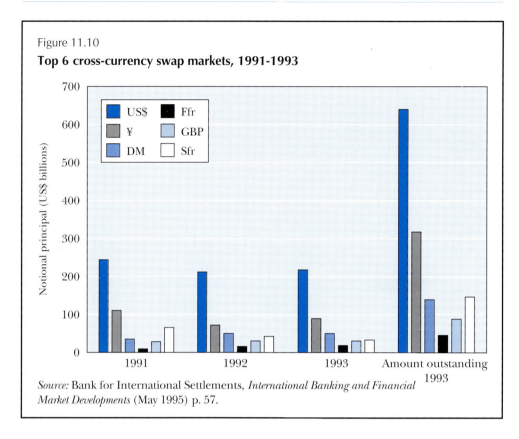

Figure 11.10

Top 6 cross-currency swap markets, 1991-1993

Source: Bank for International Settlements, *International Banking and Financial Market Developments* (May 1995) p. 57.

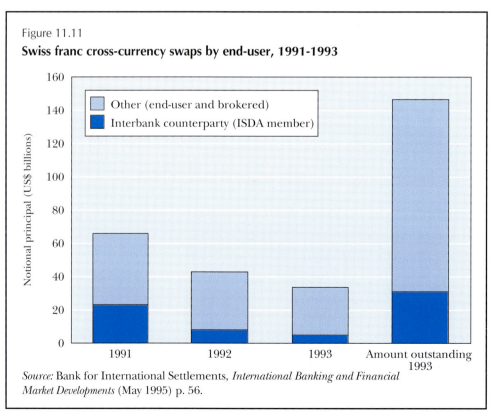

Figure 11.11

Swiss franc cross-currency swaps by end-user, 1991-1993

Source: Bank for International Settlements, *International Banking and Financial Market Developments* (May 1995) p. 56.

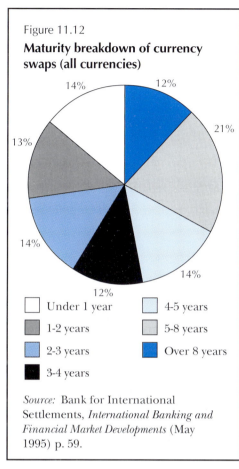

Figure 11.12

Maturity breakdown of currency swaps (all currencies)

- ☐ Under 1 year
- ▨ 1-2 years
- ▨ 2-3 years
- ■ 3-4 years
- ☐ 4-5 years
- ▨ 5-8 years
- ■ Over 8 years

Source: Bank for International Settlements, *International Banking and Financial Market Developments* (May 1995) p. 59.

is scant information on the volume and relative uses of OTC instruments such as Swiss franc interest options, forward rate agreements (FRAs) and interest rate guarantees (IRGs).[28] Options on interest rate-related Swiss franc products cover a wide range of maturities from 3 months to more than 10 years and are heavily marketed by banks to commercial customers. In 1991, they were demanded primarily by institutional investors (40 per cent), banks (30 per cent) and private investors (20 per cent). Corporations accounted for only 10 per cent of total demand.[29]

The Swiss franc FRA market was estimated in 1991 to be Sfr200 billion in size, approximately double the notional size of interest rate swaps and twenty times the size of IRGs.[30] FRAs and IRGs are mainly wholesale instruments that appear to be traded mainly among banks for the purpose of portfolio management and used by large companies for their cash management. The three largest Swiss banks accounted for approximately 35 per cent to 40 per cent of the total trading volumes in FRAs and IRGs (see Table 11.7).[31]

Table 11.12 summarizes the types and maturities of the major Swiss franc OTC and exchange-traded derivatives.

5. Summary of Swiss derivatives

The listing rules (*Kotierungsreglement*) for the Swiss Stock Exchange regarding derivative instruments are virtually identical to the rules for debt securities (see Chapter 9) and equities (see Chapter 10).[32] The only major difference is the minimum capitalization

6. Listing requirements for derivatives

---

[28] Appendix 11-A.1 outlines the information reported by banks to the Swiss National Bank.

[29] Marcel Erni, *Derivative Swiss Franc Interest Rate Instruments: Pricing, Market Structure, Market Potential* (Bern: Verlag Paul Haupt, 1992) p. 127.

[30] Erni, p. 101. On an exposure-equivalent basis (ie, adjusted for duration), FRAs were estimated to be Sfr100 billion, about a quarter the size of interest rate swaps and two and a half times the size of IRGs.

[31] Erni, p. 124.

[32] A fuller discussion of the listing requirements for equity, debt and derivatives can be found in Appendix 1 at the end of this book.

Table 11.12

Type & maturity structure of Swiss OTC- and exchange-traded derivatives, November 1995

	Months			Years										
	0-3	3-6	6-9	1	1½	2	3	4	5	6	7	8	9	10+
Equity-related derivatives														
I. Options														
A. Covered options (Stillhalter optionen)														
• On selected Swiss shares	⇨	⇨	■	■	■	■	■	■	■	■				
B. OTC traded options														
• Options on major Swiss companies	■	■	■	■	■	■								
• Options on the SMI Index	■	■	■	■	■	■								
C. Exchange-traded options														
• SOFFEX Short-term option on Swiss companies	■	■	■											
• SOFFEX Long-term options on Swiss companies	⇨	⇨	■	■	■									
• SOFFEX Low exercise price option	■													
• SOFFEX Short-term SMI option	■	■	■											
• SOFFEX Long-term SMI option	⇨	⇨	■	■	■	■								
II. Futures														
A Exchange-traded futures														
• SOFFEX SMI futures	■	■	■											
Interest rate-related derivatives														
I. Swaps, FRAs and IRGs														
A. Swaps	⇨	■	■	■	■	■	■	■	■	■	■	■	■	■
B. Forward rate agreements	■	■	■	■	■	■								
C. Interest rate guarantees	⇨	■	■	■	■	■	■	■	■					
II. Options														
A. OTC-traded options														
• On short-term interest-earning assets	■	■	■	■	■	■								
• On medium-term interest-earning assets					■	■	■	■	■	■				
• On long-term interest earning-assets											■	■	■	■
B. Exchange-traded options														
• LIFFE 3-month Euro-Swiss franc future	■	■	■											
• CONF-futures (federal bond futures)	■	■	■											
III. Futures														
A. Exchange-traded futures														
• LIFFE Sfr-3-month Euro Swiss franc future	■	■												
• CONF-future (federal bond futures)	■	■	■	■										
Foreign exchange-related derivatives														
I. Swaps														
A. Cross-currency swaps	■	■	■	■	■	■	■	■	■	■	■	■	■	■
II. Options														
A. OTC-traded options														
• Foreign exchange options offered by major banks	■	■	■	■	■	■	■	■	■	■	■	■		
B. Exchange traded options														
• PHLX – Option on spot market	■	■	■	■	■									
• PHLX – UCOM (united cross currency option)	■	■	■	■	■									

Table 11.12 *continued*

Type & maturity structure of Swiss OTC- and exchange-traded derivatives, November 1995 *continued*

	Months			Years										
	0-3	*3-6*	*6-9*	*1*	*1½*	*2*	*3*	*4*	*5*	*6*	*7*	*8*	*9*	*10+*
• LIFFE	■	■	■	■	■									
III. Futures														
A. Exchange-traded futures/forwards														
• CME Swiss franc future	■	■	■											
• CME Swiss franc forward contract	■	■	■											

⇨ Means the time period over which the underlying contract is implicitly covered by the derivative.

requirement for new issues. When options are issued by a company other than the original security issuer, the minimum capitalization must be either Sfr10 million or a variable amount dependent on the total capitalization of the underlying securities (see Appendix 1).

7. Some trends in the derivative markets

So long as Swiss franc exchange rates, interest rates and stocks continue to fluctuate, demand for, and the proliferation of, derivative instruments will grow. Some individual derivatives will die early deaths (like the Sfr3-month Euro-Swiss franc futures contract on SOFFEX) due to a lack of general interest or because of the dominance of one exchange over another, but the one constant in this process of planting and pruning will be the drive to provide better, more flexible and more liquid Swiss franc instruments.

The Swiss derivative exchanges and OTC markets will continue to complement and substitute. They will complement to the extent that they provide overall liquidity for both buyers and sellers to hedge positions in one market by taking opposite positions in the other market.[33] They will compete in as far as exchanges move toward product customization and OTC providers offer greater counterparty security and standardization.

SOFFEX must respond to the challenges ahead of it in a competitive manner. In particular it must take full advantage of the clear trend in the derivative markets toward linking exchanges (especially between different time zones) and extending trading hours. CME and SIMEX formed a mutual offset trading link in 1984. LIFFE and TIFFE signed an agreement in 1995 that enabled Euroyen futures contracts to be listed on LIFFE – effectively extending the trading day of the Euroyen to 16 hours. LIFFE and the Chicago Board of Trade, as well as the Philadelphia Stock Exchange and Hong Kong Futures Exchange have agreed to trade each other's contracts on the respective trading

---

[33] In 1995, the Chicago Mercantile Exchange announced a new facility called a "Swaps Collateral Depository" (an agreement with SunGuard Capital Markets and S.W.I.F.T.) to increase the stability and security worldwide of OTC derivative transactions among commercial banks, investment banks and securities firms. The service includes receiving swap transactions from banks, marking them to market and reporting collateral positions.

205

floors. Moreover, CME, MATIF and Reuters launched the GLOBEX system in June 1992, on which contracts of exchanges from around the world are traded after hours.[34]

In 1993, France's MATIF and Germany's DTB exchanges were linked in an effort to reduce the dominance of LIFFE in England. In early 1995, a working group comprised of the European Union's stock exchanges, plus those of Norway, Sweden and Switzerland worked on a proposal to link and electronically trade Europe's blue-chip stocks. Furthermore, the European Community Investment Services Directive should come into force in 1996, permitting cross-border stock trading. The process of harmonizing such factors as admission regulations, trading rules and other technical matters will not be easy, but there is a trend in this direction. Switzerland will have to participate in these activities or lose its position as one of the global leaders in the derivative markets. To this end in 1995, SOFFEX has been discussing ways to link with the Deutsche Börse AG in Frankfurt.[35]

In the future, the issue of capital backing for off-balance sheet derivatives will be addressed once more. The 1988 Basel Accord recommended 8 per cent backing against risk-weighted assets with the risk weighting varying from 0 per cent to 100 per cent. The required derivative backing was calculated by converting them into credit equivalents and then weighting them. For exchange-traded derivatives, the default risk was so low that the risk weighting was set at 0 per cent. All other derivatives carried a risk-weighting of 50 per cent (ie, Sfr4 of capital had to be held to back for every Sfr100 of derivatives because this equals 50 per cent of the 8 per cent equity requirement).

The problem with the Basel Accord was that it addressed only default risk and ignored market risk. Many observers would like to see the capital backing requirement reflect other risks. A committee of the Bank for International Settlements has been studying this issue in order to make recommendations for the implementation of such a market risk-adjusted system. One of the major problems with any system will be the inability of traditional accounting methods to quantify adequately the risks associated with these instruments.

In the end, derivative use will continue to be controversial until end-users gain experience and establish adequate internal controls. Uses must be strictly defined and excessive risk-taking avoided. Training, better risk measurement tools, control, daily marked-to-market valuations and segregating risks will all have to be accomplished in order to manage these risks successfully.

---

[34] DTB joined the GLOBEX in May 1994.

[35] The proliferation of bilateral agreements has raised the issue of whether these links would be more useful if performed on a multilateral basis. Because of their widespread use, bilateral agreements (as opposed to the multilateral GLOBEX-type arrangements) appear to have the upper hand. Regardless, there is general encouragement of such agreements because they have helped to promote global integration.

Table 11-A-1.1

Existing official data on derivatives market activity in Switzerland

Features of current derivatives business reporting to the Swiss National Bank

Entities covered	All financial institutions subject to the Bank Law
Nature of data	Statistics for monetary policy purposes
Consolidation basis	Consolidated
Valuation method	Notional value
Stock or flow information	Stocks
Periodicity of reporting	Annual
Products covered	OTC
	Exchange-traded (only foreign exchange contracts)
Breakdown domestic/ foreign currency	Only foreign exchange contracts
Counterparty breakdown	Only foreign exchange contracts for resident/non-resident category
	Only foreign exchange contracts for bank/non-bank category
	Risk weights under Basel Capital Accord not reported

Source: Bank for International Settlements, *Issues of Measurement Related to Market Size and Macroprudential Risks in Derivatives Markets: Report prepared by a working group established by the central banks of the Group of Ten countries* (Basel: 1995) Annex III, pp. 6-7.

Table 11-A-1.2

Existing official data on derivatives market activity in Switzerland
Interest rate contracts

Item	*Reporting status*
Aggregate notional value – for all contracts (stocks)	Yes
Detailed Reporting of	
Futures	No
Forwards (FRAs)	No
Swaps	Yes
of which Single currency	No
Cross currency	No
Swap related (floors, caps, collars)	No
Swaptions	No
Options (exchange-traded)	No
Options (OTC)	No
Aggregate replacement cost – for all contracts	No
Detailed reporting of	
Futures	No
Forwards (FRAs)	No
Swaps	No
Swap Related (floors, caps, collars)	No
Swaptions	No
Options (exchange-traded)	No
Options (OTC)	No
Maturity	
Less/more than 1 year	No
More detailed	Yes
Currencies	
Domestic/other	No
More detailed	No

Source: Bank for International Settlements, *Issues of Measurement Related to Market Size and Macroprudential Risks in Derivatives Markets: Report prepared by a working group established by the central banks of the Group of Ten countries* (Basel: 1995) Annex III, pp. 8-9.

Table 11-A-1.3

Existing official data on derivatives market activity in Switzerland
Foreign exchange contracts

Item	Reporting status
Aggregate notional value – for all contracts (stocks)	Yes
Detailed reporting of	
Futures	Yes
Forwards	No
Treasury swaps	No
Currency swaps (principal exchange)	No
Options (exchange-traded)	No
Options (OTC)	No
Aggregate replacement cost – for all contracts	No
Detailed reporting of	
Futures	No
Forwards	No
Foreign exchange swaps	No
Currency swaps	No
Options (exchange-traded)	No
Options (OTC)	No
Maturity	
Less/more than 1 year	Yes
More detailed	No
Currencies:	
US$/DEM	No
US$/JPY	No
US$/Domestic	Yes
DEM/Domestic	Yes
JPY/Domestic	Yes

Source: Bank for International Settlements, *Issues of Measurement Related to Market Size and Macroprudential Risks in Derivatives Markets: Report prepared by a working group established by the central banks of the Group of Ten countries* (Basel: 1995) Annex III, pp. 10-11.

Table 11-A-1.4

Existing official data on derivatives market activity in Switzerland
Equity contracts

Item	*Reporting status*
Aggregate notional value – for all contracts (stocks)	No
Detailed reporting of	
Futures	No
Swaps	No
Options (X-traded)	No
Options (OTC)	No
Replacement cost	No
Detailed reporting of	
Futures	No
Swaps	No
Options (exchange-traded)	No
Options (OTC)	No
Maturity	
Less/more than 1 year	No
More detailed	No
Underlying share prices	
US	No
Japanese	No
German	No
UK	No
French	No
Other	No

Source: Bank for International Settlements, *Issues of Measurement Related to Market Size and Macroprudential Risks in Derivatives Markets: Report prepared by a working group established by the central banks of the Group of Ten countries* (Basel: 1995) Annex III, pp. 12-13.

Table 11-A-2.1

SOFFEX short-term option on shares
Contract specifications

Characteristics	Description
Contract size	5 underlying shares
Tick size	Depending on option prices: Sfr0.10-9.90 minimum tick = Sfr0.10; Sfr10.00-19.80 minimum tick = Sfr0.20; Sfr20.00-99.50 minimum tick = Sfr0.50; Sfr100+ minimum tick = Sfr1.00
Contract months	Current month, the two following months plus next month of the A-Cycle (January, April, July, October)
Exercise prices	At least 3 exercise prices per contract month such that there is a call and a put in-, at- and out-of-the-money. Additional strike prices are introduced on the next trading day if the daily settlement value of the underlying instrument has reached or exceeded (gone below) the average of the highest (lowest) and second highest (lowest) exercise price on the previous day and the residual term is at least 5 trading days.
Trading hours	10am until approximately 5 minutes after close of Zürich Stock Exchange (approximately 4:15pm). Break: 1:00pm until 1:55pm. (No break after the introduction of EBS, and closing time at approximately 4:35pm.)
Last trading day	Third Friday of the expiration month, if this is a working day in Zürich (otherwise previous trading day).
Option style	American
Settlement method	Physical delivery three banking days after the exercise date.
Margin	Premium plus percentage rate of the underlying: – For at/in-the-money options: 10 per cent. – For out-of-the-money options: 5 per cent.
Starting date	May 19, 1988
Automatic exercise	No
Position limits	Yes
Daily settlement value	Base equity: last paid price; Option: last paid contract price. SOFFEX will fix a price if no transaction took place within the hour preceding the close of trading or if the last paid contract price does not reflect the actual market conditions.
As of	June 1995
Category	Equity

Table 11-A-2.2

SOFFEX long-term options on shares
Contract specifications

Characteristics	Description
Contract size	5 underlying securities
Tick size	Depending on option prices: Sfr0.10-9.90 minimum tick = Sfr0.10; Sfr10.00-19.80 minimum tick = Sfr0.20; Sfr20.00-99.50 minimum tick = Sfr0.50; Sfr100+ minimum tick = Sfr1.00
Contract months	January and July with a maximum term of 12 and 18 months.
Exercise prices	At least 3 exercise prices per contract month such that there is a call and a put in-, at- and out-of-the-money. Additional strike prices may be introduced (SOFFEX decision) on the next trading day if the daily settlement value of the underlying instrument has reached or exceeded (gone below) the average of the highest (lowest) and second highest (lowest) exercise price on the previous day and the residual term is at least 5 trading days.
Trading hours	10am until approximately 5 minutes after close of Zürich Stock Exchange (approximately 4:15pm). Break: 1:00pm until 1:55pm. (No break after the introduction of EBS, and closing time at approximately 4:35pm).
Last trading day	Third Friday of the expiration month, if this is a working day in Zürich (otherwise previous trading day).
Option style	American
Settlement method	Physical delivery three banking days after the exercise date.
Margin	Premium plus percentage rate of the underlying: – For at/in-the-money options: 10 per cent – For out-of-the-money options: 5 per cent.
Starting date	June 7, 1995
Automatic exercise	No
Position limits	Yes
Daily settlement value	Base equity: last paid price. Option: last paid contract price. SOFFEX will fix a price if no transaction took place within the hour preceding the close of trading or if the last paid contract price does not reflect the actual market conditions.
	Very attractive to private and institutional investors due to long time horizon and the longer roll over times.
Remarks	As the maturity of these instruments decreases (to 6 months or less), they are integrated into the cycle of short-term options. In fact, the contract was designed to be similar to the short-term contract for that purpose.
As of	June 1995
Category	Equity

Table 11-A-2.3

SOFFEX low exercise price option
Contract specifications

Characteristics	Description
Contract size	5 underlying securities
Tick size	Depending on option prices: Sfr0.10-9.90 minimum tick = Sfr0.10; Sfr10.00-19.80 minimum tick = Sfr0.20; Sfr20.00-99.50 minimum tick = Sfr0.50; Sfr100+ minimum tick = Sfr1.00
Contract months	Nearest 2 months of A-Cycle (January, April, July, October)
Exercise prices	Fixed at Sfr1.00
Trading hours	10am until approximately 5 minutes after close of Zürich Stock Exchange (approximately 4:15pm). Break: 1pm until 1:55pm. (No break after the introduction of EBS, and closing time at approximately 4:35pm)
Last trading day	Third Friday of the contract month, if this is a working day in Zürich (otherwise previous trading day).
Option style	American
Daily price limits	No
Settlement method	Physical delivery 3 banking days after the exercise date
Margin	Premium plus 10 per cent of the underlying
Starting date	May 21, 1991
Automatic exercise	No
Position limits	Yes
Daily settlement value	Base Equity: last paid price; Option: last paid price of underlying share minus Sfr1.00.
Remarks:	Only calls are traded
As of	June 1995
Category	Equity

Table 11-A-2.4

SOFFEX short-term options on SMI Index
Contract specifications

Characteristic	Description
Contract size	Sfr5.00 per index point
Tick size	Depending on option prices: Sfr0.10-9.90 minimum tick = Sfr0.10; Sfr10.00-19.80 minimum tick = Sfr0.20; Sfr20.00-99.50 minimum tick = Sfr0.50; Sfr100+ minimum tick = Sfr1.00
Contract months	Current month, the two following months plus next month of A-Cycle (January, April, July, October)
Exercise prices	At least 5 exercise prices per contract month such that there is one call and one put, at-the-money and two calls and two puts in- and out-of-the-money. Additional strike prices are introduced on the next trading day if the daily settlement value of the SMI has reached or exceeded (gone below) the second highest (lowest) strike price on the previous day and the residual term is at least 5 trading days.
Trading hours	10am until approximately 5 minutes after closing of Zürich Stock Exchange (approximately 4:15pm). Break: 1pm until 1:55pm. (No break after the introduction of EBS, and closing time at approximately 4:35pm).
Last trading day	Third Friday of the contract month, if it is a trading day in Zürich; (otherwise, the previous trading day). Trading ends at 11:30am.
Option style	European
Settlement method	Cash settlement 3 days after the exercise date
Margin	Premium plus a percent of the underlying: – For at/in-the-money options = 5.0 per cent – For out-of-the-money options = 2.5 per cent
Starting date	December 7, 1988
Automatic Exercise	No
Position limits	No
Daily/final settlement value	Base equity: *Daily settlement:* Calculated value of the SMI-Index after the close of the Swiss Stock Exchanges. *Final settlement:* Average of 31 SMI values calculated at 1 minute intervals between 11:00 and 11:30 on the last trading day. Option: *Daily settlement:* Last contract price. SOFFEX will fix a price if no transaction took place within the hour preceding the close of trading or if the last paid contract price does not reflect the actual market conditions.
As of	June 1995
Category	Index

Table 11-A-2.5

SOFFEX long-term options on SMI Index
Contract specifications

Characteristic	Description
Contract size	Sfr5.00 per index point
Tick size	Depending on option prices: Sfr0.10-9.90 minimum tick = Sfr0.10; Sfr10.00-19.80 minimum tick = Sfr0.20; Sfr20.00-99.50 minimum tick = Sfr0.50; Sfr100+ minimum tick = Sfr1.00
Contract months	January and July with a maximum term of 12 and 18 months. Those contracts with maturities 6 months or less remaining are integrated into the short-term option cycle.
Exercise prices	At least 3 exercise prices per contract month such that there is a call and a put in-, at- and out-of-the-money. Additional strike prices may be introduced (SOFFEX decision) on the next trading day if the daily settlement value of the underlying instrument has reached or exceeded (gone below) the average of the highest (lowest) and second highest (lowest) exercise prices on the previous day.
Trading hours	10am until approximately 5 minutes after closing of Zürich Stock Exchange (approximately 4:15pm). Break: 1pm until 1:55pm. (No break after the introduction of EBS, and closing time at approximately 4:35pm).
Last trading day	Third Friday of the expiration month, if it is a trading day in Zürich; (otherwise, the previous trading day). Trading ends at 11:30am.
Option style	European
Settlement method	Cash settlement 3 banking days after the exercise date
Margin	Premium plus a percent of the underlying: – For at/in-the-money options = 5.0 per cent – For out-of-the-money options = 2.5 per cent
Starting date	May 2, 1994
Automatic exercise	No
Position limits	No
Daily/final settlement value	Base equity: *Daily settlement:* Calculated value of the SMI-Index after the close of the Swiss Stock Exchanges. *Final settlement:* Average of 31 SMI values calculated at 1 minute intervals between 11:00 and 11:30 on the last trading day. Option: *Daily settlement:* Last paid contract price. SOFFEX will fix a price if no transaction took place within the hour preceding the close of trading or if the last paid contract price does not reflect the actual market conditions.
As of	June 1995
Category	Index

Table 11-A-2.6

SOFFEX SMI futures
Contract specifications

Characteristics	Description
Contract size	Sfr50.00 per index point
Tick size	*Size:* 0.1 index points *Value:* Sfr5.00
Contract months	Current month, the two following months plus next month of A-Cycle (January, April, July, October)
Trading hours	9:30am until approximately 5 minutes after closing of Zürich Stock Exchange (approximately 4:15pm). Break: 1pm until 1:55pm. (No break after the introduction of EBS, and closing time at approximately 4:35pm).
Last trading day	Third Friday of the expiration month, if it is a trading day in Zürich; (otherwise, the previous trading day). Trading ends at 11:30am.
Option style	European
Settlement method	Cash settlement one banking day after the last trading day
Margin	Initial margin: Sfr5,000 Spread margin: Sfr200.00
Starting date	November 9, 1990
Position limits	No
Daily/final settlement value	Base equity: *Daily settlement:* Calculated value of the SMI-Index after the close of the Swiss Stock Exchanges. Final Settlement: Average of 31 SMI values calculated at 1 minute intervals between 11:00 and 11:30 on the last trading day. Future: *Daily settlement:* Last paid contract price. SOFFEX will fix a price if no transaction took place within the hour preceding the close of trading or if the last paid contract price does not reflect the actual market conditions.
As of	June 1995
Category	Index

Table 11-A-2.7

SOFFEX CONF futures (futures on Swiss government bonds)
Contract specifications

Characteristics	*Description*
Contract size	Sfr100,000 nominal of a 6 per cent synthetic long-term government bond
Tick size	*Size:* 0.01 per cent of nominal; *Value:* Sfr10.00
Contract months	Nearest 4 months of C-Cycle (March, June, September, December)
Trading hours	8.30am to 5pm . No break.
Last trading day	Two days prior to the third Wednesday of the contract month if it is a Zürich Stock Exchange working day (otherwise previous trading day). Trading ends at 11:00am.
Daily price limits	No
Settlement method	Physical delivery 3 banking days after the exercise date
Margin	Initial margin: Sfr1000; Spread margin: Sfr250
Starting date	May 29, 1992
Automatic exercise	No
Position limits	No
Daily/final settlement value	Future: *Daily settlement:* Last paid contract price. SOFFEX will fix a price if no transaction took place within the hour preceding the close of trading or if the last paid contract price does not reflect the actual market conditions. *Final settlement:* Average of all paid prices of the expiring contract between 10:00 and 11:00 on the last trading day.
Remarks:	SOFFEX is publishing a list of bonds that are accepted for delivery
As of	June 1995
Category	Interest rate

Table 11-A-2.8

SOFFEX options on CONF-futures
Contract specifications

Characteristic	Description
Contract size	1 CONF futures contract
Tick size	*Size:* 0.01
	Value: Sfr·10.00
Contract months	Nearest 2 months of the C-Cycle (March, June, September and December).
Exercise prices	At least 5 exercise prices per contract month such that there is one call and one put, at-the-money and two calls and two puts in- and out-of-the-money. Additional strike prices are introduced on the next trading day if the daily settlement price of the underlying CONF future with the same contract month has reached or exceeded (gone below) the average of the second highest (lowest) and third highest (lowest) exercise prices and the residual term is at least 5 trading days.
Trading hours	8:30am until 5pm. No break.
Last trading day	5 trading days prior to the last trading day of the CONF-Futures contract if it is an exchange day in Zürich. (Otherwise the previous trading day.) Trading ends at 5pm.
Option style	American
Settlement method	Opening a CONF futures position
Margin	Premium plus a percent of the underlying:
	– For at/in-the-money options = 1.0 per cent
	– For out-of-the-money options = 0.5 per cent
Starting date	January 28, 1994
Automatic exercise	No
Position limits	No
Daily settlement value	Base future: daily settlement price of corresponding future contract.
	Option: last paid contract price. SOFFEX will fix a price if no transaction took place within the hour preceding the close of trading or if the last paid contract price does not reflect the actual market conditions.
As of	June 1995
Category	Interest rate

Table 11-A-2.9

Philadelphia Stock Exchange cross Swiss franc currency option
Contract specifications

Characteristics	Description
Contract size	Sfr62,500
Quotation	US$ per Swiss franc
Tick size	*Size:* US$ 0.0001
	Value: US$ 6.25
Contract months	*Regular options:* March, June, September, December plus two near term month-end options.
	Month-end options: Three nearest months.
	Long-term options: 18, 24, 30 and 36 months (June and December).
Exercise prices	Three nearest months: At increments of 0.5 cents;
	6, 9 and 12 months: At increments of 1.0 cents;
	Over 12 months: At increments of 2.0 cents.
Trading hours	2:30am- 2:30pm. New York time
Expiration date	*Regular options:* Friday before the third Wednesday of expiration month.
	Month-end options: Last Friday of the month.
	Long-term options: Friday before the third Wednesday of the expiration month.
Last trading day	Providing it is a business day, otherwise the day immediately prior:
	Regular options: Friday preceding the third Wednesday of the contract month.
	Month-end options: Last Friday of the month.
	Long-term options: Friday before the third Wednesday of the expiring month.
Option style	Regular and month-end options: American and European; long-term options: European.
Daily price limit	None
Position limits	100,000 contracts in aggregate
Minimum price fluctuation	US$0.0001 equals US$6.25
Settlement method	Physical delivery of Swiss franc currency.
Margin	Premium plus 4 per cent of contract value less out-of-money amount, to a minimum of premium plus 3/4 of contract spot value, paid in US$ and marked to market daily.
Starting date	January 26, 1983
Automatic exercise	No.

Table 11-A-2.10

**Options on LIFFE 3-month Euro-Swiss franc interest rate futures
Contract specifications**

Characteristics	Description
Contract size	Sfr1,000,000. One three-month Euro-Swiss franc futures contract
Quotation	100 minus rate of interest Multiple of 0.01 (ie, 0.01 per cent)
Tick size	*Size:* 0.01; *Value:* Sfr25
Contract months	March, June, September, December
Exercise prices	At increments of 0.25 (ie, 0.25 per cent), nine exercise prices are listed for new series. Additional prices are introduced on the business day after the 3 month Euro-Swiss franc futures contract settlement price is within 0.12 of the fourth highest or lowest existing strike prices.
Trading hours	08.12am-4.05pm
Last trading day	11.00am – last trading day of the underlying three month Euro-Swiss franc futures contract: two days prior to the third Wednesday of the delivery month.
Option Style	American
Minimum price fluctuation	0.01 equals Sfr25
Settlement	Assignment of Three Month Euro-Swiss franc futures contracts for the delivery month at the exercise price
Margin	SPAN margined. Initial margin charged by the clearing house for long and short positions is consolidated with reference to daily published risk factors and the level of initial margin for the related futures contract (Sfr600), which it cannot exceed.
Starting date	October 15, 1992
Automatic exercise	Fully automatic exercise of in-the-money options on last trading day.
Daily Price Limits	No
Position Limits	No
Exercise	Exercise by 5pm on any business day prior to the last trading day.
Expiry date	Expiry at 12.30pm on the last trading day.
Delivery day	Delivery on the first business day after the exercise day.

Table 11-A-2.11

CME Swiss franc futures
Contract specifications

Characteristic	*Description*
Contract size	Sfr 125,000
Tick size	*Size:* US$0.0001 per Sfr
	Value: US$12.50 per contract
Contract months	January, March, April, June, July, September, October, December and spot month on the first day preceding contract month
Trading hours	7:20am to 2pm (Central time), except on last day of expiring contract when close is 9:16am.
Last trading day	Futures trading shall terminate at 9:16am on the second business day immediately preceding the third Wednesday of the contract month
Minimum price fluctuation	Multiples of US$.0001 per Swiss franc or US$12.50 per contract
Settlement method	Delivered in the country of issuance at a bank designated by the Clearing House. Delivery shall be made on the third Wednesday of the contract month. If that day is not a business day in the country of delivery, delivery shall be made on the next business day immediately succeeding.
Margin	Initial margin: US$2,970 per contract outright positions
Daily price limit	Yes
Starting date	May 1972

Table 11-A-2.12

LIFFE three-month Euro-Swiss franc interest rate futures
Contract specifications

Characteristic	Description
Contract size	Sfr1,000,000
Quotation	100 minus rate of interest
Tick	*Size:* 0.01
	Value: Sfr25
Contract months	March, June, September, December
Trading hours	8:10am-4:05pm London time
APT trading hours	4:24pm-5:55pm London time
Last trading day	11am London time. Two business days prior to the third Wednesday of the delivery month
Minimum price fluctuation	Multiples of 0.01 or Sfr25 per contract
Settlement method	Cash settlement based on the Exchange Delivery Settlement Price (EDSP). EDSP is based on the British Association Interest Settlement Rate (BBAISR) for three month Euro-Swiss franc deposits at 11am London time on the last trading day. The settlement price will be 100.00 minus the BBAISR rounded to two decimal places.
Initial margin	Sfr600.00 per contract
Daily price limit	No
Starting date	February 7, 1991

12

MAJOR SWISS TAXES ON INVESTORS[1]

The Constitution gives the Swiss federal government the right to impose and collect indirect taxes such as customs duties, stamp taxes, the value-added tax and excise taxes, and, since 1940, these rights have been extended to permit the imposition and collection of direct taxes on income. Cantons and municipalities have the right to impose and collect direct taxes on income and capital. The assessment and collection of the federal direct taxes are the responsibility of the cantons, but the Federal Tax Administration retains supervisory powers.

Because of the overlap among federal, cantonal and municipal taxes,[2] the Swiss Federal Constitution empowered the federal government to harmonize the basis of these taxes. In 1993, laws were passed to achieve horizontal harmonization among the cantons,[3] and on January 1, 1995, the government implemented legislation to achieve vertical harmonization between the cantons and federal government.

By international standards, Switzerland is not a tax haven. Swiss taxes are moderate and relatively stable (but with a definite positive trend), reflecting the nation's steady political, economic and social climate. Because of Switzerland's federalist structure, federal, cantonal and municipal governments receive tax income of roughly equal proportions. Just as there are tax laws at the federal level, parallel laws exist for each of the 26 cantons and half cantons. As a result, the after tax return an investor or company earns depends upon the choice of cantonal and municipal residence.

Overview of major Swiss taxes for investors

Investors in the Swiss money and capital markets must pay a variety of different taxes.

1. Important Swiss taxes for investors

Federal withholding tax

The federal government imposes a 35 per cent withholding tax (*Quellensteuer*) on all Swiss capital income: dividends of domestic companies, interest payments of domestic

---

[1] This chapter is based on Swiss-American Chamber of Commerce, *Swiss Value-Added Tax: Ordinance*, English Translation of the Official Text, June 22, 1994. Swiss-American Chamber of Commerce, *Swiss Stamp Tax Legislation* English Translation of the Official Text, 2nd ed., 1993. Arthur Anderson, *Swiss Stamp Tax on the Issuance and Transfer of Securities* December 1993. Price Waterhouse, *Corporate Taxes: Switzerland* 1995. STG Coopers & Lybrand, *Taxation in Switzerland* 6th ed., 1995. Revisuisse Price Waterhouse, *... and now let's sort out the Value-Added Tax: The definitive regulations* 1994. STG Coopers & Lybrand, *Swiss value-added tax 1995: An Overview.* Moore Stephens Refidar Treuhand-Gesellschaft, *Basic concepts of corporate taxation in Switzerland* February 1995.

[2] This overlap is with direct taxes and not indirect taxes.

[3] The process of harmonization is expected to be completed by the year 2000.

borrowers, bonus shares, interest on Swiss bank accounts[4] and even lottery prizes.[5] There is no withholding tax on revenues from foreign sources such as foreign bonds and notes.

For Swiss residents, withholding tax payments are not lost, since they are either reimbursed by the government or go toward the payment of personal tax liabilities. By contrast, non-Swiss residents are unable to reclaim any part of this tax unless their county of residence has a double tax treaty with Switzerland. In 1995, forty countries had negotiated such treaties (see Appendix 12-A-1). Relief from the Swiss withholding tax for interest income is normally equal to, or greater than the relief for dividend income. The only countries that have negotiated exceptions to this rule are France and South Africa. Though complete relief from withholding tax may not be available, in most countries it is possible to apply any non-reimbursed tax payments against local income taxes.

Regardless of their existence, the real value for investors of these double-taxation treaties depends critically upon how rapidly and reliably the authorities refund taxes. Experience has taught many investors that it is preferable to avoid investments where withholding tax duties are involved, if only to save costs.

Stamp duties (issue taxes and transfer taxes)

Swiss stamp duties are taxes on the issuance of securities (*Emissionsabgabe*), their transfer of ownership rights (*Umsatzabgabe*) and insurance premiums (see Appendix 12-A-2). In a September 1992 referendum, the Swiss electorate voted to abolish the stamp duty on money market transactions[6] and to impose taxes that vary with the maturity of domestic notes and bonds. Focusing on bond and money market transactions (rather than equities), the new law imposed tax rates on new issues (capital injection tax) that were different from the taxes on secondary market transactions (the security transfer tax). In addition, the new stamp duty legislation expands the definition of taxable security dealers to include banks, brokers and companies with taxable securities worth more than Sfr10 million, as well as "the managers" of mutual funds.

Table 12.1 highlights the Swiss financial instruments affected by the Swiss stamp tax reforms, and Table 12.2 shows the rates for both new issues and secondary sales.[7]

Stamp duty on the issue of new securities

A 3 per cent issue tax is imposed on corporations wishing to tap the Swiss capital market by either increasing the nominal value of their existing shares, or issuing new bonds, notes, shares, non-voting equity securities, certificates of participation and dividend right certificates.[8] No issue tax is levied against share transactions of foreign companies, nor is

---

[4] Unlike many countries, Switzerland taxes the income on Swiss-domiciled savings accounts regardless of currency denomination.

[5] The tax is imposed only on prizes exceeding Sfr50.

[6] Money market instruments included under this rule are mutual fund certificates, investment certificates and security trading positions of dealers.

[7] Also see Appendix 12-A-3.1 to 12-A-3.4.

[8] If dividend right certificates or non-voting equity shares are issued free of charge, a Sfr3 per certificate stamp tax is imposed.

Table 12.1

Major changes in the stamp tax regulations

Transactions on which the stamp tax has been removed

Capital injection tax	*Security transfer tax*
1. Issues of shares in Swiss investment funds	1. Issues of corporate and cooperative company shares, participation certificates, shares of investment funds and money market instruments by Swiss and non-Swiss debtors in any currency denomination
2. Domicile transfers from abroad to Switzerland	2. Trading money market instruments of Swiss and non-Swiss debtors
3. Issues connected to mergers, spin-offs and corporate transformations	3. Security dealers' trading activities related to their commercial portfolios
	4. Trading of foreign bonds between or among foreign domiciled parties arranged by Swiss dealers
	5. Debenture issues by foreign debtors denominated in a foreign currency or Swiss francs or participation rights in foreign companies[9]
	6. Subscription right transfers
	7. Return of securities for cancellation

New stamp duties

Capital injection tax	*Security transfer tax*
1. Bond issues by Swiss debtors	1. None
2. Money market instruments issued by Swiss debtors.	

Source: "Switzerland shakes up tax code," *International Tax Review* (June 1993) pp. 6-8.

it levied in cases where rights are gained as a result of mergers, changes of legal form, domicile transfers by foreign corporations to Switzerland or conversion of participation certificates into shares.[10]

For bonds, the Swiss stamp tax is assessed at rates of 0.12 per cent for each year or part year of the maximum term to maturity. Medium-term notes are taxed at a 0.06 per cent rate for each year or part year of the maximum term to maturity. Finally, money market paper has a pro-rated, 0.06 per cent tax based on a 360-day year.

---

[9] Share issues by foreign investment funds (Swiss franc-denominated or foreign exchange-denominated) are still subject to the stamp tax.

[10] For PC conversions to be tax free, there must be proof that the stamp tax was paid previously.

Table 12.2

Stamp duty: capital issue tax and security transfer tax

Capital issue tax (Primary market)	Stamp duty
Shares	3%
Long term bonds	0.12% per year
Medium term bonds	0.06% per year
Money market paper	Pro rated based on 0.06% per 360-day year
Insurance premiums	5% per year (1.25% for third party liability and comprehensive vehicle insurance)

Securities transfer tax (Secondary market)	Stamp duty
Swiss securities	0.15%
Non-Swiss securities	0.30%
If one party is a foreign bank or broker	0.15%
If both parties are foreign banks or brokers	0.00%

Source: STG Coopers & Lybrand, *Steuern in der Schweiz* (1995).

On shares of co-operative corporations, the issue tax is due 30 days after their official assessment. On participation rights, notes and money market papers issued continuously, payment is due 30 days after the end of the quarter during which the tax claim arose. In all other cases, payment is made 30 days after the tax claim arose.

Stamp duty on secondary market trading of shares and other equities

The stamp tax must be paid whenever a change in ownership of securities occurs with the help of Swiss security dealers. It is due 30 days after the end of the quarter during which the tax claim arose and irrespective of whether the trades are transacted over a formal stock exchange. For the purchase or sale of foreign securities, a rate of 0.3 per cent is imposed on the Swiss franc value of the security. A rate of 0.15 per cent is imposed on domestic security transfers when the debtor is a resident of Switzerland and the bank is acting as a pure intermediary. Whereas the law requires the dealer to pay, usually the buyer and seller each pay half of the tax. Bonds, bank cash bonds, mortgage bonds, shares, co-operative participation certificates and investment fund certificates are also subject to this tax.

Stamp duty on insurance premiums

In general, a 5 per cent duty (1.25 per cent for third party liability and comprehensive vehicle insurance) paid by the insurer is levied on insurance premiums. There are many exemptions (eg, life insurance along with sickness, accident, transport and compulsory social security insurance) and special applications in this area. The stamp tax is levied on the payment of insurance premiums that are part of the Swiss portfolio of an insurer subject to Confederation supervision or when the Swiss insurer has public-law status. It is also levied in those cases where the Swiss insurer makes insurance premium payments to a foreign insurer not subject to Confederation supervision.[11]

Capital gains tax

The Swiss Confederation and all cantons except Graubünden impose no taxes on capital gains associated with securities (ie, the capital gains associated with moveable property) by private individuals.[12] However, capital gains are taxed as regular income if they are associated with a business activity. Similarly, these earnings are heavily taxed if they involve short-term earnings associated with real estate.

Taxes on savings

Saving by Swiss residents for old age retirement is tax-deductible so long as the funds are invested in certified, restricted-access accounts. Moreover, these funds are not subject to wealth taxes and, until they are paid out, their returns are free from Swiss income taxes. These funds must remain invested until the applicant is at least five years short of the qualifying age for state, old age pension benefits, emigration, early withdrawal for self-use-housing or leave for self-employment. Deductions are limited and depend on whether the individual already belongs to an occupational pension plan.

For saving in non-restricted accounts, both cantons and the federal government provide some relief in the form of deductions (eg, in 1995, Sfr1,300 for individuals, Sfr2,600 for married couples and Sfr500 for each child were permitted as deductions against direct federal taxes[13]). By contrast, the income from free-access savings is taxable at normal income tax rates unless it is part of a retirement plan. In this case, the charge at the federal level amounts to 20 per cent of the normal tax rate, but there are exceptions under Article 204 "Direkte Bundessteuern", Issue 1995 under the heading "Transitional Provisions".

2. Corporate taxes

Income taxes

For all Swiss-domiciled corporations, profits are taxed at the federal, cantonal and municipal levels. The tax rates for Swiss-domiciled companies are based on world-wide income except for earnings from non-domestic real estate and permanent foreign establishments. Since the rates in each canton and municipality vary, the tax burden a corporation carries depends on where the company's headquarters are located. In general, the maximum statutory rates on before-tax income vary between 17 per cent and 32 per cent.

Almost half of all cantons base their income taxes on the ratio of profits to capital and taxed reserves. The other half impose progressive tax or various flat duties. The

---

[11] Swiss-American Chamber of Commerce, *Swiss Stamp Tax Legislation* English Translation of the Official Text, 2nd ed., 1993, p. 12.

[12] Graubünden's tax is imposed if the assets are held less than 10 years, and the sale resulted in gains of more than Sfr5,000.

[13] Even larger deductions are permitted if the individual did not contribute to any other form of occupational pension scheme or restricted-access savings. Married couples must legally and actually live in a state of undivided marriage. The child deduction can also be claimed for a supported person when Article 35, para 1(a) and (b) can be claimed.

Table 12.3

Federal corporate tax

Tax	*Tax rate*
Basic tax	3.63 per cent on all total taxable net income
Supplement	3.63 per cent on all taxable net income exceeding a 4 per cent return on capital
Additional supplement	4.84 per cent on all taxable net income exceeding an 8 per cent return on capital
Total tax liability	**Sum of above taxes (maximum 9.8 per cent)**

municipal tax is typically a fixed multiple of the cantonal tax. In 1995, the direct federal income tax on after-tax profits ranged from 3.63 per cent to 9.8 per cent (see Table 12.3).

Each corporation in Switzerland is taxed as a separate legal entity – the parent and affiliates are taxed separately. The parent company is taxed only on its own income and the dividends received from affiliates.[14] So long as the transactions between a Swiss branch and foreign head office are at arm's length, Switzerland imposes no withholding tax on profit transfers to the head office.

At the federal level, losses from seven business years preceding the tax period may be deducted from net profit. Cantons and municipalities vary their treatment of carry-forward provisions. Loss carry-back provisions are not permitted at the federal level and, among the cantons, only Thurgau sanctions it.

Withholding taxes

In 1995, the 35 per cent federal withholding tax on Swiss-earned income was the only Swiss duty applied at the source level on the Swiss capital market.[15] Its primary purpose is to ensure that individuals who should pay taxes actually pay them. This tax does not apply to royalties, rents, management fees, interest on private loans and foreign profit repatriation.

Relief from withholding tax must be applied for and is given by means of refunds. For Swiss residents (individuals and companies), a complete, 100 per cent refund can be claimed when their income taxes are declared. By contrast, foreign residents may recover

---

[14] According to Article 53 of the "Direct Federal Tax Law", legal entities that are subject to taxation on only a portion of their profits and capital pay taxes on the assets taxable in Switzerland at the tax rate corresponding to their total profits and capital. An entity subject to taxation and with a registered office and place of effective management abroad pays taxes on business operations, permanent establishments and real estate in Switzerland at a minimum rate calculated on the profit earned in Switzerland and the capital invested in Switzerland.

[15] Salaries and wages of foreign labour are also subject to withholding taxes. According to Articles 83 ff of the *Direct Federal Tax Law*, foreign employees without long term residence permits from the immigration control authorities are subject to a withholding tax on all income from the employment relationship. The employer is liable for the tax and deducts it from the employee's wages. Based on economic affiliations, persons domiciled abroad are subject to a withholding tax on earned income if they are engaged in a gainfully-employed activity in Switzerland as a border commuter or with a weekly residence permit. A withholding tax is also levied on the Swiss income paid to artists, athletes, lecturers, members of corporate management, pensioners (on the basis of a prior public employment relationship) and employees in connection with international transport.

the withholding tax only to the extent their countries have double taxation treaties with Switzerland. In most nations, this unrecoverable portion of the withholding tax can be deducted from gross income for tax purposes. Appendix 12-A-1 shows the countries with which Switzerland has a double taxation treaty and the unrelieved portions of Swiss withholding tax that residents of these countries must bear.

Corporate capital tax

A corporation's net worth (ie, capital plus disclosed and hidden reserves) is taxed on the federal level at 0.08 per cent and by the canton and municipality at rates between 0.2 per cent and 0.7 per cent.

Value-added tax[16]

On 1 January 1995, Switzerland abandoned its turnover tax and introduced a value-added tax (VAT).[17] Unless they are expressly exempted from the tax (as postal services and hospitals are), this 6.5 per cent tax is imposed on the value added portion of all transactions in Switzerland involving goods and services. The VAT is reduced to 2 per cent for basic goods such as water, food and medication.

VAT is a tax on domestic consumption. As a result, it is imposed on all imports, but not on exports.[18] In this way, international competition is made more even. Domestic products are able to compete in the international markets without the added burden of this tax, and foreign producers must bear the same VAT burden as domestic Swiss companies.

Capital gains tax

With minor exceptions, virtually all income earned by corporations (including capital gains) is classified as direct income and subject to taxation at the standard rates. The tax on real estate is often treated differently from canton to canton and within a canton, the rate can also vary depending on how long the asset has been held. The capital gains on certain special-purpose companies are not taxed at the cantonal and municipal levels.

Inter-company dividends

For any Swiss joint stock company or cooperative owning at least 20 per cent of the original or ordinary share capital of another company or participation with a current market value of at least Sfr2 million, the profits tax is abated in proportions corresponding to the ratio between the net earnings on such participations and total net profit (see Article 69, "The Direct Tax Law", 1995).

Holding companies

Holding companies are companies whose main activities are the administration of their holdings in other companies or in the shares of such companies. At the federal level, holding companies pay no Swiss taxes on the profit distributions they receive from their

---

[16] See Appendix 12-A-4 for a fuller discussion.

[17] Because this tax was approved by executive ordinance rather than an act of parliament, it can (and has) been challenged by various groups.

[18] Companies must still report all exports.

holdings. Any additional income (such as royalties, interest and capital gains from the sale of shares held in portfolios) is taxed at preferential rates (see Article 69, "The Direct Tax Law", 1995). At the cantonal level, tax rules vary but with two exceptions (Appenzell Ausserrhoden and Neuchâtel), no profit taxes are imposed on these companies, and the net worth tax is imposed at a reduced rate.

Companies with substantial equity interests

A company engaged in a commercial or industrial activity (ie, not a portfolio holding) has a substantial interest in another company (Swiss-domiciled or foreign-domiciled) if it owns 20 per cent or more of that company's nominal share capital or has a shareholding in it valued at least Sfr2 million. To avoid triple taxation (ie, at the corporate, holding company and individual levels), normally, the Swiss federal profits tax (not taxable profit)[19] is abated in proportions corresponding to the ratio between the net earnings on such participations (ie, earnings after administration costs and interest on associated debts) and total net profit.[20]

Domiciliary companies

Under cantonal law, domiciliary companies are companies that are domiciled in Switzerland, but own no real estate, conduct no business and have no business premises in Switzerland. At the federal level, in spite of earning their revenues from foreign sources, they are taxed as if they were normal operating companies. At the cantonal level, domiciliary companies normally pay no profits tax and pay a reduced capital tax (most cantons extend tax concessions to these companies).

Foreign income received

The federal and cantonal tax rate applied to Swiss resident corporations is based on their world-wide income (including real estate income). Foreign-based income itself is not taxed; only income transferred to Switzerland. Dividends, interest and royalties may be handled slightly differently. Unrecoverable foreign withholding taxes in countries with which Switzerland has double tax treaties typically can be deducted from Swiss corporate taxes. The withholding taxes of non-treaty countries can not be set against corporate taxes, but they are deductible for income tax purposes.

Stock dividends

Stock dividends received are not taxable if there is no change in the company's income statement as a result of the transaction. Typically, this means that the stock's book value is recorded at original cost. Stock dividends paid by Swiss corporations are taxable and treated as cash dividends.

---

[19] STG Coopers & Lybrand, *Taxation in Switzerland* 6th ed., 1995, p. 52.
[20] In 2001 after cantonal taxes are harmonized, the same rules will apply to all cantons.

Table 12-A-1.1

Effective tax rate[21] on foreign recipients of Swiss-based investment income that are resident in countries having double taxation treaties with Switzerland

Recipient	Portfolio (%)	Substantial participations[1] (%)	Interest (%)[2]	Royalties (%)[3]
All resident corporations & individuals	Nil[4]	Nil[4]	Nil[4]	
Non-resident corporations & individuals				
Non-treaty countries	35	35	35	Nil
Treaty countries				
1 Australia	15	15	10	
2 Austria	5	5	5	
3 Belgium	15	10	10	
4 Bulgaria	15	5	10	
5 Canada	15	15	15[5]	
6 China, P.R.	10	10	10	
7 Denmark	Nil	Nil	Nil	
8 Egypt	15	5	15	[6]
9 Finland	10	5	Nil	
10 France	5	5/15[7]	10	
11 Germany (profit-sharing bonds)	15[8]	5	Nil	30
12 Greece	15	5	10	
13 Hungary	10	10	10	
14 Iceland	15	5	Nil	
15 India	15	15	15/10[9]	
16 Indonesia	15	10	10	
17 Ireland, Rep. of	15	10	Nil	
18 Italy	15	15	12.5	
19 Ivory Coast	15	15	15	
20 Japan	15	10	10	
21 Korea, Rep. of	15	10	10	
22 Luxembourg	15	0/5[10]	10	
23 Malaysia	15	5	10	
24 Mexico	15	5	15/10[11]	
25 Netherlands	15	Nil	5	
26 New Zealand	15	15	10	
27 Norway	15	5/15[12]	0	
28 Pakistan	35	15	15[13]	
29 Poland	15	5	10	
30 Portugal	15	10	10	
31 Romania	10	10	10	
32 Russian Federation	35	35	35	
33 Singapore	15	10	10	
34 South Africa	7.5	7.5	35[14]	
35 Spain	15	10	10	
36 Sri Lanka	15	10	10/5[15]	
37 Sweden	15	Nil	5	

[21] Tax rate after relief from double taxation.

Table 12-A-1.1 *continued*

Effective tax rate[21] on foreign recipients of Swiss-based investment Income that are resident in countries having double taxation treaties with Switzerland *continued*

Recipient	Portfolio (%)	Substantial participations[1] (%)	Interest (%)[2]	Royalties (%)[3]
38 Trinidad and Tobago	20	10	10	
39 United Kingdom	15	5	Nil	
40 United States	15	5	5	

[1] A substantial holding is considered to arise where the recipient company holds at least the following percentages of the Swiss company's voting power of shares:

Trinidad & Tobago 10%

Finland, France & Germany 20%

Belgium, Bulgaria (not yet in force), Egypt, Greece, Iceland, Indonesia,
Ireland, Japan, Korea, Luxembourg, Malaysia, Netherlands, Norway,
Poland, Portugal, Singapore, Spain, Sri Lanka, Sweden, United Kingdom 25%

Pakistan 33.33%

United States, with some other requirements. 95%

[2] Withholding tax is levied only on the interest on bonds, bond-like loans and interest paid by banking institutions.

[3] At present, there is no withholding tax on royalties or on license and similar fees payable by Swiss individuals or corporations.

[4] The statutory rate of 35 per cent is levied but refunded, provided the respective earnings are declared as income for tax purposes.

[5] Full relief is granted for interest on federal, cantonal, and communal bonds and for interest payments on loans granted or secured by the Canadian export promotion agency.

[6] Full relief is granted for interest paid in connection with sales on credit and for interest on loans granted by a bank.

[7] Relief is 30 per cent, leaving a tax of 5 per cent, except where the French company is foreign-owned and the shares of either the dividend-paying Swiss company, or the recipient foreign-owned French company are not quoted on a stock exchange or traded over-the-counter. In that issuance the relief is restricted to 20 per cent, leaving a tax of 15 per cent.

[8] If the payer is a hydroelectric power company operating under joint concession of Switzerland and Germany, relief is 30 per cent, leaving a tax of 5 per cent.

[9] Interest on loans granted by a bank as from the year 2000 is 10 per cent; otherwise 15 per cent.

[10] Relief is 30 per cent, leaving a tax of 5 per cent if the holding period of the dividend-paying Swiss company is less than two years.

[11] 10 per cent tax on interest paid to a bank or a company owning at least 20 per cent of the paying company's shares.

[12] As long as dividends paid by a Norwegian company are deductible from the company's profit, the tax rate is 10 per cent.

[13] No relief is available for individual recipients.

[14] No relief as long as interest from foreign sources is not subject to South African tax in the hands of South African recipients. If it is taxed in South Africa, relief of 25 per cent is granted, leaving tax of 10 per cent.

[15] The 5 per cent rate is applicable if the recipient of interest is a bank or other financial institution resident in Sri Lanka.

Source: Price Waterhouse, *Corporate Taxes 1995: Switzerland.*

Because it increases Switzerland's issue and transactions costs above average international levels, the Swiss stamp tax has been singled out as one of the most important reasons for the anaemic development of the country's money market. Furthermore, critics feel these duties are responsible for Switzerland's loss of mutual fund business to Luxembourg (which now handles a major share of the Swiss bank mutual funds) and the loss of a significant equity and Eurobond business to London.

To reduce and reverse the outflow of capital from Switzerland to countries with lower taxes, the stamp tax was repealed in 1993. Its abolition immediately increased the liquidity of the Swiss equity markets. Within a few weeks of the referendum, Swiss share trading volume doubled on the Swiss markets. At the same time the trading of Swiss shares in London fell by half.[22] Increased transactions involving bank Nostro dealings were especially noticeable. Fiscally, the abolition of stamp taxes was expected to reduce Swiss tax revenues by an estimated Sfr400 million, but analysts expect that the imposition of new taxes on bonds will partially offset this decline.[23]

The prognosis for the development of a strong Swiss money market is brighter as a result of the stamp tax reform, but foreign competition for Swiss equity trading will continue to be keen, especially for the shares of Swiss multinationals. Offshore trading of Swiss stocks is well-developed, and, in spite of the reforms, stamp duties still apply to about 80 per cent of Swiss securities transactions and will continue to be imposed on all client-related equity transactions conducted in Switzerland.

Appendix 12-A-2

The Swiss stamp tax

---

[22] Economic Intelligence Unit, "Stamp duty changes increase securities trading in Switzerland," *Country Report* August 3, 1994.

[23] *OECD Economic Surveys: Switzerland* (1991/92) p.65, and "Poised to Reveal More," *Euromoney* (August 1992) p. 78.

Appendix 12-A-3

Stamp tax

Table 12-A-3.1

Primary market transactions of foreign bond issues and shares as well as mutual fund parts of foreign investment funds

Domestic stockholders	Sfr bonds w/ foreign non-banks &/or brokers	Sfr bonds w/ foreign banks &/or brokers	Mutual fund parts issued by foreign investment funds	Foreign shares issued by foreign banks or stock brokers
Direct underwriting of the issuer	2 x 1.5%	1 x 1.5%	2 x 1.5%	1 x 1.5%
Placed with:				
Domestic stockbroker	2 x 1.5%	2 x 1.5%	2 x 1.5%	2 x 1.5%
Foreign banks &/or stockbroker	2 x 1.5%	2 x 1.5%	2 x 1.5%	2 x 1.5%
Domestic customers	2 x 1.5%	2 x 1.5%	2 x 1.5%	2 x 1.5%
Foreign customers	2 x 1.5%	2 x 1.5%	2 x 1.5%	2 x 1.5%
Placed on commission for:				
Domestic underwriters	2 x 1.5%	1 x 1.5%	2 x 1.5%	1 x 1.5%
Foreign banks &/or stockbrokers	0	0	1 x 1.5%	0
Domestic customers	2 x 1.5%	1 x 1.5%	2 x 1.5%	1 x 1.5%
Foreign customers	0	0	2 x 1.5%	1 x 1.5%
Own account	2 x 1.5%	1 x 1.5%	2 x 1.5%	1 x 1.5%

Note: Eurobonds in foreign currencies, foreign shares in any currency, money market paper in Swiss francs or foreign currency, that are issued by foreign businesses, banks or stockbrokers are exempt from the stamp tax.

Source: Calculated by authors.

Table 12-A-3.2

Secondary market transactions for domestic and foreign securities: domestic stock brokers as agents

Domestic stockbroker as agent for:	Domestic stockbrokers	Foreign banks and/or stockbrokers	Domestic customers	Foreign customers
With domestic securities:				
Domestic stockbrokers	0	1 x 0.75%	1 x 0.75%	1 x 0.75%
Foreign banks and/or stockbrokers	1 x 0.75%	2 x 0.75%	2 x 0.75%	2 x 0.75%
Domestic customers	1 x 0.75%	2 x 0.75%	2 x 0.75%	2 x 0.75%
Foreign customers	1 x 0.75%	2 x 0.75%	2 x 0.75%	2 x 0.75%
With foreign bonds:				
Domestic stockbroker	0	0	1 x 1.5%	1 x 1.5%
Foreign banks or stockbrokers	0	0	1 x 1.5%	0
Domestic customers	1 x 1.5%	1 x 1.5%	2 x 1.5%	2 x 1.5%
Foreign customers	1 x 1.5%	0	2 x 1.5%	0
With foreign shares and mutual fund shares:				
Domestic stockbrokers	0	0	1 x 1.5%	1 x 1.5%
Foreign banks or stockbrokers	0	0	1 x 1.5%	1 x 1.5%
Domestic customers	1 x 1.5%	1 x 1.5%	2 x 1.5%	2 x 1.5%
Foreign customers	1 x 1.5%	1 x 1.5%	2 x 1.5%	2 x 1.5%

Source: Calculated by authors.

Table 12-A-3.3

Secondary market transactions for domestic and foreign securities: domestic stockbrokers as contract parties

Domestic stockbroker acting as: fund manager, agent and all other stockbrokers as contract party with:*	Domestic stockbroker	Foreign banks and stockbrokers	Domestic customers	Foreign customers
Domestic securities	1 x 0.75%	2 x 0.75%	2 x 0.75%	2 x 0.75%
Foreign bonds	1 x 1.5%	1 x 1.5%	2 x 1.5%	2 x 1.5%
Foreign shares & mutual fund shares	1 x 1.5%	1 x 1.5%	2x 1.5%	2 x 1.5%

Domestic stockbrokers: banks, brokers as contract party with:				
From trade position				
Of domestic securities	0	1 x 0.75%	1 x 0.75%	1 x 0.75%
Of foreign bonds	0	0	1 x 1.5%	1 x 1.5%
Of foreign shares and mutual funds shares	0	0	1 x 1.5%	1 x 1.5%
From own shares or positions with investment character				
Of domestic securities	1 x 0.75%	2 x 0.75%	2 x 0.75%	2 x 0.75%
Of foreign bonds	1 x 1.5%	1 x 1.50%	2 x 1.50%	2 x 1.50%
Of foreign participations and fund shares	1 x 1.5%	1 x 1.50%	2 x 1.50%	2 x 1.50%

* All other stock brokers, domestic corporations, businesses and cooperative societies that have securities as of their last balance sheet valued at more that Sfr10 million.

Source: Calculated by authors.

Table 12-A-3.4

Stamp duty on issues and turnover of syndicate loans and sub-participations

	Debtors with Swiss residence	*Debtors with foreign residence*
Domestic creditors issue and place with more than 10 non-bank sub-participants in any currency	Premium 1.2%/0.6%	
Foreign creditors issue and place with more than 10 non-bank sub-participants in any currency	Stamp tax approximately according to the regulations for placement against commission	
Domestic stockbrokers issue and place with more than 10 non-bank sub-participations for more than one year in any currency		Stamp tax = 2 x 0.75%
Foreign creditors' issues and placements by means of domestic stockbrokers with more than 10 non-bank sub-participations for more than one year in Swiss francs		Stamp tax approximately according to the regulations for placement against commission
Foreign creditors' issues and placements by means of domestic stockbrokers with any subscribers in any amount of sub-participation in a foreign currency		0

Source: Calculated by authors.

Appendix 12-A-4

Swiss value-added tax[24]

The Swiss value-added tax took effect on January 1, 1995. This tax is imposed on the Swiss consumption of goods and services (domestic-produced and foreign-produced). In 1995, the rate on most goods and services was 6.5 per cent. A lower 2 per cent rate was imposed on basic goods such as water, food, non-alcoholic beverages, medication and newspapers.

Since each company is entitled to reclaim the tax payments it makes on inputs, the effective tax rate paid is only on the value added at each stage of production. The turnover tax is imposed on any company that sells goods and services or self-uses goods and services worth more than Sfr75,000 per year. With minor exceptions, imports (even duty free imports) are subject to this tax.

Businesses with annual turnover not exceeding Sfr250,000 and having net taxes (after deductions) not exceeding Sfr4,000 or producing non-VAT-taxable goods are exempt from this tax, as are farmers, foresters, market gardeners, livestock dealers, painters and sculptors. Capital companies, cooperatives, foundations and permanent establishments of foreign companies are afforded special consideration. Domestic firms purchasing foreign services are taxed when the value of such services exceeds Sfr10,000 per year. If closely-related affiliates of a company are considered for tax purposes to be a group, their internal transfers are not subject to the value-added tax. Cantonal and municipal authorities are exempt from the tax-except in those instances where professional or commercial activities are performed.

Exemptions from the value-added tax

The Value-Added Ordinance stipulates that all federal exemptions from the value-added tax are automatically exempted at the cantonal and municipal levels. Examples of businesses (usually services) that have such exemptions are the postal service, health and medical services, welfare and social services, social security transactions, charities, educational, religious and cultural activities, insurance, real estate trading and rental, as well as games of chance and sales of non-profit organizations. Sales revenues generated abroad are also exempt, as are imported goods held under customs control until their re-export, telecommunication services from foreigners, air service to or from foreign destinations, travel agent services if they involve foreign travel and intermediary services for tax-exempt and foreign activities. A limited 50 per cent tax deduction is available for expenses such as accommodations, board and beverages, transport for business trips and all private car expenses.

---

[24] This section is based on Swiss-American Chamber of Commerce, *Swiss Value-Added Tax: Ordinance, English Translation of the Official Text*, (June 22, 1994) and Price Waterhouse, ... *and now let's sort out the Value-Added Tax: The Definitive Regulations* (1994).

13

A REVOLUTION IN AUTOMATION: "FINANZPLATZ SCHWEIZ"

Over the past decade, the Swiss financial markets have been extensively reformed in a transformation without parallel in Swiss history. Laws have been changed, institutions modified, technology improved and out-moded traditions abandoned. In 1996, Switzerland expects to completely implement the world's first national, fully-integrated, electronic security network, and to catapult itself into a technology leadership position in the handling of security market transactions. The new system integrates all the salient aspects of the Swiss securities markets: equities, bonds, derivatives, mutual fund units, fund transfers, trading, clearing, market information and settling.

These changes substantially increase the efficiency of the Swiss securities markets, making them even more internationally cost-competitive and adding a new dimension to the traditional sources of Swiss competitive advantage, such as banking secrecy, quality services and a sound currency image. The improvements are also significant because they support a subtle change of emphasis in Switzerland, from private banking customers to institutional clients. While Swiss financial institutions will still cater to a large private customer base, the efficiencies of the new system will attract large customers that are more interested in low costs, rapid transaction execution and quality reporting than access to investment advice, market research and customized banking services.

The "Swatch effect" has been used to describe the impact of the new financial reforms, analogizing them to the Swiss watch industry's rebirth after SMH broke from tradition by producing a colourful and popular plastic watch. There are compelling similarities between the two. Like the Swatch, the Swiss financial community did not develop any new technologies, but rather combined existing technologies in a state-of-the-art fashion. The innovation came from masterful integration, creating a system that was worth more than the sum of its parts.

In spite of their similarities, one area where the Swatch analogy falls short is the price/quality comparison. The Swatch is a well-built plastic time piece with a competitive price aimed at the low end of the watch industry. In contrast, Swiss financial services (once functioning at significant levels) are aimed to satisfy the most sophisticated needs of the market players at extremely competitive prices compared to other markets. If SMH were able to produce Rolex watches at the cost of a Swatch, the analogy would be complete.

239

1. Components of Swiss financial reform

The new Swiss financial system was constructed with the firm understanding that, to make it work, three major gears had to be built and synchronized (see Figure 13.1); namely, the efficient use of the latest technologies, the creation of modern financial institutions and regulatory reforms governing its financial markets. The development of any one of these components would have been useful by itself, but the only way to unleash Switzerland's true potential was by the coordinated interaction of all three.

Technology and new financial institutions

The Swiss institutional reforms have four major components: SEGA/Intersettle, SOFFEX, Swiss Interbank Clearing and the electronic stock exchange (EBS). SEGA was created in 1970 to handle domestic security transactions. SOFFEX, the Swiss Options and Financial Futures Exchange, started its operations in May 1988, modernizing and developing the Swiss derivatives market. Also in 1988, Intersettle began operations as SEGA's counterpart to handle international (ie, cross-border) transactions. Intersettle was put into operation in 1994, more than one year before the launch of the electronic stock exchange, the final jewel in Switzerland's financial setting. On the securities side of the Swiss markets, the combination of the electronic stock exchange, Intersettle, SEGA and Swiss Interbank Clearing (SIC) provides an unmatched level of sophistication for trading and custody services. On the derivative side of the market, the combination of SOFFEX and SIC provides equal world class sophistication.

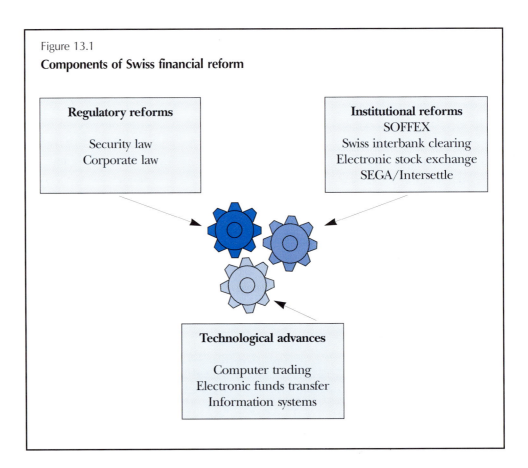

Figure 13.1

Components of Swiss financial reform

Regulatory reforms

Security law
Corporate law

Institutional reforms
SOFFEX
Swiss interbank clearing
Electronic stock exchange
SEGA/Intersettle

Technological advances

Computer trading
Electronic funds transfer
Information systems

Elektronische Börse Schweiz (EBS) is Switzerland's non-profit,[1] centralized, electronic, order-driven system for trading, clearing and safeguarding both domestic and foreign securities.[2] The new exchange will permit the continuous trading of all listed securities, improve Switzerland's compatibility with leading international exchanges and add an important dimension to Switzerland's international capital market position. At an estimated cost of Sfr120+ million, the new exchange is the culmination of many Swiss legislative and institutional changes.

EBS adds substantial liquidity to the Swiss markets not only because it merges all of Switzerland's former exchanges into one, but also because it increases the attractiveness of Switzerland relative to its international competitors. Having broad and deep markets is one of the keys to the future success of EBS. Many investors lost substantial sums during the stock market crash of 1987 because they could not sell their shares quickly on the Swiss exchanges.[3] For many, the memories will take considerable time to erase.

Earnest efforts to reform the antiquated Swiss stock exchanges began in 1988 when trading rules were modified. Daily trading sessions were lengthened; the number of continuously-traded stocks was expanded; the handling of non-continuously traded stocks was improved, and the trading practices of Switzerland's major stock exchanges were coordinated.

Two year's later, a reporting system was introduced to monitor the daily trading volumes on both the stock exchanges and OTC markets. At that time, Switzerland had seven stock exchanges (Zürich, Basel, Geneva, St. Gallen, Lausanne, Neuchâtel and Bern) – clearly sub-optimal in terms of efficiency and liquidity. By contrast, the US had eight stock exchanges and seven futures exchanges. The need for consolidation was clear, and in 1991, the seven exchanges were reduced to three, leaving only the Zürich, Basel and Geneva exchanges still functioning.[4]

This consolidation was only an interim measure. Three exchanges were still too many for a nation of 7 million people. The ultimate goal was to create a unified national exchange. Toward this end, in May, 1993, the Swiss Stock Exchange Association (SSE) was established as the unitary authority for the three remaining exchanges. The SSE ended centuries of fragmentation in the administration of Swiss security trading. The development of the SSE was also significant because it moved the locus of supervision from a regional to a centralized level (as of January 1, 1994), and thereby created the need for national (federal) stock exchange laws.

With the SSE to oversee the three exchanges, attention turned to the most obvious impediment blocking stock exchange reform; the open outcry system of trading. Abolishing open-outcry meant changing the way stock trading business had always been performed. The complete introduction of EBS in 1996 will mean that traders will no longer shout buy and sell orders from a trading pit on the exchange floor. Rather, they

---

[1] The Swiss Stock Exchange charges its members an annual fee to cover costs.

[2] Foreign shares have been traded on EBS since December 8, 1995. It is expected that Swiss shares, Swiss options and all bonds will be traded beginning the latter part of 1996.

[3] "Can Zürich keep up its zip?" *Institutional Investor* (October 1989) p. 338. (Interview with Pierre Mirabaud, partner in Geneva's Mirabaud & Co.)

[4] Floor trading at the Bern exchange was stopped and replaced by telephone trading. The Lausanne exchange was merged with Geneva, and both the Neuchâtel and St. Gallen exchanges were closed.

Table 13.1

Major European exchange trading systems, 1995

Exchange	Country	Products	Market-making	Self-regulation
EBS	Switzerland	Stocks, bonds & options	No[a]	Yes
SOFFEX	Switzerland	Futures & options	Yes	Yes
IBIS	Germany	Stocks, bonds & options	No[a]	Yes
DTB	Germany	Futures & options	Yes	Yes
Super CAC	France	Stocks, bonds & options	No[a]	Yes
SAX	Sweden	Stocks[b]	No[a]	Yes

[a] Voluntary market-making possible

[b] Convertible debt instruments, premium bonds and options.

will sit behind electronically-linked computers (that could be anywhere in the country or for that matter, anywhere in the world). Trades are entered into EBS and the computer system automatically matches the buy and sell orders, fixing the transaction prices.

Once the orders are matched, custody services (settlement, clearing, registration and safeguarding) are electronically channelled through automated clearing facilities. For domestic securities, these functions are handled by *Schweizerische Effekten und Giro AG* (SEGA). International securities and foreign purchases (and sales) of Swiss franc securities are handled by Intersettle. Transferring, safekeeping and managing Swiss securities is simplified significantly because most of them are in dematerialized form (book entries in a computer rather than physical pieces of paper), making settlement virtually instantaneous.

Fund transfers associated with security transactions are handled by an equally automated system. Both SEGA and Intersettle are linked to Swiss Interbank Clearing, a clearing system of the Swiss National Bank. Domestic security transactions that are done through SEGA require only the debiting and crediting of bank balances. International transfers require the additional step of clearing transactions with foreign correspondent banks of Intersettle.

EBS is run on the principles of transparency and non-discrimination. Members have the duty to report spot trades that are done both on and off the exchange,[5] as well as futures trades.[6] Trades are executed on the basis of arrival time, giving small members equal access to the market. In a similar sense, all members receive the same information, at virtually the same time.[7] As a result of EBS, security information quality, completeness and access have taken a quantum jump forward.

---

[5] Off exchange transactions must be reported within 30 minutes of completion. There is an exemption from reporting for shares traded on foreign exchanges for which Switzerland is not the home exchange.

[6] Futures trades for individual shares are done off the exchange and are limited to 12 month maturities.

[7] Because it is technologically impossible to contact everyone at exactly the same time, the order of notification is randomized.

SOFFEX (the Swiss Financial Futures and Options Exchange) has the distinction of being the world's first totally electronic, national exchange for trading, clearing and settling option contracts. It was one of the key building blocks for Switzerland's integrated financial system. In October 1993, SOFFEX became a wholly-owned subsidiary of the Swiss Stock Exchange Association (SSE), allowing for a common organizational structure with EBS.

Though trading volumes on SOFFEX were disappointingly low in its initial years, they have since increased to levels that have made the exchange one of the largest derivative markets on the European continent. In 1994, SOFFEX traded nearly 28 million option and futures contracts. This derivative activity has been helped by a new fee schedule that was introduced in 1993 and its revision implemented in 1995. Not only were fees reduced by an estimated 66 per cent, but they were simplified, as well. The competitive arena for international capital transactions has been constantly changing, and to stay in front of other marketplaces, Switzerland has no option but to produce better, more efficient services. Table 13.2 shows the contracts traded on SOFFEX.

Many analysts feel that a single European market is inevitable. Not only are other nations developing systems that will eventually be every bit as automated as Switzerland's, but they are taking steps to link their domestic markets in order to increase liquidity, expand investment options and coordinate supervision.[8] The process of harmonizing such factors as admission regulations, trading rules and other technical matters will not be easy, but the trend is clearly in this direction. Switzerland will have to participate in these activities or see its financial importance fade.

Table 13.2

Derivatives traded on SOFFEX: traded contracts (as of January 1995) and volumes (1994)

Contract	Volume 1994
Short-term options on Swiss shares	18,315,391
Short-term options on the SMI	6,667,211
Futures on the SMI	1,694,260
CONF-futures (futures on confederation bonds)	949,657
Long-term options on the SMI	120,569
Low exercise price options on shares (LEPO)	50,738
Options on CONF-futures	49,748
Long-term options on Swiss shares	Not offered in 1994
Total contracts	**27,847,574**

Source: Swiss Options and Financial Futures Exchange, Jahresbericht 1994 pp.16 and 28.

[8] In February 1995, Barings International, the oldest merchant bank in the world, failed as a result of derivative losses amounting to almost US$1.24 billion incurred by Nicholas Leeson, a trader in Singapore. Leeson accumulated combined positions amounting to nearly ¥ 30 trillion on both the Japanese and Singapore exchanges. Many analysts feel that such risks could have been avoided if the two exchanges had better-communicated trader positions.

3. Swiss interbank clearing

Swiss Interbank Clearing (SIC) was introduced on June 10, 1987 to speed the clearing of financial transactions among Swiss banks. Immediately, the new system had a substantial effect. By one estimate, 'the velocity of Swiss payments [increased] from three times to 50 times (and occasionally 90 times)'.[9] With speedier payments, banks were better able to optimize their reserve positions and consequently, excess reserves in the Swiss banking system fell. The new system had the additional advantage of materially enhancing the Swiss National Bank's ability to both control and manage bank reserves and the monetary base. In 1995, the daily transactions on SIC were estimated between Sfr140 million and Sfr150 million.

4. SEGA and Intersettle

EBS sends all transaction details through the SECOM system (short for SEGA Communication System) to SEGA and Intersettle for settlement and clearing.[10] Both SEGA and Intersettle are linked directly to the Swiss Interbank Clearing system (SIC) of the Swiss National Bank.

SEGA

Since the early 1960s, Swiss banks have cooperated to reduce the cost of handling securities traded both on the stock exchange and the over-the-counter market. In 1970, *Schweizerische Effekten und Giro AG* (SEGA), the Swiss Securities Clearing Corporation, was founded by 175 banks. SEGA clears, settles and collectively stores securities involving transactions between residents within Swiss borders. Settlement is on a book-entry basis with an almost completely dematerialized security depot.[11] In 1995, SEGA conducted daily payments amounting to about Sfr4 billion.

Since 1982, SEGA has settled its transactions on a delivery-versus-payment basis,[12] and since March 27, 1995, funds have been transferred on a transaction-by-transaction basis via Swiss Interbank Clearing (SIC) through bank accounts with the Swiss National Bank. Simultaneous settlement eliminates many of the risks associated with clearing delays and slow clearing times. Typically, counterparties include ownership transfer and payment instructions with their transaction details.

SEGA's settlement system requires instructions by both the seller and the buyer, as well as the proof of availability of securities and cash. Daily statements from SEGA provide the basis for immediate control by the banks involved. New issues can also be handled through the same system.

---

[9] The Economic Intelligence Unit, *Financing Foreign Operations*, (November 1, 1992) Section 4.2.

[10] SECOM is the electronic data processing system that links SEGA, Intersettle and Swiss Interbank Clearing. It gives one day settlement and provides security settlement and management services.

[11] There is serious discussion in Switzerland over abolishing all paper securities – just as France has done. However, with transaction costs at US$1.95 per transaction, the pressure is not too great to make a quick decision.

[12] Delivery-versus-payment transactions are effective when payment is made rather than after a specified contract period. As a result, they reduce the risk put on custody institutions because they diminish the need for security lending and, therefore, reduce exposure to default risk.

Intersettle was founded on March 31, 1988 with an initial capital of Sfr10 million and more than 130 shareholders. Among these shareholders were the Switzerland's Big Banks,[13] brokerage firms, almost all the regional banks and a large number of foreign banks based in Switzerland. It took six years to establish this clearing system at a cost of approximately Sfr100 million. It was recognized that, because of its highly competitive transaction fees, the only way Intersettle could pay for itself was through large volumes of trades.

In Switzerland, SEGA handles intra-Switzerland transactions and Intersettle handles cross border transactions. Banks and other financial institutions wishing to buy or sell Swiss or foreign securities (denominated in Swiss francs or foreign currencies) settle their transactions through Intersettle. As a result, Intersettle has both Swiss franc-denominated and foreign currency-denominated security holdings and bank accounts.[14] Due to the dominance of Switzerland in the private investment area, Intersettle is positioned to take considerable clearing market share in both international equities and bonds.

Intersettle acts as the bargaining agent for its members (see Figure 13.2), and has established affiliations with 16 major international custodians (see Table 13.3). With an increasing number of users, it will be able to extract economies of scale for its members by negotiating discounts on international custodial service fees.

Intersettle

Table 13.3

Intersettle's global custodial agents

	Country or region	Custodial agents
1	US	Brown Brothers Harriman
2	South America	Citibank
3	Germany	Dresdner Bank
4	France	Société Générale
5	The Netherlands	ABN-Amro Bank
6	Europe*	Citibank
7	*Italy*	*Banca Commerciale Italiana*
8	*Spain*	*Banco Bilbao Vizcaya*
9	*Portugal*	*Banco Commercial Portugues*
10	Africa*	Barclays Bank
11	*South Africa*	*First National Bank of Southern Africa*
12	Japan	Mitsubishi Bank
13	Australia	ANZ
14	Asia	HSBC
15	Canada	Toronto-Dominion Bank
16	UK	Barclays Bank

* Exceptions are listed on the lines below in italics.

---

[13] Today, Swiss Bank Corporation, Union Bank of Switzerland and Credit Suisse own nearly 60 per cent of Intersettle.

[14] Foreigners wishing to purchase or sell non-Swiss securities can transact business through Intersettle. However, such transactions may be at a competitive disadvantage relative to more direct channels.

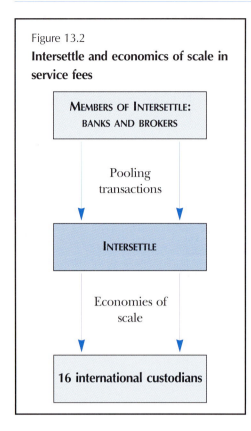

Figure 13.2

Intersettle and economics of scale in service fees

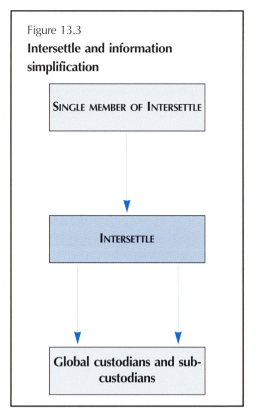

Figure 13.3

Intersettle and information simplification

In addition to offering its members low custodial fees, Intersettle allows its users to streamline their international clearing networks. Without Intersettle, Swiss banks would use dozens or even hundreds of foreign correspondents as local custodians at a considerable cost in terms of redundant overhead. Rather than establish computer or communication links with an assortment of foreign custodians, Swiss members need only connect to Intersettle for their information flows (see Figure 13.3).

It is hoped that the network established by Intersettle will gradually take over the basic international custody services consisting of safe keeping, settlement and clearing of its affiliated members. With its enormous pool of security assets, Intersettle will have significant capacity to offer borrowing and lending services to help dealers and investors avoid settlement failures.

Intersettle is run as a service centre rather than a profit centre. Fees are competitive and at the present time, there are no plans to initiate price-cutting wars or to cross-subsidize transactions. Similarly, Intersettle does not intend to build expertise in repurchase agreements. Until April 1993, the turnover tax (stamp duty) severely restricted the repurchase agreement market in Switzerland. However, further changes in the stamp tax laws could encourage repo activity.

Intersettle does not deal directly with private customers (see Figure 13.4), but rather with banks and brokers. In 1994, it was linked to SEGA through SECOM, an electronic data processing network that is a part of Swiss Interbank Clearing (SIC). As a result, a nationwide electronic web has been created that permits the efficient and accurate clearing of domestic transactions involving funds, securities and cash management services, as

Figure 13.4

Clearing and settlement

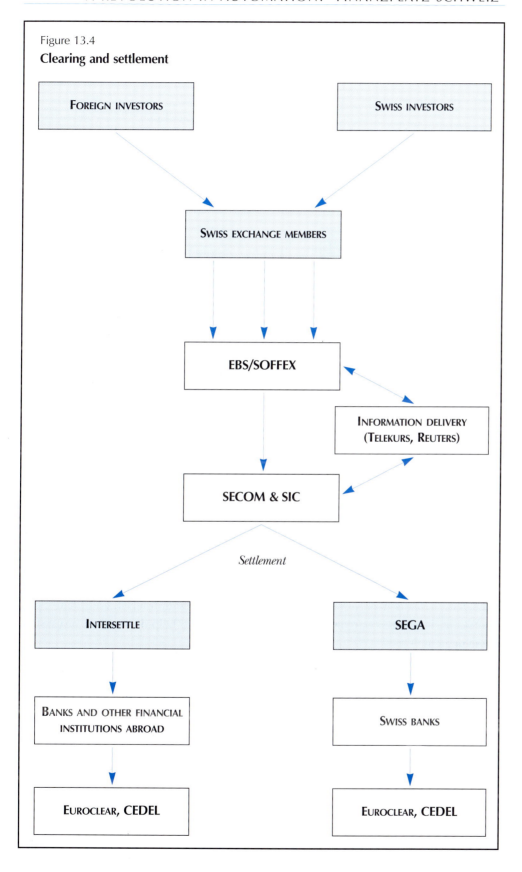

well as borrowed and lent securities. Through SECOM, the same is achieved for world-wide transactions. The Swiss goal is to establish a seamless electronic system with low transaction costs that will make Intersettle an increasingly important player in the clearing world.

Switzerland's forceful move into the clearing and custodial business coincides with an on-going legal battle in Europe to prevent large investors from dealing directly with clearing organizations. If institutional investors win the right to settle their transactions directly through clearing agents and custodial organizations, Switzerland will benefit. In 1994, Swiss institutions had over Sfr2.1 trillion under management. These funds are projected to grow considerably over the next decade.[15] As a result, an efficient custodial system should provide the Swiss financial community with a means of accessing the rapidly growing institutional investor market while maintaining or improving its position with private clients. Even if the institutional business never materializes, quality custodial services are needed to service existing customer needs.

Rivalry among Intersettle, Euroclear and Cedel

Cedel and Euroclear began as international clearing houses for Eurobonds, but have moved into global custody and associated services because of customer demand. Intersettle claims that it will not compete head-to-head against Euroclear and Cedel in the Eurobond market. In fact, it has advised clients with large Eurobond holdings and considerable daily transaction volumes to maintain their Cedel and Euroclear relationships. Rather, Intersettle intends to focus on Swiss domestic bonds and international equities. Regardless of these positioning statements, Intersettle is offering virtually the same services as Euroclear and Cedel, so competition is likely to grow more fierce among these three rivals in the future.

Table 13.4 compares the charges by Euroclear, Cedel and Intersettle at the beginning of 1996. The cost of using Intersettle was substantially above the cost of using either Euroclear or Cedel mainly because of Intersettle's relatively low transaction volumes. It is anticipated that as EBS develops and matures, transactions will increase driving Intersettle's costs closer to those of Euroclear and Cedel.

5. Regulatory reforms to create Finanzplatz Schweiz

Introduction

Having a technologically-advanced financial infrastructure without a modernized tax and regulatory system is a bit like owning a Lamborghini Diablo, but refusing to drive it above second gear. Switzerland made critical changes in its financial system during the late 1980s and early 1990s, but many of theses changes would never have had a chance to realize their full potential unless a host of supporting legislation was passed, with more still to come.

---

[15] Stefan Hepp, *The Occupational Pension Schemes in Switzerland – An Emerging Institutional Investment Force* Dissertation Nr. 1149, Verlag Paul Haupt, (Bern/Stuttgart, 1990) Ch. 3. Also see, B. Gehrig, "Ausländische Privatkundschaft spielt eine dominierde Rolle", *Finanz und Wirtschaft* No. 76, September 25, 1993. Other estimates put the figure closer to Sfr1-1.5 trillion. See, L. Schuster, "Die Rolle der Schweizer Banken im internationalen Finanzwesen", *Oesterreich. Bankarchiv*, No. 7, 1987. Also, see L. Koenig, "Can the UBS Colonels Win the Overseas Battle?", *Euromoney* July 1989, Vontobel, "Schweizer Börsen in internationalen Wettbewerb", *NZZ*, Jan 27, 1990 and, "Switzerland: World Equity Markets", *Euromoney Supplement* June 29, 1994.

Table 13.4

Snapshot of the fee structure among Intersettle, Euroclear and Cedel, January 1996

Transaction cost	Intersettle[a] (US$)	Euroclear (US$)	Cedel(US$)
Transfer of securities between members of the system (per transaction)	8.33[b]	0.50	1.50
Transfer of securities against payments between members of the system (per transaction)	8.33[b]	0.50	1.50
Transfer of securities against payments between Euroclear and Cedel (per transaction)	12.50[b]	1.00	1.50
Deposit of equities[c]	0.065-0.50% p.a.	0.2-0.50% p.a.	0.175-0.25% p.a.
Removal of security from system (per transaction)	8.33[b]	0.50	1.50

[a] Assumes an exchange rate of Sfr1.20/US$.
[b] For Swiss shares and Swiss franc denominated bonds, discounts on these basic fees of up to 50 per cent are possible depending on the number of transactions.
[c] Fees related to custodian domicile, size and market value of the positions (safekeeping with the most efficient markets).

Federal laws were needed to regulate transactions on the newly-created national stock exchange. To enhance Switzerland's attractiveness to international investors (especially institutional investors), regulatory changes had to be made in such areas as shareholder rights, permissible takeover defence tactics and stock exchange admission rules.

To bring the nation into closer alignment with other highly-developed financial markets, attention had to be paid to the growing problems associated with white collar crime in the form of insider trading, money laundering and membership of organized crime groups. Finally, tax reforms were – and still are – among the most important changes needed to globalize Switzerland's financial system. Even with the most technologically-advanced and judiciously regulated financial system in the world, Switzerland's efforts to modernize the financial system will suffer if its tax system acts as a disincentive for dealing on it.

Swiss company law

Reform of Swiss company law took over 30 years to accomplish, but in the minds of many analysts, it was one of the most significant legislative changes in this particular field since St. Gallen enacted the first Swiss trading regulations in 1639. The new legislation revised the company law section of the Swiss Code of Obligations[16] and aligned Switzerland's policies more closely with those of the European Community.[17] Formerly, Swiss company

[16] Obligationenrecht, articles 620-763.
[17] Though its reporting provisions were enacted on July 1, 1992, companies were granted a grace period until 1994 to comply with its requirements.

Table 13.5

Representative stock splits in 1992

	Company/share category	Split ratio	New par value (Sfr)
1	Bär Holding B/R	1:10	50/10
2	Berner Allgemeine R	1:5	100
3	Cementia B	1:5	20
4	Ciba Geigy B/R	1:5	20
5	Helvetia R	1:5	50
6	Logitech R	1:10	20
7	Maag B	1:4	50
8	Merkur R	1:5	25
9	Phoenix Mecano B	1:10	10
10	Sulzer R	1:10	100
11	Surveillance B/R	1:5	100/20
12	UBS B/R	1:5	100/20
13	Warteck Invest R500	1:5	100
14	Warteck Invest R1000	1:10	100

Abbreviations
Note: B = Bearer share; R = Registered share; P = Participation certificate

law was written to protect the rights of creditors (especially banks). The new law is more balanced and focuses on shareholder (especially minority shareholder) rights.

The revised Swiss Company Law materially improves the transparency of Swiss company operations. For the first time in the nation's history, a law exists mandating listed companies to publish audited and consolidated financial reports. Furthermore, the law strengthens shareholder protection, reduces the chances of corporate trading abuses, simplifies the means of securing capital and limits takeover defence tactics.

Many of the changes were made to broaden Switzerland's appeal to international investors, but retail also benefitted from the new regulation. The new law permits companies to issue shares with minimum nominal values as low as Sfr10 per share (down from the previous threshold of Sfr100 per share). Soon after the change, numerous companies split their shares, thereby reducing share prices with the intention of making them more appealing to small investors (see Table 13.5).

To address the criticism that Switzerland was unappealing because of its wide variety of stock instruments (especially for small companies),[18] share categories were reduced by some companies to accommodate the investment community.[19]

Although the investment community had already turned against PCs, they were more stringently regulated causing many public companies to abandon them. Prior to the new Swiss Equities Law, corporations could freely choose the total nominal value of shares relative to the total nominal value of their other securities (eg, participation certificates).

[18] This view was expressed by Pierre Mirabaud in "Can Zurich keep its zip?" *Institutional Investor*, (October 1989) pp. 337-338.

[19] The share categories remained the same by law.

The new rules limit the amount of equity a company is able to issue in the form of participation certificates to a maximum of 200 per cent of the share capital in the form of bearer or registered shares.[20] Moreover, the new rules permit new voting shares (ie, shares that have the same voting rights but a lower par value) to be issued only if the nominal value of the common stock does not surpass ten times the nominal value of the "voting shares".[21]

Shareholder disclosure has also been made more transparent. Unless company articles of incorporation stipulate a lower reporting level, corporations are now required under Article 663c of the new Law to publish in their annual reports the identity of shareholders (individuals or groups) who own more than 5 per cent of their shares. In practice, this obligation of the company will be complemented by the investors' obligation to report such 5 per cent plus holdings under the new stock exchange law.

The new Swiss company law also enhances the rights of minority shareholders who allegedly have been refused pertinent business information by a company's board of directors. In cases where the board of directors refuses such requests and the General Meeting supports the minority shareholder position, a majority vote of the shareholders can trigger a court-appointed special auditor to collect the information.

If the General Meeting does not support the petition, minority shareholders controlling at least ten per cent of the share capital or owning shares with a nominal value of at least Sfr2 million can ask a competent judge to appoint an independent special auditor. In these cases, the minority shareholders must substantiate the allegation that the company has violated either a law or the articles of incorporation. Information obtained through these means can be used only for the specific purposes petitioned.

Under the old law and also under the new one, Swiss companies with registered shares are able to prevent takeovers by making the transfer of stock subject to the approval of their boards. Under the old law, no justification was required when such transfers were refused.[22] The new laws constrain corporations' ability to refuse share registration with voting power. In the case of a listed company, such a refusal is permitted only when its articles of association provide for a percentage limit or the acquirer does not expressly declare that he/she bought the shares in his/her own name and for his/her own account or under certain circumstances, only if registration would violate another Swiss federal law (eg, Lex Friedrich or the Banking Laws).

Corporate restrictions on voting are permitted if a company's articles of association provide that no shareholder should be allowed to vote more than a certain percentage of total votes (regardless of whether he owns them or acts as a proxy).[23] As a result, companies have a *de jure* ability to restrict takeovers by writing restrictive articles of association.

---

[20] Prior to this Act, PCs were a virtual no man's land in the Swiss capital markets, varying from company to company. They had no standard nominal value relative to the voting shares and at some companies, holders had no right to attend annual shareholder meetings. (See "Non-Voting Shares; Swiss Companies Find PCs a Convenient Vehicle for Raising Fresh Capital Without Having to Worry About Losing Management Control", *Euromoney Corporate Finance* (November 17, 1986) p. 83.

[21] Peter Kurer, Heinz Schärer and Eveline Oechslin, "International M&A Supplement: Switzerland," International Financial Law Review (September 1992) pp. 57-62.

[22] In these cases, the ownership was vested in the buyer and the voting rights remained with the seller. See, Carlo Lombardini, "Swiss stock exchanges: what does the future hold?", *International Financial Law Review* (August 1989) pp. 33-36.

[23] Peter Kurer, Heinz Schärer and Eveline Oechslin, "International M&A Supplement: Switzerland," *International Financial Law Review* (September 1992) pp. 57-62.

Similarly, Article 659SS of the Swiss Company Law addresses a company's ability to purchase its own shares. The new rules permit such purchases, but limit them, under normal conditions, to 10 per cent of the total outstanding shares and to 20 per cent in connection with a takeover defence, and require that they be disclosed in the Annual Report.[24]

One area of weighty concern has to do with the quality of figures reported by Swiss companies. Under the new law, figures must meet the test of reliability rather than the "true and fair" criterion.

Securities Trading Law (a.k.a. stock exchange law)

In 1995, both houses of Parliament passed the Federal Securities Exchanges and Trading Act (SEA) in order to regulate the Swiss stock exchange and securities trading, thereby bringing Switzerland closer to the trading practices of the US and well ahead of most other nations with highly-developed capital markets. The final version of the law was passed in April 1995 by the Swiss legislature, and enactment is scheduled for 1 January 1997.

The purpose of this law is to regulate: the national Swiss stock exchange, brokers and security dealers, public takeovers and the rights of minority shareholders and the disclosure of investor information. It is notable that the codification of these rules has followed rather than led the general Swiss trend of the past decade toward greater disclosure and stronger shareholder rights.[25] Passage of the law will ensure more equal treatment among all holders of the same shares in a takeover bid.[26]

It will replace the separate cantonal regulations that existed in the past, and it will create national standards of protection for investors.[27] With no federal securities trading regulations until 1995, there was no federal authority to oversee the securities trading. In addition to the cantonal supervisors, some limited control was exercised by the Swiss Banking Commission, but its jurisdiction extended only to banks. The provisions of the Federal Securities Exchanges and Trading Act (SEA) do not provide for a large national regulatory body equivalent to the US Securities and Exchange Commission. Rather, a lean oversight body within the Swiss Banking Commission will take on such responsibilities. Matters dealing with admission of new stocks, as well as the surveillance of transactions and the organization of trading, will be handled by the respective Admissions Board.

The old securities trading laws had clear and visible shortcomings. Among them were the lack of capital requirements for security-trading firms; absence of information disclosure when individual shareholders controlled a significant portion of the stock and a paucity of rules governing tender offers. The new SEA is a milestone in a series of regulatory efforts that began in Switzerland during the late 1980s.

---

[24] The extra 10 per cent, that is allowed in a takeover defence, must be resold within two years, or be declared void.

[25] In 1988, Nestlé dropped restrictions on foreign ownership of its shares. Since then other large multinationals have followed. In 1990, Roche Holding AG, which had no restrictions, introduced International Accounting Standards.

[26] The Act was stimulated, in part, by Klaus Jacob's private sale of Jacobs Suchard Corporation shares to Phillip Morris. Jacob received Sfr3,645 per share while minority shareholders received Sfr1,660 per share. Interestingly, a company has the possibility to avoid the appliance of the respective provisions of the new law if its articles of incorporation exclude them.

[27] Zurich, Basel and Geneva had laws regulating their stock exchanges, but, in Bern, Lausanne, Neuchâtel and St. Gallen, the exchanges were self-regulating.

In 1986, Basel, Geneva and Zurich began to homogenize the regulations for admission to their stock exchanges. The new rules defined the amount of share capital needed and established disclosure requirements. In 1989, the Swiss Stock Exchanges initiated the Swiss Takeover Code. The Code is a private and voluntary agreement among stock exchange members with respect to handling public takeovers. It mandates disclosure requirements, as well as a minimum and maximum offer duration.[28] The Code imposes restrictions on withdrawing and altering bids, counter offers and waiting periods after an unsuccessful bid. In 1991, the Code was extended to include participation certificates. Furthermore, it tried to impose the requirement that all shareholders receive equal treatment. Included are rules that stipulate *pro rata* allocations for tender offers and the obligation to purchase all tendered shares if a takeover offer becomes unconditional and the purchase increases the acquirer's control to over 50 per cent of the target company's voting rights.

Under Article 30 of SEA and those following, anyone acquiring stocks is required to make a public tender offer if their participation exceeds the threshold level of 33.3 per cent of the voting rights. There is an exception to this rule when organized groups of shareholders are acting contractually. Under Article 51, shareholders owning more than one-third of a company's stock, but less than half, are required to make a public offer to all shareholders if they acquire enough shares to take them above the 50 per cent threshold. Moreover, the price offered for such shares may not be more than 25 per cent below the highest price paid by the offering party over the preceding 12-month period. Articles 30 and 51 do not apply to companies that opt out of these provisions by incorporating exclusionary language in their articles of association within two years after this law became effective. [29]

Disclosure is another major issue addressed by the new law. In the past, Swiss companies had to abide by Swiss Code of Obligations (old Article 631) requirement that only a prospectus be filed before a new stock issue. Because foreign companies were not subject to these rules, they fell under the harsher restrictions imposed by the stock exchanges. The new law provides equal treatment of domestic and foreign companies.

Two other dimensions of the SEA deal with shareholder disclosure rules and stock price manipulation. Under the new law, a declaration of shareholder identity must be made when his/her voting rights reach 5 per cent. In addition, it outlaws explicitly price manipulations by means of false information on trades and authorizes regulatory cooperation with foreign supervisory authorities.

---

[28] Peter Kurer, Heinz Schärer and Eveline Oechslin, "International M&A Supplement: Switzerland," *International Financial Law Review* (September 1992) pp. 57-62

[29] See Jan Atteslander, "Investor Relations: Changing the rules," *swissBusiness*, (July/August 1994) pp. 10-13.

Appendix 1

MAJOR RULES FOR LISTING SECURITIES ON THE SWISS STOCK EXCHANGE[1]

In 1996, the unification of Switzerland's three remaining stock exchanges and the introduction of EBS should be accompanied by new listing rules (*Kotierungsreglement*, expected to enter into force in spring 1996) for shares, debt securities and derivatives on the Swiss Stock Exchange. The purpose of listing rules is to ensure that all qualified issuers (and all other market players) have unrestricted and equal access to the Swiss capital markets. They should protect investors and all other market players, by providing transparent and sufficient information, without overburdening issuers with excessive costs. For the investors, it is essential to make their decisions on the basis of complete information.

Overview

Supported by the new Federal Stock Exchange Law (entering in legal force by 1997) and the Swiss Stock Exchange Statutes, the Admissions Board (*Zulassungsstelle*) of the Swiss Stock Exchange determines the rules for admitting securities to the exchange and ensures that issuers adhere to these rules. The Swiss Admissions Board rules on such matters as admission expiry, suspension, cancellation and sanctions.[2] Moreover, it has the power to refuse a listing application if it is deemed not to be in the interest of the public, the exchange or the market participants.

1. Swiss Admissions Board

Each potential issuer is required to publish a prospectus that gives sufficient information for any investor to make well-founded decisions about the security being listed and offered. Disclosures must provide a true and fair view of the company's actual position with respect to assets, liabilities and the other aspects of the actual financial situation, as well as profits and losses. Moreover, the accounts must be in compliance with the rules

2. Conditions for listing

---

[1] This information is based on Swiss Admission Board, Complete Revision of the Listing Rules: Consultative Document, Draft Version 1.0 13.02.95, January 1995.

[2] The Admission Board has the power to ask for information above the minimum requirements published in *Kotierungsreglement*.

255

governing accounting standards (eg, regarding consolidation, foreign exchange translation, valuation, cash flow accounting, provisions and notes to accounts).

Within the broad boundaries established by the Swiss Admissions Board, companies have considerable flexibility in how they comply with reporting requirements. For instance, issuers have the option to make disclosures following non-Swiss accounting rules or guidelines (eg, IAS, EU-4 or EU-7), so long as these rules meet Swiss standards. Consequently, companies have a certain liberty to select, present and structure the information they make public. Furthermore, issuers can publish their prospectus either in German, French, Italian or English by means of two or several nationally-circulated newspapers.[3] Alternatively, disclosure can be made by means of a free brochure or pamphlet with a public announcement of its availability.

Listing notices must be made in German and French in two or more national newspapers, and must contain the following minimum information:

- name and address of the issuer and/or third party guarantor,
- class, nominal amount, number and denomination of the issue,
- summary information of the offer's main conditions,
- any material deviations from normal market practices or other important information needed for an informed investment decision,
- relevant new information subsequent to the initial disclosures,
- disclosure of any other stock exchanges where the stock is already listed or applied for,
- the security's number and ISIN code,
- specifics about where additional information is available,
- caveats that only the prospectus is relevant for the listing,
- date of publication, and
- caveat that the listing notice is not a prospectus according to the law.

The disclosure conditions for maintaining a security's listing on the Swiss Stock Exchange involve the publication of an annual report and auditor's report as well as interim reports on financial standing. The annual report must be published within six months of the end of the financial year and filed with the Admissions Board at latest, on the date of its publication. It must include a status report, balance sheet, profit and loss statement and cash flow statement, as well as notes to the accounts. These reports must be made available to anyone who requests them. The interim report is a semi-annual statement of a company's business activities and financial condition during the first six months of the financial year. It must be published within four months of the end of the relevant period.

Though there are slight variations in the Swiss Listing Rules for equities, debt securities and derivatives with respect to minimum capitalization, distribution and security

---

[3] Exemptions from publication apply in cases where the increase in share capital is less than 10 per cent of outstanding nominal or market value, or equity allotments are made to employees or previous publication was made within three months and gives the same quality of information.

information disclosures, for the most part, the requirements are the same.[4] The Swiss Admissions Board requires that debt securities have a minimum nominal value equal to Sfr20 million and that publicly-disclosed information for listing purposes cover a period of three complete financial years. Exceptions can be made by the Admissions Board.

When a company wishes to list its securities (debt, equity or derivative) on the Swiss Stock Exchange, it must provide in the listing prospectus:

- **general information on the issuer**, including the registered and head office, date of incorporation, legislation and legal form under which the company operates, principal objects, register and date of inscription as well as published ratings, if available.

- **information on groups**, (if the issuer is the parent undertaking of a group) including business activities and investment policy on a consolidated basis;

- **capital and voting rights**, including such information as amount, number and class of equity securities, dividend rights, preference rights, voting rights and restrictions, the number of shares and total nominal value of capital not fully paid in, maximum amounts of authorized and conditional capital, number and characteristics of profit sharing certificates, characteristics, amount and maturity of outstanding loans,[5] convertible loans and warrants along with exercise prices, and conversion ratios,[6] any unusual provisions regarding articles of association, description of all capital changes over the past three years, main shareholders[7] and cross-company holdings to the extent they are known;

- **business activities**, including, principal operations, major products/services sold, new products and/or activities, net turnover during the past two financial years[8] broken down by activity and geographic markets, location and size of principal establishments,[9] notable real estate owned, exploitable reserves (in cases of raw material producers such as mining and energy), as well as summary information on material patents, licenses, contracts and/or new manufacturing processes;

- **new business activities**, such as R&D of new products and processes over the past three years, pending legal actions or arbitration, business interruptions and employment numbers over the past three years;

- **investment policies**, including equity investments over the past three

---

[4] For instance, there is no difference among the three types of securities with respect to negotiability, denomination, documentation, publication, listing contents, notification, charges for sponsoring and maintaining listings, accounting provisions, expiry, suspensions, cancellations, sanctions and means of legal redress.

[5] For equity issues, the amount, maturity, exercise price and conversion ratio of outstanding convertible debt and warrants by the issuer or subsidiary must also be reported.

[6] Loan information may be summarized by giving average interest, value date and currency.

[7] Main shareholders are individuals or groups with voting rights above 5 per cent of the total. Company articles of association can stipulate lower percentages.

[8] For new equity issues, the net turnover information must be provided for three financial years.

[9] A principal establishment contributes more than 10 per cent of total turnover.

years, principal investments along with geographical distribution, method of financing and principal future investments;[10]

- **balance sheet, profit and loss statement and cash flows** for the past two financial years;[11]

- **corporate information**, including names and functions of administrative, management and supervisory individuals, partners with unlimited liability and founders, if the company was founded less than 5 years before the issue;

- **holdings, interests and loans owned by members of management and supervisory bodies**, including rights granted to these individuals on the basis of such financial transactions, potential conflicts of interest in transactions between the issuer and these individuals as well as loans by the issuers to members of management or to supervisory bodies;

- **the terms of the loan (for debt issues)**, including the nominal amount or its variable nature, currency denomination, issue and redemption prices, interest rate,[12] duration, method of repayment, early retirement possibilities, due dates, allocation procedures for advantages, if any, explanations of all guarantees[13] and subordination of securities to other debt, place of jurisdiction, legislation under which the securities were issued and information on the trustees in an intermediary role, if any;

- **security information**, including the nature of the issue,[14] lead underwriter,[15] nominal value and number of rights created and/or issued, conditions for options, if applicable and exercise agent, nominal value and number of rights created and/or issued, paying agents, tax information, security form (ie, bearer or preference), transfer information and restrictions of other stock exchanges on which securities are listed (or applied for) and persons responsible for the particulars listed in the offering;

- **information on underlying securities of derivatives,** including price movements during the past five years and restrictions on the purchase of the underlying securities,[16] permanent global certificate restrictions, if applicable, and information on transferring uncertificated securities.

- **Convertible issues** may be listed on the Swiss Stock Exchange if the underlying shares have already been admitted or if they are simultaneously being admitted to the Swiss Stock Exchange. There are multi-

---

[10] Anticipated acquisitions need not be disclosed.

[11] For new equity issues, this information must be provided for three financial years.

[12] For variable rate loans, the periods and conditions for fixing must be included.

[13] Guarantees or indemnities or keep-well agreements of a third party must be published literally and in their entirety.

[14] For options issued by third parties, mention must be made of whether it is for own account or the account of a third party,

[15] For debt and derivative issues, reserved blocks for simultaneous foreign issues must also be reported, as must price movements over the past five years, if available.

[16] Shares already listed only need furnish a statement that up-to-date information is available free of charge. Foreign issues not listed on the main exchange must provide all information required to list the security.

tiered disclosure hurdles that such instruments must overcome before they can be listed. The issuers of convertible securities must conform to the information requirements for equity securities; the convertible debt issue itself must conform to the requirements for debt securities and, finally, the conversion options must conform to the information requirements for derivatives.[17]

- When the options are issued by a company other than the original security issuer, the minimum capitalization requirements must meet the following criteria at the time of issue or listing:

Special listing rules for options

1. The minimum total option capitalization must be Sfr10 million, or
2. The minimum capitalization of the underlying securities must amount to at least:
    A. Sfr100 million in the case of loans, or
    B. Sfr50 million for Swiss equities that are part of the SMI, or
    C. Sfr25 million for Swiss equities that are not part of the SMI, or
    D. Sfr50 million for foreign equity securities, or
    E. Sfr2 million for shareholders' options on further issues of the same issuer, or
    F. For options on debt security issues with warrants, the aggregate capitalization of the loans is used for determining the minimum capitalization required.

- Information must be provided on total amount, denomination, rights attached to options (especially whether cash settlement), duration, exercise methods, exercise date and time, exercise limitations, anti-dilutive provisions, conditions for adjusting option conditions, securities pledged to option writers, methods of making shares available by companies issuing options on own shares, description of guarantees, if any, legislation under which the securities are issued, applicable law and jurisdiction. For the issuer of shareholder options, information disclosures must conform to the requirements for equity securities and the disclosures for the options themselves must conform to the rules for derivatives.
- In addition to the above-mentioned rules, warrants face multi-tiered disclosure requirements, as well.

---

[17] Moreover, if the subscription rights to equity of another issuer are any part of the conversion options, then information about that issuer must be provided in accordance with the information requirements for equity securities.

Appendix 2

SWISS SECURITY LENDING

Securities lending began in Switzerland in 1983, when Swiss domestic securities (subject to withholding tax) were exempted for this purpose from the federal turnover tax (*Umsatzabgabe*) by the Federal Tax Administration.[1] The most rapid growth has occurred since 1990. Typically, institutional investors and private investors with substantial holdings of securities are offered these services in connection with derivative and arbitrage transactions or as a means of ensuring that trades are executed smoothly.

Overview

Under Swiss federal law, borrowers obtain full title to securities. While lenders lose ownership rights, they retain a claim to have the same security or securities of equal kind and value returned at the contract termination date. Contractually, the borrowers are usually required to cover fully or guarantee the value of the transferred securities with collateral in cash, securities and/or bank guarantees. Should the securities rise in value, borrowers are required to increase their collateral or guarantees.

1. Legal conditions of security lending

For securities borrowed by third parties, banks prefer to act as agents rather than principals, thereby permitting them to carry the transactions off balance sheet as contingent assets and liabilities. Banks lend the securities to borrowers who in turn re-lend them to third parties. As a rule, banks have the added responsibility to act as the lenders' trustees. In addition, they serve as marketing agents, finding borrowers with good financial standing, as well as providing financial services, such as marking-to-market and ensuring that securities are covered by sufficient collateral.

By pooling customers' securities, banks are able to meet large customers' needs. At the same time, this enables small customers to share in transactions that may otherwise be out of their reach. These lending pools do not have independent ownership rights. Individuals retain full ownership until the securities are transferred to the borrower. At that point, borrowers acquire the voting rights, as well as the dividends, interest and other financial returns. The lenders are usually entitled to receive compensation from the borrowers.

Should the borrower declare bankruptcy, Swiss federal law requires that the liability be converted into a pecuniary claim of equivalent value.[2] After bankruptcy has been

---

[1] There is no transfer of ownership, only a transfer of legal title.
[2] Regardless, the bankruptcy office (*Konkursverwaltung*) may choose to have the obligation converted into money terms.

261

declared, lenders and borrowers are prohibited from entering into agreements that would offset claims and/or counterclaims. Since lenders are entitled to receive full compensation for the securities lent, banks usually offer a guarantee to make up the difference if there is any deficiency.

2. Federal cantonal and local restrictions on security lending

Under Swiss federal, cantonal and local laws, few restrictions apply to security lending activities. Because these transactions are classified as loans of fungible objects rather than security transactions, they are regulated by Swiss property law rather than the federal stock exchange rules. Exceptions do occur in cases dealing with insurance companies and pension funds where regulatory authorities have specific rules prohibiting or controlling these transactions. For instance, mutual funds are prohibited from engaging in security lending, unless they include this function in their fund regulations. These regulations are subject to the Federal Banking Commission's approval.

3. Security lending and taxes

Security lending transactions are not subject to the Swiss Security Transfer Tax, but the dividends, interest and other financial returns (such as commissions) are considered income and fully taxable. These transactions (lending and returning of securities) do not trigger realization of capital gains, therefore, both at the federal and cantonal levels, no capital gains taxes are assessed.[3]

---

[3] According to Federal Tax Authorities, it is not 100 per cent clear whether all the capital gains realized when securities are returned to private owners are free from taxes, because a component of (taxable) income might be in this capital gain.

THE CO-PUBLISHERS

JB^{co}B

THE JULIUS BAER GROUP

A PRIVATE BANK FOR
INSTITUTIONAL INVESTORS

Dr. G. Sellerberg, Senior Vice
President, Bank Julius Baer, Zurich

The Julius Baer Group, whose key company – Bank Julius Baer & Co. Ltd. – was founded in 1890, holds a leading position in the Swiss and international portfolio management business. With well over US$40 billion of client assets (excluding global custody), it ranks 22nd in Europe and 5th in Switzerland (banks only).

The success story of the Julius Baer Group is closely linked with its experience, spanning more than one hundred years, in global private banking and in securities and foreign exchange trading. Our institutional business, which has also been intensively fostered for decades, accounts for roughly one-third of our client assets. The Group also holds a strong market position in brokerage for foreign institutional investors in Switzerland and Germany and is one of the leading Swiss companies in the international investment fund business. The experience gained in these diverse businesses is offered to institutional clients as a comprehensive and professional service in the form of Baer Custodian Service.

Institutional portfolio management

The two key companies of the Julius Baer Group in the field of institutional portfolio management are Julius Baer Investment Management in New York/London and Julius Baer Asset Management in Zurich. The strong market position of these companies reflects the high quality of their client-oriented services and their competitive performance results.

As part of the Group's strategic expansion of its institutional business into new markets, Julius Baer Investment Management Inc. (JBIM) was founded in New York in 1983. This SEC-registered company manages more than US$3 billion, focusing primarily on international bond portfolios. In this segment JBIM ranks 5th among all portfolio managers of US tax-exempt institutions.

JBIM's first-class list of clients comprises about 30 organizations, including seven US federal states which account for approximately three-quarters of total client assets. Its marketing success in the intensely competitive US institutional business is mainly attributable to repeated overperformance in the past decade. JBIM follows an active expansion strategy in its core business, in the management of equity mandates for US clients and in the build-up of client relationships in Europe.

Julius Baer Asset Management Ltd. (JBAM), which assumed new duties on 1

January 1995, is responsible for institutional portfolio management in Switzerland, for the management of most of the investment funds of the Julius Baer Group and for the execution of special mandates with institutional requirements. With about US$9 billion of client assets and Sfr22 million of share capital, JBAM is one of Switzerland's leading portfolio management companies.

The company offers a tailor-made selection of mandates: balanced mandates according to BVG (Swiss occupational pension fund) guidelines or specific client requirements, Swiss/international equity mandates and Swiss/international bond mandates. Special mention should be given to the expertise in the management of Swiss equity funds (Swiss Stock Fund for primary stocks and Special Swiss Stock Fund for secondary stocks) and Swiss bond funds, which regularly receive high marks in the performance rankings by the international rating agencies. These activities receive substantial support from a skilled Swiss research team which is highly respected in Switzerland and abroad.

Additional institutional portfolio management activities are located in London and Frankfurt. London-based Julius Baer Investments Ltd. specializes in international bond mandates as well as in the management of international and European equity portfolios. Baer Capital GmbH in Frankfurt is the portfolio management company for the institutional money of Bank Julius Baer (Deutschland) AG. It manages more than 500 million German marks, primarily in investment funds of the Julius Baer Group.

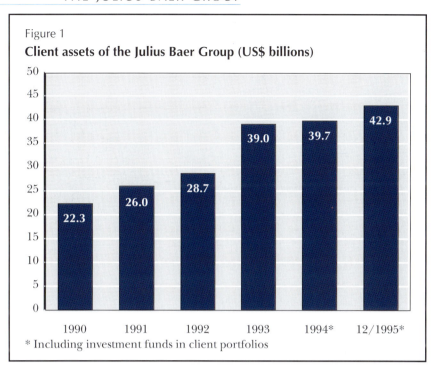

Figure 1

Client assets of the Julius Baer Group (US$ billions)

* Including investment funds in client portfolios

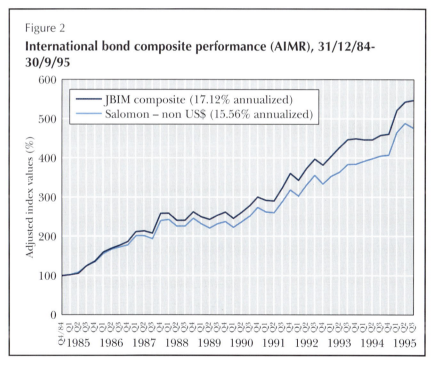

Figure 2

International bond composite performance (AIMR), 31/12/84-30/9/95

The companies of the Julius Baer Group possess vast experience in global securities trading, own stock exchange seats in Zurich, Frankfurt, Philadelphia and Chicago and have an international research team. This combination of professional capabilities results

International brokerage network

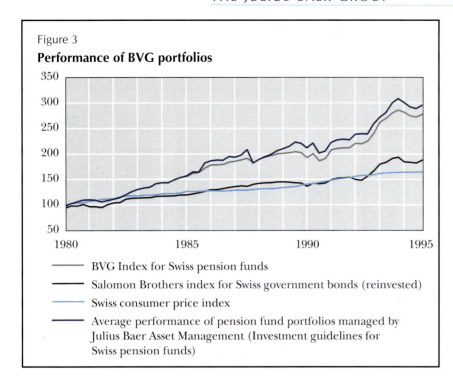

Figure 3

Performance of BVG portfolios

············· BVG Index for Swiss pension funds

———— Salomon Brothers index for Swiss government bonds (reinvested)

············· Swiss consumer price index

———— Average performance of pension fund portfolios managed by Julius Baer Asset Management (Investment guidelines for Swiss pension funds)

in a significant position in the global brokerage business.

Bank Julius Baer in Zurich is one of the three largest local brokers for Swiss equities, while our Bank in Frankfurt, founded only in 1989, already ranks among the top 10 brokers on the German stock market. First-class fundamental research is complemented by an active sales team. Comparable services are offered by Julius Baer Securities in New York.

In the institutional brokerage business, the Group's solid position in foreign exchange trading also deserves mention. These activities are concentrated in Zurich and New York but are also conducted in Geneva and London. Julius Baer is a niche player and position taker and offers its clientele around-the-clock trading through a specialized trading team.

A broad range of investment fund activities

The Julius Baer Group established its first investment funds more than 25 years ago. It now manages a range of 40 investment funds with total assets of around US$4 billion, covering the key investment sectors and the leading equity and bond markets worldwide.

Over half of our investment fund assets relate to EU-concordant UCITS funds domiciled in Luxembourg. These funds in particular have also been placed mainly with third parties outside the Julius Baer Group through a successful collaboration strategy with European distribution partners. Julius Baer Investment Funds Services Ltd., Zurich, the company in charge of our investment fund activities, also places its know-how at the disposal of fund promoters who do not belong to the Julius Baer Group. The services related to the founding and management of offshore mutual funds in Grand Cayman are a unique and rapidly growing segment in the investment fund business. These instruments are particularly suitable for independent private portfolio managers, enabling them to achieve improved implementation of their investment policy and substantial rationalization effects in portfolio administration. We had already reached a business volume of more than US$700 million US dollars in this new area at the end of 1995.

Baer custodian service for the global custody business

Despite entering the custody business only in 1993, Bank Julius Baer already has a mandate volume of more than US$4 billion and a market share of 3 per cent in Switzerland. Our key client groups are Swiss pension funds, insurers and finance companies as well as foreign-domiciled banks and brokers.

Our global custody services include worldwide securities administration, processing of securities and foreign exchange transactions, account management in all major currencies and detailed reporting. The comprehensive know-how of the Julius Baer Group can be used efficiently and intensively by professional business partners.

Our activities in Securities Lending & Borrowing represent an additional service for institutional investors. We offer sound technical processing in accordance with international practices.

Summary

A private bank for institutional investors – this title is only contradictory at first glance. At the Julius Baer Group, the steady development of our service structures is a business policy that has been successfully followed for decades. The mutual enrichment of service quality, personal client counselling and professional know-how is clearly evident in the day-to-day business. All client groups can benefit from our broad range of services, the close relationships made possible through our extensive international presence, and our first-class financial position.

The contact persons at the individual Group companies listed in the following tables will gladly provide you with information on the services of the Julius Baer Group.

Address List

1) Julius Baer Investment Management Inc., New York/London
Contact New York: Jay A. Dirnberger
Tel. +1 (212) 297 3850
Fax +1 (212) 557 7839
Contact London: Jonathan Minter
Tel. +44 (171) 626 3561
Fax +44 (171) 283 6146

2) Julius Baer Investments Limited, London
Contact: Michael Anthony
Tel. +44 (171) 623 4211
Fax +44 (171) 283 6146

3) Julius Baer Asset Management Ltd., Zurich
Contact: Dr. Urs Baltensweiler
Tel. +41 (1) 287 68 00
Fax +41 (1) 287 53 21

4) Baer Capital GmbH, Frankfurt am Main
Contact: Dr. Harald Fuchs
Tel. +49 (69) 75696-0
Fax +49 (69) 743 2511

5) Brokerage Switzerland
Bank Julius Baer & Co. Ltd., Zurich
Contact: Martin Eberhard
Tel. +41 (1) 228 51 11
Fax +41 (1) 211 25 60

6) Brokerage Germany
Bank Julius Baer (Deutschland) AG, Frankfurt am Main
Contact: Patrick Bettscheider
Tel. +49 (69) 75696-0
Fax +49 (69) 743 25 11

7) Julius Baer Securities Inc., New York
Contact: Bernard Spilko
Tel. +1 (212) 297-3800
Fax +1 (212) 557-7839

8) Julius Baer Investment Funds Services Ltd., Zurich
Contact: Mathias Brüschweiler
Tel. +41 (1) 228 57 65
Fax +41 (1) 202 41 61

9) Offshore Mutual Funds
Bank Julius Baer & Co. Ltd., Zurich
Contact: Roland Eberhard
Tel. +41 (1) 228 51 11
Fax +41 (1) 211 25 60

10) Baer Custodian Services/Securities Lending & Borrowing
Bank Julius Baer & Co. Ltd., Zurich
Contact: Jürg Ryffel
Tel. +41 (1) 228 51 11
Fax +41 (1) 211 25 60

Client focus with a global perspective

Over the course of two decades, J.P. Morgan has reforged its capabilities with a sole purpose: to excel globally in serving clients with complex financial needs. From a foundation of leadership in commercial banking, we have built a global financial firm of unprecedented scope and strength. We meet a wider variety of client needs around the world today than we have at any other time in our history. We offer a complete range of sophisticated financial services to companies, institutions, and individuals, from advising on corporate structure to raising equity and debt capital to managing complex investment portfolios.

At J.P. Morgan, relationships have always taken precedence over transactions. Striving to offer the most informed, objective advice, we will counsel a client against a course of action if we believe it is not in their interest. And when decisive execution is required, Morgan marshals solid experience and unequaled energy.

Drawing on investment, commercial, and merchant banking tradition as markets and client needs change, we intend to keep breaking the mould. Our objective remains simply this: to provide services of the highest quality that help our clients achieve their goals.

JPMorgan

A tradition of global service

J.P. Morgan has long served as advisor, underwriter, and lender to an extensive roster of major companies. During the late nineteenth and early twentieth centuries, the firm was instrumental in the initial structuring and financing of U.S. Steel, General Electric, American Telephone & Telegraph, and several other prominent corporations. Most of those early clients still maintain relationships with Morgan today, as do a wide variety of promising new companies, which rely on the firm to help formulate business strategies, determine optimal capital strategies, and increase long-term shareholder value.

In world financial markets, Morgan has long been an important intermediary, linking issuers and investors around the globe. In addition, Morgan has forged a solid reputation as an investment manager of institutional assets. The firm has also served the investment and fiduciary needs of many of the great personal and family fortunes amassed during the past century – a role it continues to play as a leading financial advisor to wealthy individuals.

As a financial advisor to national governments, Morgan established its reputation in 1870, when it extended a daring £10 million loan to the besieged government of France during the Franco-Prussian War. The firm served as a financial representative for the French and British governments during the two World Wars and provided major financing for reconstruction after both conflicts. In 1988 Morgan developed a landmark program to enable the Mexican government to issue US$2.6 billion in bonds to creditor banks in exchange for existing debt – a model widely used afterward in restructuring the debt of developing countries. More recently Morgan arranged a US$5.5 billion syndicated loan to help the government of Kuwait rebuild its nation after the Persian Gulf War. In emerging markets, the firm is advising a number of governments in their efforts to privatize industries and nurture free market economies.

Our philosophy and character – how we work – are as important as our capabilities and services. We work within the context of a few long-standing, fundamental beliefs and strategic strengths:

Objectivity

We always put our clients' long-term interests first. We examine their situation impartially and recommend the best strategic options.

Teamwork

A team approach gives our clients the benefit of the breadth of our capabilities, functionally and geographically, as well as our most creative thinking. Our team-oriented culture also makes Morgan a rewarding and collegial place to work.

Ethics and integrity

We always operate with the belief that our reputation for fair dealing is our greatest asset; we are committed to maintaining the highest standards of conduct.

Global perspective

We bring an international reach and local touch to problem solving that comes from the years of experience we have gained from operating in all the major financial markets of the world.

Capital strength

Our solid capital base and high credit rating often translate into added financial stability and flexibility for our clients.

In the development of modern global finance, few institutions have played a more prominent role than J.P. Morgan.

J.P. Morgan around the world

North America

New York
J.P. Morgan & Co. Incorporated
Morgan Guaranty Trust Company of
   New York
J.P. Morgan Securities Inc.
Morgan Guaranty private banking offices
Tel. (1 212) 483 2323
J.P. Morgan Investment Management Inc.
Tel. (1 212) 837 2300
J.P. Morgan Futures Inc.
Tel. (1 212) 648 6560
Morgan Guaranty International Finance
   Corporation
Tel. (1 212) 648 3755

Boston
J.P. Morgan Securities Inc.
(1-617) 428-4777

Chicago
J.P. Morgan & Co. Incorporated
J.P. Morgan Securities Inc.
J.P. Morgan Futures Inc.
Tel. (1 312) 541 3300

Houston
J.P. Morgan Securities Inc.
Tel. (1 713) 655 9995
J.P. Morgan Investment Management Inc.
Tel. (1 713) 655 0086

Los Angeles
Morgan Guaranty representative office
J.P. Morgan Investment Management Inc.
J.P. Morgan California
Tel. (1 213) 489 9300

Palm Beach
J.P. Morgan Florida, FSB
J.P. Morgan Securities Inc.
Tel. (1 407) 838 4600

San Francisco
J.P. Morgan & Co. Incorporated
Morgan Guaranty representative office
J.P. Morgan California
J.P. Morgan Securities Inc.
J.P. Morgan Futures Inc.
Tel. (1 415) 954 3200

Wilmington
J.P. Morgan Delaware
Tel. (1 302) 651 2323
J.P. Morgan Services Inc.
Tel. (1 302) 634 1000

Toronto
Morgan Bank of Canada
J.P. Morgan Securities Canada Inc.
Tel. (1 416) 981 9200

Nassau
Morgan Guaranty banking office
Morgan Trust Company of The Bahamas
   Limited
Tel. (1 809) 326 5519

Cayman Islands
J.P. Morgan Delaware banking office
Morgan Fonciere Cayman Islands Ltd.
Morgan Trust Company of the Cayman
   Islands Ltd.
Tel. (1 809) 949 8666

Latin America

Buenos Aires
Morgan Guaranty banking office
J.P. Morgan Argentina S.A.
Tel. (54 1) 325 8046

Caracas
J.P. Morgan Venezuela, S.A.
Tel. (58 2) 925 401

Mexico City
J.P. Morgan Grupo Financiero, S.A.
   de C.V.
J.P. Morgan Casa de Bolsa, S.A. de C.V.
Banco J.P. Morgan, S.A.
Tel. (52 5) 540 9333

Rio de Janeiro
Morgan Guaranty banking office
JPM Corretora de Cambio, Títulos e
   Valores Mobiliários S.A.
J.P. Morgan Investimentos e Finanças Ltda.
Banco J.P. Morgan S.A.
Tel. (55 21) 297 1257

Santiago
J.P. Morgan Chile Ltda.
Tel. (56 2) 206 6474

São Paulo
Morgan Guaranty banking office
JPM Corretora de Cambio, Títulos e
   Valores Mobiliários S.A.
J.P. Morgan Investimentos e Finanças Ltda.
Banco J.P. Morgan S.A.
Tel. (55 11) 281 3700

Europe

London
Morgan Guaranty banking office
Tel. (44 71) 600 2300
International Private Banking
Tel. (44 71) 839 9211
J.P. Morgan Securities Ltd.
J.P. Morgan Sterling Securities Ltd.
Tel. (44 71) 600 2300
J.P. Morgan Investment Management
Tel. (44 71) 451 8000

Amsterdam
J.P. Morgan Nederland N.V.
Tel. (31 20) 676 7766

Brussels
Morgan Guaranty banking office
Tel. (32 2) 508 8211
J.P. Morgan Benelux S.A.
Tel. (32 2) 513 4903
Euroclear Operations Centre
Tel. (32 2) 224 1211

Channel Islands
J.P. Morgan Jersey Limited

Frankfurt
Morgan Guaranty banking office
J.P. Morgan GmbH
J.P. Morgan Investment GmbH
Tel. (49 69) 7124 0

Geneva
J.P. Morgan (Suisse) S.A.
Tel. (41 22) 731 5800

Madrid
Morgan Guaranty banking office
J.P. Morgan España S.A.
Morgan Gestion, S.A.
J.P. Morgan Sociedad de Valores y
   Bolsa, S.A.
Tel. (34 1) 435 6041

Milan
Morgan Guaranty banking office
Tel. (39 2) 77441
J.P. Morgan S.p.A.
J.P. Morgan SIM S.p.A.
Tel. (39 2) 796149

Paris
Morgan Guaranty banking and private
   banking offices
J.P. Morgan & Cie S.A.
Société de Bourse J.P. Morgan S.A.
Tel. (33 1) 4015 4500

Prague
J.P. Morgan International Ltd.
Tel. (42 2) 526 845

Rome
Morgan Guaranty representative office
Tel. (39 6) 8530 1236

Warsaw
J.P. Morgan Polska Sp. z o.o.
Tel. (48 22) 630 6304

Zurich
Morgan Guaranty banking office
Tel. (41 1) 206 8111
J.P. Morgan (Suisse) S.A.
Tel. (41 1) 208 9111
J.P. Morgan (Switzerland) Ltd.
Tel. (41 1) 206 8511
J.P. Morgan Securities Ltd.
Tel. (41 1) 206 8686

Asia / Pacific

Tokyo
Morgan Guaranty banking and private
   banking offices
Tel. (81 3) 5573 1100
J.P. Morgan Securities Asia Ltd.
Tel. (81 3) 5573 1111
J.P. Morgan Trust Bank Ltd.
Tel. (81 3) 5573 1110

Beijing
J.P. Morgan & Co. representative office
Tel. (86 1) 500 2255 ext. 2763
or (86 1) 500 8483

Bombay
ICICI Securities and Finance Company
   Limited
Tel. (91 22) 283 7014

Hong Kong
Morgan Guaranty banking and private
   banking offices
J.P. Morgan Securities Hong Kong Ltd.
J.P. Morgan Securities Asia Ltd.
Tel. (852) 2841 1311

Jakarta
Morgan Guaranty representative office
Tel. (62 21) 323 368

Manila
Morgan Guaranty representative office
Tel. (63 2) 810 0361

Melbourne
Morgan Guaranty banking office
J.P. Morgan Australia Limited
J.P. Morgan Australia Securities Limited
Tel. (61 3) 623 8300
J.P. Morgan Investment Management
   Australia Limited
Tel. (61 3) 623 8400

Osaka
J.P. Morgan Securities Asia Ltd.
Tel. (81 6) 205 4800

Seoul
Morgan Guaranty representative office
Tel. (82 2) 732 2300

Shanghai
J.P. Morgan & Co. representative office
Tel. (86 21) 279 7301

Singapore
Morgan Guaranty banking and private
   banking offices
J.P. Morgan Securities Asia Ltd.
J.P. Morgan Investment Management
Tel. (65) 220 8144
J.P. Morgan Futures Inc.
Tel. (65) 225 1011

Sydney
Morgan Guaranty banking office
J.P. Morgan Australia Limited
J.P. Morgan Australia Securities Limited
Tel. (61 2) 551 6100

Taipei
Morgan Guaranty representative office
Tel. (886 2) 712 2333

Swiss Bank Corporation

SWISS BANK CORPORATION: GLOBALLY ACTIVE, CUSTOMER FOCUSED

Swiss Bank Corporation, founded in Basle in 1872, has, over the years, developed into a dynamic, innovative and future-oriented Swiss bank. In Switzerland, it is one of the three big banks and a leading bank offering a full range of services to all customers. Swiss Bank Corporation's SBC Warburg Division, created in July 1995 when SBC's former International and Finance Division joined with the investment banking business of the London-based S.G. Warburg Group, is a leading European investment bank with a focus on global activities in corporate finance, equities, rates, foreign exchange, the related risk management and global institutional asset management.

Swiss Bank Corporation has total assets of US$240 billion; in terms of equity, SBC was ranked 3rd in Switzerland and is among the 20 best-capitalised banks in the world. It has a workforce of over 27,000 in over 400 offices in 47 countries. With a market value of around Sfr18 billion or 4 per cent of the total Swiss stock market capitalisation, SBC shares are among the most highly capitalised and traded Swiss stocks.

It has been SBC's consistent goal to belong to the world's top-tier banks in terms of professionalism, profitability and market position. Return on equity and efficient risk management are priority concerns. Our approach is completely customer oriented – involving the building up of an effective management structure, technical expertise in the development of new products and the highest degree of quality and attention when advising customers.

To attain these goals, over the past two years Swiss Bank Corporation has seen a reorganisation that clearly and consistently differentiated between corporate and business management. On the one side, the Corporate Centre is exclusively entrusted with corporate management; the various business areas on the other side are each wholly accountable for their results.

Swiss Bank Corporation's activities are based on three core businesses:

- We are one of the world's leading asset managers for private and institutional investors. We are about to strengthen and globalize our asset management capabilities and substantially expand our franchise with institutional investors. We have made an important step in this direction with the acquisition of Brinson Partners in 1995, one of America's leading asset managers for institutional customers.

- In **global investment banking** we have created a prominent platform thanks to our leadership position in advisory, financial structuring and risk management. With the help of SBC Warburg, this enables us to develop and deepen our relationship with major international clients.

- In **domestic retail and corporate banking** we are strengthening our market position to achieve a sustained improvement in earnings.

In SBC Warburg the leadership positions of both partners involved complement each other : SBC's leadership in capital markets, interest rates, foreign exchange and risk management technology is a perfect match for the former S.G.Warburg's excellent position in corporate finance, equity research, primary equity and equity distribution.

SBC Warburg's origins are European; the orientation, however, is global, with a strong presence in the Americas and Asia Pacific. SBC Warburg not only has two strong home markets, Switzerland and the United Kingdom, but also has a significant investment banking presence in a number of European countries and in South Africa, in the form of domestic and cross-border businesses. It is also a leading adviser and intermediary of cross-border banking activities in North and South America. It has a strong position in domestic and cross-border business in Asia Pacific and is a leading investment bank in Australia and New Zealand.

SBC Warburg is organised into five principle businesses, headed by one member of the executive board who is globally responsible and wholly accountable for its results:

- In **corporate finance** SBC Warburg is a leader in UK and Continental European M&A and has executed some of the most complex and innovative corporate restructurings;

- In **equities** SBC Warburg is one of the leading international equity underwriters and among the largest players in the European secondary cash market. We have a significant market share in global cross-border institutional flows and conduct the largest share of foreign equity trading in the USA. This strong position is based not only on the quality of our global sales and advisory force but also on the particular strengths of our equity research and our dominant position in risk management;

- In the **rates business** the depth and breadth of the product range, especially in the area of exchange-traded and OTC derivatives, is one of SBC Warburg's decisive strengths; this is supported by our superior distribution skills, our pre-eminent position as an underwriter and as a provider of risk management products;

- In **foreign exchange**, the dominance in the option market, with daily volumes averaging US$7 billion across a hundred different currency pairs, allows SBC Warburg to execute large transactions for its clients without alerting the market place to any unusual activity;

- In the **global institutional asset management** the acquisition of Brinson Partners in 1995 was an important strategic step. With assets under management of more than US$40 billion, this globally active company, which operates under the Brinson name, belongs to the leading houses in the USA.

The **domestic division**, which became operational as such on 1 January 1994, consists of four business areas, each headed by a member of the executive board who is fully accountable for the results. This structure reflects the consistent focus of the Bank's business activities to the needs of its customers:

- **Private investors and asset management** is serving the Group's high net worth private client franchise internationally. In Switzerland, the Bank successfully expanded its leadership position in the investment fund sector in 1995, and with Sfr56 billion under management in mutual funds only and a diversified range of 91 funds, managed to increase its market share to 31 per cent. This makes Swiss Bank Corporation the undisputed number one in Switzerland.

- **Domestic retail banking** realigned its structures and its branch organisation in 1995 in order to achieve more efficient internal processes. Together with a range of innovative products such as the "Key Club" that systematically rewards customer loyalty, SBC maintains its strong position in the Swiss retail market.

- **Corporates and institutionals** offers the Bank's global services through 47 locations in Switzerland to a wide range of public entities, corporations, banks and pension funds. Additional relationship management units are located in New York and London as well as in Asia, so that foreign subsidiaries of Swiss companies can also be assisted locally in these important economic regions.

- **Logistics** comprises the Domestic Division's entire infrastructure, human resources, information technology, support services and production.

Swiss Bank Corporation supports you with all of its resources. Client focus is one of the leading principles of this organisation, as stated in our mission statement: "Our concepts and our internal structures are customer-oriented". Consequently, our range of products and our activities are driven by the requirements of the markets. The quality of our services as perceived by the customer must meet the highest standards.

Please contact us; we are looking forward to a successful business partnership with you.

Swiss Bank Corporation
Headquarters Basel: Tel: +41 61 288 2020
Fax: +41 61 288 9923
Investor Relations: Tel: +41 61 288 7574
Fax: +41 61 288 9099

☼ SBC Warburg
A DIVISION OF SWISS BANK CORPORATION

SBC Warburg
A Division of Swiss Bank Corporation
SBC Warburg, Zurich: Tel: +41 1 239 1111
Fax: +41 1 238 7606
SBC Warburg, London: Tel: +44 171 606 1066
Fax: +44 171 382 4800
SBC Warburg, Hong Kong: Tel: +852 2971 8888
Fax: +852 2868 1510